AMERICA'S SECURITY IN THE 1980s

The security of the US is of vital importance to us all. If we are to avoid increasing tension in this 'dangerous decade' we must address the conflicts which affect that security. The IISS chose America's security as the theme of their prestigious annual conference which was held in late 1981 in Williamsburg, Virginia. America's alliances with the West and Asia, domestic factors influencing defence policy, strategic and conventional capabilities and attitudes towards the Soviet Union are some of the issues examined in this book.

In addition, overviews are provided in essays by distinguished authors such as Barbara Tuchman on the historical context, by Henry Kissinger on the current international context, and by Laurence Martin on the strategic context.

This is an important publication for all who are concerned with the future of the international security system and the part the United States will play in that system.

The editor
Christoph Bertram

The other contributors
William Bader
Pierre Hassner
William Hyland
Henry Kissinger
Jan Lodal
Laurence Martin
Tom B. Millar
Philip Odeen
Barbara Tuchman
David Watt
Thomas R. Wheelock

America's Security in the 1980s

Edited by

CHRISTOPH BERTRAM

St. Martin's Press   New York

© The International Institute for Strategic Studies 1982

ISBN 0–312–02199–2

Library of Congress Cataloging in Publication Data

Main entry under title:
America's security in the 1980s.

1. United States – National security – Addresses,
essays, lectures.   2. United States – Military policy –
Addresses, essays, lectures.   3. United States –
Defenses – Addresses, essays, lectures.   I. Bertram,
Christoph, 1937–
UA23.A6635   1982   355'.033073   82–16814
ISBN 0–312–02199–2

CONTENTS

Introduction

CHRISTOPH BERTRAM

It is necessary to start with two observations not of the proceedings of the Conference at which the papers published here were first presented, but of the theme and the place. For the first time in over 20 years, the Institute held an Annual Conference in the United States from 10 to 13 September 1981, in Williamsburg, Virginia. It was an appropriate setting for a discussion of America's security in the 1980s. Americans retain the ability not only to discuss their own problems in the open but welcome others to join them in this discussion as if by right. It is this same characteristic which for the rest of the world makes America the largest simulator of problems which are not exclusively American; in talking about America's security, we talked therefore about that of many other countries as well – and not only because of the shadow that American power casts all over the globe. If our meeting produced any lessons, they are not only for Americans to learn. In fact, we discussed, within the context of US security, most themes of *international* security.

Four features marked this discussion: uncertainty about the security environment at home and abroad; a tendency to concentrate on the means not the ends; the need to define security objectives coherently; and that of maintaining domestic and alliance support for their pursuit.

Prevailing Uncertainties

The first, the sense of uncertainty, pervades all contributions. There is uncertainty over the depth of the 'new consensus' in the United States – how long will it last, particularly when economic prospects are cloudy? There is uncertainty over the ability of the Executive to regain leadership in defence and foreign policy from a Congress that not only – to use William Bader's graphic term – has had its Spring but that is reluctant, and perhaps unable, to proceed to a less activist, more serene and passive Autumn. More important, there is uncertainty over priorities. The question-marks are not only imposed by financial and other resource constraints, so ably analysed in Philip Odeen's Paper; more fundamentally, they are imposed by uncertainty over concepts and requirements. There are among strategists today almost as many recipes as there are experts, and the general consensus that military force will continue to be relevant and that miltary strength needs to be improved, quickly evaporates when it comes to translating the principle into practice.

Not even the effects of nuclear weapons can be measured with certainty. The missiles in the arsenals have been tested but not fired in anger, their technical performance is measured in the artificial world of test ranges and simulators but – thank God – not in the reality of war. What people lack in evidence, they often make up for in conviction, and precise consequences are drawn on a shaky basis of reliable data. These Papers avoid such temptation. Jan Lodal's thoughtful assessment of the requirements for American nuclear forces set a tone which was followed throughout our discussions. The 'window of opportunity' which has haunted the meetings of strategists for a number of years, seems if not to close, at least to fade away as a usable concept. ICBM vulnerability was put in the overall context of the nuclear forces – not, as so often in the past, analysed in isolation. While there were different views on the controllability of nuclear exchanges – from those who, like Desmond Ball in his Adelphi Paper *Can Nuclear War Be Controlled?*, are highly sceptical about any such prospect, to those who believe that it might become technically feasible some time in the future – it is clear that, at the moment, survivable robust command and control for complicated nuclear exchanges do not exist. The list of uncertainties does not stop there. Political uncertainty lies over America's Alliances. Are they affected, as David Watt's Paper suggests, by no more than the familiar strains of a close coalition of states, or are they facing today a qualitatively new and fundamental challenge of compatability? Uncertainties, finally, over the nature of and response to crises in the Third World and the role of military force in such response, and over how to cope with the other super-power, the Soviet Union.

If a distinction exists between American and non-American strategists, it is not so much over the recognition that these uncertainties exist as in the spirit in which they are accepted. Most countries have been taught by history to live with uncertainty. The United States, however, has made history by believing that certainty is attainable, that problems are there to be solved rather than endured. It is this which gives America her vitality. But it also makes the adjustment to the age of uncertainty more painful for her than to many of her Allies.

Means and Ends
Uncertainty is probably also a major reason why so much of the strategic debate in recent years has tended to be concerned with means rather than ends. Strategic forces are often discussed without the concepts that should guide them; arms sales and technology transfers are recognized as an instrument of policy in the Third World, but the objective of that policy is rarely spelt out and economic leverage in dealing with the Soviet Union is advocated without defining what it is that ought to be achieved.

Perhaps understandably, we take refuge from the uncertainties of outcomes in the certainties of inputs. But tools cannot define the task; they must be able to serve it. What will be the objective of US policy toward the Soviet Union once military strength has been restored? What should be the rules that America wants the Soviet Union to respect and what would be incentives for Soviet restraint? There is a 'means/ends' confusion in current military doctrines such as 'flexible response' and 'massive retaliation'. In dealing with third-world crises, merely to call for the Rapid Deployment Force cannot provide the answer. And only if the concepts of military power are clear, can arms control be pursued with clear objectives. Strategy is not the study of means but of the application of means to an end. Not only governments but the analytical community as well have perhaps too often allowed the analysis of the means to overshadow the definition of the objectives they should serve.

The Need for a Strategy
Henry Kissinger's is the most forceful contribution to this collection of Papers to demand a more conceptual, a more strategic notion of policy for the United States and the West, and to identify some of the major elements of such a policy. To call for a coherent strategic concept as many of these Papers do – on deterrence, on relations with the Soviet Union, on order in the Third World – is, on the surface at least, no more than logical. But in an untidy world the call for concepts can also be both dangerous and disabling: dangerous because it risks pressing a disorderly reality under the supposed tidiness of prescriptive analysis; disabling because the difficulty of getting there could provide an alibi for doing nothing – witness the European call for a 'comprehensive concept' after the Soviet invasion in Afghanistan. In today's world, a 'comprehensive concept' may well be a contradiction in terms.

There are many doubts and they are voiced here. In the nuclear field, a strategy often has only the function of declaratory policy; after all, the composition and targeting list of American nuclear forces has been largely immune to the periodic changes in nuclear doctrines announced by successive Secretaries of Defense. Perhaps, in the light of that experience, we should be grateful to the new Administration that it has refrained from pronouncing another doctrine. And would the spelling out of specific priorities not invite opposition from a Congress of special interests? (As William Bader's Paper suggests, the controlling devices born in the 'Congressional Spring' could be used to produce the ultimate unpredictability of US foreign and security policy.) William Hyland's Paper on the American view of the Soviet Union shows the particular American problem with strategies: that they have to be over-presented, even over-sold, to gain political support and thus carry within them the seeds of their own destruction since the promised results of specific policies are not always easy to demonstrate. Nor are non-Americans immune from the temptation of fudging the issues in order to make them politically less divisive. The integration of theatre nuclear forces into West European defence has only been made acceptable in the past to Americans and Europeans alike by pretending to the former that the weapons would not entail the risk of an attack on the United States and to the latter that they deter because of that risk. The arguments against attempting to spell out the objectives of policy are persuasive indeed, not only in the American context. But they are not convincing, at least not in democracies which have to depend on sustained popular support for sustainable, defined policies.

Only if an Administration knows what its priorities are can it present a convincing case over the time span it needs to implement them; and only if it can show that it has done its sums correctly, as Philip Odeen points out in his Paper, can it resist the ever-present temptation for cutting or stretching military programmes. Predictability of policies is not an accident but the result of hard work in gaining and maintaining respect and support – from one's own populace, from one's allies and from one's adversaries.

That this must be more than the pronouncement of general principles is evident. Most of these Papers present policy, and while it would be over-ambitious to expect that between them they could come up with a coherent concept, some elements emerge:

– On nuclear versus conventional forces: there is a clear need to strengthen conventional forces as the highest priority;
– On nuclear doctrine: in spite of many doubts expressed over the concept of 'war-fighting', there can be little disagreement over the need for the United States to have more options than merely that of massive response if deterrence is to be effectively extended to America's Allies. The question will be not whether, but which options for limited use are essential for effective deterrence – an exercise very different from the blind addition of more and more sophisticated strike packages;
– On conventional forces: while it would be desirable to restructure US conventional forces to make them more flexible to cope with the range of conflict contingencies in Europe, Asia and third-world areas, governments will have to make do with what they have got. *This* will have to be the framework for developing more effective conventional force options for the future;
– On third-world contingencies: the globalist/regionalist dichotomy is probably both misleading and misguided – misleading because global generalities have to take into account regional specifics; misguided because the countries in the Third World can and will no longer be pressed effectively into the matrix of global super-power competition;
– On relations with the Soviet Union: there is no alternative to what Pierre Hassner calls 'variations on Mr.X': containment, together with military balance, crisis management, and arms-control efforts. But containment can scarcely be achieved when strains between the United States and her Allies and with the Third World offer the Soviet Union chances to sow discord among her opponents. One of the most important elements of US policy toward the Soviet Union would therefore seem to lie in good relations with Allies and third-world countries.

Public Support
That these or other policies cannot be devised and pursued in quasi-isolation from domestic political concerns and constraints is emphasized by Barbara Tuchman's historical review at the beginning of this collection. It is repeated in Henry Kissinger's assessment of future choices. It is a theme that runs consistently through all the Papers, bringing out what strategic analysts in and out of government have perhaps often tended to forget at their peril: that without acceptance by the public there can be no sustainable policy. This is also a matter for the presentation of policy; words *do* count – the new US Administration remains largely judged not by what it has done but by what its spokesmen have been saying. Nowhere is this responsibility more marked than in the nuclear field; the depth of feeling and support behind the anti-nuclear movement in Western Europe shows the consequences that can follow if nuclear planners and their political masters forget this basic rule. There is a thin membrane between the acceptable – deterrence – and the unacceptable – the fighting of wars with nuclear weapons.

This is not merely a matter of presentation; even if the term 'war-fighting' were to be removed from the vocabulary, the direction of strategic thinking which lies behind the term would sooner or later again strain public tolerance. If the West wants a sustainable nuclear doctrine, it must be acceptable not only in its presentation but also in its substance, or else the balance abroad will not balance at home.

Will it balance in the United States of the 1980s? There can be no one who, after reading Barbara Tuchman's review of 200 years of American history, will not ask: what will be the consequences of failure, what the effects of disappointment on the mood of America, if the results promised by the Reagan Administration do not materialize? The new consensus in the American body politic remains fragile; one reaction to failure could be a US retrenchment to 'hemispheric defence'; the lure of Mrs Tuchman's idyllic nineteenth-century America, confident because isolated, might then be difficult to resist. Indeed, the very reluctance of the present Administration to produce a coherent policy could also indicate a more traditional American abhorrence of becoming embroiled in the complexities of a messy world, and the renewed attention to threats in Latin America a nostalgic return to one's own back yard. Yet one important reason why this is not a realistic option lies in America's links with the world: of the major powers, the United States is the only one with strong domestic constituencies directly affected by the most likely crises of the 1980s – in Europe, in the the Middle East, in Latin America, and in Southern Africa. While this may limit America's margin of manoeuvre, it will also rule out isolationist abstinence.

Yet the lure of turning inward is a powerful one, and again it is not only an American phenomenon. The provincialization of modern society is a general trend on both sides of the Atlantic. It is particularly costly for America's Allies; while the *United States* may get by without a strategy, *the West* will not. David Watt is, I believe, right: the cut-rate Alliance that he depicts will not last because it would be an alliance of mutual suspicion and pettiness and it could open up again the divisive German issue in the centre of Europe. America has, for the past 30 years, provided the confidence and generosity that made this Alliance so unprecedentedly successful as a framework for political accommodation and co-operation. Today, the crisis is so serious because there is deep doubt in Europe (and elsewhere) about the wisdom of US political leadership, and, as Pierre Hassner points out in his Paper, it may be the United States' attitude towards the Third World even more than disappointment over the state of US–Soviet relations which feeds these doubts and the thoughtless anti-Americanism that accompanies them.

The only way I can see to arrest this slide into what would be a totally unnecessary progressive estrangement is for America's allies to move to David Watt's 'de luxe alliance' – away from the tradition of simultaneously criticizing, and waiting for American leadership, to the confident and considerate initiation of policies that make sense for the Alliance as a whole, perhaps, as some suggested and others doubted, in closer co-operation with the other chief American ally, Japan. That – a responsible input in the formation of common policies – would be both a more difficult and more important contribution of America's allies to American and their own security than all the familiar dreams of burden sharing and division of labour.

The American People and Military Power in an Historical Perspective

BARBARA TUCHMAN

Change in the sphere of military power and international relations has been so radical since 1945 as to raise a question whether the past is relevant. Probably it is because, while the national experience of the last two centuries may be totally inapplicable and unusable in the world of the 1980s, it has formed certain American characteristics which I think will continue to operate.

The outstanding feature of our military experience has been its paradox. We have been anti-militarist in thought and sentiment while remarkably combative in character and practice. At the start, the single common principle on which all thirteen colonies could agree was absolute rejection of an organized army in peacetime. This sentiment appeared in the Declaration of Independence, which made one of its chief accusations against George II that 'he kept among us in time of peace, Standing Armies without the Consent of our legislatures' and 'has effected to render the Military independent of and superior to the Civil Power.' In fear of engendering a regular army, the united colonies hampered their own fight for independence by refusing to require enlistment for the duration of the War. After independence, they began nationhood by rejecting a national army in favour of local militias under state control, and in their Constitution firmly established the principle of civilian control of the military.

America's active record has been more belligerent. The greatest western war of the nineteenth century in scope, violence, numbers engaged, duration and military influence was fought here in the United States – our Civil War. In the two centuries since independence, US regulars have gone to battle in 69 Indian campaigns not counting innumerable skirmishes, two wars on this continent (the War of 1812 and the Civil War) and seven foreign wars (Tripoli, Mexican, Spanish–American, World Wars I and II, Korea, Vietnam) not counting various forays in Latin America and China. From Washington to Eisenhower we have had ten presidents who have been generals in the same period that England had one as prime minister – the Duke of Wellington. Only three of the Americans were professionals; the rest were lawyers (inevitably), and politicians whose battlefield service brought them the popularity and prominence that carried them to the White House. A military exploit too put Theodore Roosevelt on the path to the Presidency, although he was never a general. In addition, two notable soldiers, General Winfield Scott and the first Union commander, General McClellan, were nominated for the Presidency; two others, Admiral Dewey and General MacArthur, wanted to be; and one is presently eyeing the spot from close proximity, although not quite as close as he originally believed.

Three Principles

Along with this bellicosity, Americans have shown their dislike of organized war by a desperate attachment to three principles: unpreparedness until the eleventh hour; the quickest feasible strategy for victory regardless of political aims; and instant demobilization, no matter how inadvisable, the moment the hostilities are over. These are the three characteristics that can still affect our conduct – as they have done before. In 1783, within two months of the signing of a preliminary peace, the Continental Army had largely evaporated. A year later Congress voted to disband the national army which then consisted of 700 men, retaining only 80 privates to guard ammunition stores with no officer allowed to be over the rank of captain. After victory in World War II, demobilization was so rapid as to endanger the continued occupation of conquered territory. General Eisenhower had to exert every pressure available to him to get Congress to extend the draft for another year, otherwise, he wrote in his diary, 'the thing is chaos'. The same phenomenon took place after each of our wars in between.

The standing army phobia derived not from any aversion to fighting but from the passion for liberty that infused the eighteenth century. Drawn out of the great political struggles of seventeenth-century England, a permanent army was seen by Englishmen as well as by their transplanted brethren as the great menace to free men, the sure instrument of so-called 'slavery' whose possession would transform any state into tyranny. This was the principle behind our effort to forgo the awful institution, to rely on a citizen's army, to spread the burden by short enlistments as widely as possible, to end any organized war as quickly as possible and to maintain no regular armed force of any size in advance of need.

Once the fight is on, the American preference is for aggressive offensive actions followed by going home and back to normal as soon as possible. Both South and North in the Civil War expected one decisive clash to settle the issue; no-one anticipated the four-year-long agony that ensued. It might have been spared if the aged Winfield Scott's proposed strategy of strangling the Confederacy by economic blockade until superior armies could be trained and equipped had been adopted, but that was too slow for the American nature. Or had there been an army in being at the start, it might have smashed the Southern rebellion at its outbreak. In our time, containment of the Soviet Union would have been a very different matter if Churchill's strategy of invading Europe from the South-east had prevailed – and of course succeeded – but this likewise was too indirect and protracted for American taste. 'A Democracy cannot fight a Seven Years War', General Marshall said.

Whatever the mood of today (which is none too clear), anti-militarism has been a fundamental sentiment in our history. The suppression of 'militarism' personified by the Kaiser was widely regarded as an aim of World War I. Combining with isolationism and neutrality, which I shall come to shortly, anti-militarism has generated more genuine passion than any but the most momentary pro-war sen-timents. One need only think back to the American Peace Societies of the 1840s, to the ideals and hopes aroused by the two Hague Disarmament Conferences, to the public re-vulsion in the 1930s at the Senate's revelations about the munitions industry, to the emotions aroused against the Vietnam War, and to the repugnance to the draft which Americans seem to exhibit so much more vigorously than Euro-peans.

Warlike no; violent yes. That we are a violent people is undeniable, and the reason for this too goes back to the beginning. The first settlers of the American wilderness bore arms on their own behalf. Every man owned a gun to defend his home and family against Indian attack as well as to provide game for food; each community appointed a captain for the com-mon defence. Military action was personal and vital, not imposed in drilled ranks and chalked white pantaloons for some remote dynastic or territorial ambition of a monarch.

As a cause of violence on both sides, the displacement of the country's native inhabitants was a matter of greater moment and the conflict more intense, prolonged and fierce than is generally remembered today. The red men's sudden massacres and savagery were matched by white betrayals, seizures and slaughter of the red men. Which is not to say that decent and friendly relations did not also exist, as they did, but that the contest was deep and enduring and exacerbated when England and France involved the Indians in their wars on this continent.

After independence and throughout our growth as a nation, Indian fighting continued in an ineluctable expansion by the new republic and a slow tragic losing by the native inhabitants, fiercely resistant to the end. Conquest of a continent is not a gentle thing. It took seven years and used up eight commanders in two wars to harry the Seminoles out of Florida, although they never numbered more than a thousand fighters and had no outside aid or source of supply. American forces succeeded only by destruction of crops and villages, inducing starvation, and by seizure of leaders who came under a flag of truce. The difficulties of guerrilla warfare when, as a military historian has written, 'the guerrilla is animated by an intense will to independence', were never more clearly exhibited, and a good look at the Seminole War during our late adventure in Vietnam might have told policy-makers more than the Pentagon's computers. On second thought, perhaps not. Information which does not fit into the policy-maker's preconception or wish, tends to be ignored whether the source is electronic or human.

Conquest of the plains took fifty years of incessant warfare. Eventually, when the Civil War released armed men to the frontier, the struggle was won by the fort, the repeating rifle, starvation, treachery, the railroad, the reservation policy and, ultimately, the extermination of the buffalo which had provided the plains Indian with food, shelter and clothing. The last battle was fought in 1890 – less than one hundred years ago. As a profound and continuous strain in our development as a nation, Indian fighting cannot be overlooked, though it would be hard to say whether it left any imprint still carried by our present population and relevant to the 1980s.

Security for the Continent

Security in America was at first a land problem, but after the French threat from Canada was eliminated in 1763 it shifted to defence of our shores. The need became apparent during the War of Independence, when Britain's command of the seas enabled her to deliver her forces against us. As soon as the young Republic could scrape together some money, we began to build the elements of a navy of six frigates and to fortify the coasts at our principal ports. A navy did not, here or in England, carry the onus of a threat to liberty and early became the acceptable channel of strength, free of the suspicion that attached to an army.

Basically, however, to quote Washington's words from his Farewell Address, our security lay in 'Our detached and distant situation'. This alone, he said, if we remained united, would defy harm from abroad and require our neutrality to be respected. His thinking was rational but events were not. The British, as it turned out, did *not* respect our neutrality, resulting in the War of 1812, as the textbooks tell us. Actually, the belligerent impulse came equally from the American 'War Hawks' of the western territories, who harboured aggressive designs on Canada and prevailed in Congress over the bitter resistance of commercially prospering New England. 1812 was our first war for gain.

Owing to the divided spirit and incompetent land operations, we gained nothing except the humiliation of British raids on our coasts and burning of our capital. Only stiff naval actions on Lake Erie and Lake Champlain prevented major British invasion from Canada, and provided the immortal slogans needed for national pride: 'We have met the enemy and they are ours', and Captain Lawrence's dying command, 'Don't give up the ship; fight her till she sinks'. Never mind that she *was* given up. These fights and Jackson's famous if supererogatory victory at New Orleans, which inflicted 2,000 casualties on the Redcoats to 70 of our own and killed the British commander, Lord Pakenham, the great Wellington's brother-in-law, magnified American self-confidence and obscured the war's lame end in stalemate and *status quo ante*.

Yet Americans felt strengthened as a nation and somehow, in spite of New England almost seceding at the Hartford Convention in 1814, more united and renewed in the national feelings that had dwindled since the Revolution. No less important, the war confirmed, as noted by Albert Gallatin, Secretary of the Treasury, the need of permanent taxes to maintain a military establishment, but sentiment was not with him. Congress very gingerly voted for an army of 10,000, half the size recommended by President Madison, and ordered the Great Lakes armed ship stripped of equipment and laid up.

Parsimony of power, however, in no way limited self-confidence. Within the decade, and without the military means to warrant it, the United States, under President Monroe, announced to the European powers that any attempt by them to 'extend their system . . . to any portion of this hemisphere' would be considered 'as dangerous to our peace and safety'. No less forceful, though less well known, Monroe added a warning to Czar Alexander I of Russia to keep his hands off the Pacific coast, though it was not yet US territory, because 'the American continents [his plural] by the free and independent condition they have assumed and maintained are henceforth not to be considered as subjects for colonization by any European power'.

The exuberance of continental space, of un-limited resources, of a new nation with a new purpose generated the Monroe Doctrine, our first exercise in a world role. For the rest of the century confidence reigned with hardly a thought for military power. We felt confident of our ocean walls, our growing physical, geo-graphical and industrial muscle. Without the firing of a shot, the Louisiana Purchase of 1803 had doubled the area of the Republic by almost a million square miles, stretching from the Gulf of Mexico to the Rocky Mountains. 'Shall we expect some transatlantic military giant to step the Ocean and crush us at a blow?' de-claimed the young Abraham Lincoln in 1838. 'Never! All the armies of Europe, Asia and Africa combined, with all the treasures of the earth (our own excepted) in their military chest, with a Buonaparte for a commander, could not by force take a drink from the Ohio, or make a track on the Blue Ridge in a trial of a hundred years!'

In this superb security, we felt at mid-century the summons of a 'manifest destiny' to fill the continent allotted by Providence to our swelling population. Although the quarrel over Texas had been smoking for ten years, ever since the Alamo, we entered upon the war with Mexico with 4,000 men and twelve field guns. Since militia were enjoined from the foreign service, the combat forces were made up by volunteers on a one-year enlistment, which renewed the old problem of soldiers going home and requiring replacement in the midst of hostilities. Nevertheless, the war with Mexico proved to be popular, successful and lucrative.

The gain from victory, including Texas pre-viously self-annexed, was even greater than the Louisiana Purchase, amounting to over a million square miles and bringing in Cali-fornia. With that acquisition, United States territory reached the Pacific. Destiny pointed westward. Within a few years the naval arm carried Commodore Perry to the opening of Japan, again without benefit of gunfire except in the form of some rather persuasive salutes by the ships' cannon. Whether or not this can be called an employment of military power, the result was a fateful step to the Orient, bringing treaties, trade, and coaling stations for a trans-Pacific steamship service.

Security was not our problem in this robust time except in the form of internal dissension over the problem of slavery. I will not dwell on the Civil War, which is well enough known to allow me to skip to its aftermath. When it was over, energies and industries burst into a vast material rather than geographical growth – a period of railroads, steel, steam, foreign mar-kets, robber barons, and the gilded age. The national vigour of these years impelled us to-ward expansion, and thus we came at the end of the century to the great divide when the old, consciously anti-militarist America gave way to the sadder, harder generality of mankind.

The Quest for Power

By 1890, when the frontier passed from our history, a new exhilaration – the gleam of foreign adventure, of influence and territory beyond our borders – took over the American mind which had formerly believed these things to be malignancies of the old world we had left behind.

Even President Benjamin Harrison felt the stirring when he hinted in his Inaugural Ad-dress in 1889 that American interests were not 'so exclusively American that our entire in-attention to any events that might transpire elsewhere can be taken for granted'. How we might envy that 'entire inattention' today.

An important section of the public known as 'anti-imperialists' strenuously resisted the new trend and found a prominent voice, among others, in Charles William Eliot, President of Harvard, who denounced 'the abandonment of what is charcteristically American'. 'The building of a navy', he sternly said, 'and parti-cularly of battleships is British and French policy. It should never be ours'. But he spoke against the tide.

Momentous changes in history occur when they answer the *zeitgeist*; they formulate and implement something that is struggling for ex-pression. In the 1890s it was power. The prophet of the new credo was Admiral Alfred Thayer Mahan, whose discovery and epic for-mulation of the power that could be exercised through command of the seas, published in 1890 under the title *The Influence of Sea Power in History*, excited not only his country-men but, more dangerously, Great Britain and Germany. One wishes that one could do without Admiral Mahan, who has become a banality in these discussions, but it is impossible because his influence was so enormous and pivotal. A vanished American can be seen in his father, Dennis Hart Mahan, Professor of Military Science at West Point, of whom it was said that he had never seen a battle and never went outdoors without an umbrella.

Admiral Mahan's chief disciple and instrument was Theodore Roosevelt who, guided by him, energized President McKinley to annex Hawaii, who, as Under-Secretary of the Navy, coaled the Asiatic Squadron for action at Manila in advance of the war with Spain, who as President built the battleships – ten in four years – that so outraged President Eliot, who 'took' Panama to connect the oceans so that Mahan's edict, 'Never divide the fleet', could be obeyed, who sent the Atlantic Squadron to rescue a supposed American kidnapped in Morocco, who presided over the Peace Conference held in America to settle the Russo-Japanese War, who, enjoying his world influence, exerted pressure upon the Kaiser at Algeciras, and who despatched the Great White Fleet around the world to impress the nations, especially Japan. By the end of his second term in 1908, the US, with 25 battleships and 10 heavy cruisers in existence or commission, was the third naval power in the world.

In the meantime, we had fought the Spanish-American War, which is of no interest as a war but only as a use of military power for acquisition. Beneath the popular cause in aid of Cuba's insurrection (we aided popular insurrections in those days) was an appetite, as Senator Cullom of Illinois put it candidly, for 'annexing some property; we want all this northern hemisphere'. Volunteers called from the National Guard responded eagerly enough, only to meet an appalling shambles of graft, mismanagement and incompetence in supply and equipment, and of course disease, when our forces reached Cuba. Given the enemy's situation, however, the war was easy to win. Forced to cede her Caribbean possessions, Spain was eliminated from the western hemisphere, and we awoke to find ourselves a colonial power, though there was nothing approaching consensus in the development. We acquired Cuba, Puerto Rico and the Philippines which dismayingly proved antipathetic to our sovereignty. So also, in profound misgiving, were the anti-imperialists, the old believers, whose spokesmen in the Senate came within one vote of defeating the treaty with Spain confirming transfer to the US of the Philippines.

To our extreme embarrassment we now found it necessary to impose our rule by force upon a people fighting for independence, just like a wicked old European power. It should be noted, however, that we gave the Philippines a promise of future independence which has been kept and, after some foot-dragging, eventually relinquished Cuba, too, except for an area retained as a naval base. The War, not so much against Spain as against the Moros in the Philippines, sealed the great divide. It created a bitterness in public opinion, to be revived in the era of Vietnam. As the price of becoming a Pacific power, it raised the spectre of a divided fleet and, in the new naval base at Pearl Harbor in Hawaii, offered a hostage to fate.

The Lure of Isolationism

Thereafter, the American conscience wavered between acquisition and renunciation. Less predatory than Europeans and Japanese, the US took no territory in China, although willing enough to use the privileges of the Treaty Ports established by the British. After the Boxer Rebellion of 1900, we secured the right to maintain an American regiment on Chinese soil while satisfying our conscience by turning back the Boxer indemnity to support Chinese studying abroad.

We now enter the twentieth century, where problems of security and military power would never be simple again. The scandals attending the Spanish-American War could not be shrugged off or forgotten. As Secretary of War, Elihu Root shook up and reorganized the old administrative Bureaux and introduced that organ of modern professionalism, a General Staff. Given the instrument, it had to be used: planning the employment of military power now entered permanently into the American system. The last best hope of being different, of founding a non-militarist nation, had finally succumbed.

There is usually a lag in awareness of change. The American people and their leaders, President Taft and President Wilson, held to the fixed belief that the US could remain immune from the rising tensions in Europe. The Chief of Staff, General Leonard Wood, did not agree but was frustrated in his efforts to prepare an organization able to draft and train a large army for the emergency of major war. When the outbreak came in 1914, Wilson asked his countrymen 'to be neutral in fact as well as name, impartial in thought as well as in action' and, with some exceptions, they were happy to oblige. Neutrality was a premise of our nation stemming from George Washington's Neutrality Proclamation and subsequent Neutrality Act in 1794. In 1914–17 realities overcame the wish, and, five months after re-electing Wilson on the slogan 'He kept us out of war', the US became a belligerent.

Like the Black Death, the terrible suffering and punishment of the Great War did not make man better or leave a purged and better world. Disillusion was general. In the US it turned Americans back again to disgust with Europe's affairs and to isolationism which Wilson's inept handling of the League of Nations issue did nothing to mitigate. Anti-militarism flourished in the 1920s, expressed in the naval limitations of the Washington Conference and in the Kellog-Briand Pact, nobly, if impractically, renouncing war as an instrument of policy. It reached a peak in the 1930s during the appeasement era, combining with an insistent public demand for another Neutrality Act like Washington's to keep us uninvolved.

The new demand was fuelled by the Senate Munitions Investigation Committee, headed by Senator Nye, which in 1934–36 spread before the public 18 months of testimony on the cartels, trade, financing and profits of the arms industry. The result was an outcry for legislation to embargo arms to all belligerents and to take the profits out of war by drastic taxes and income ceilings. Nye was himself genuinely horrified to discover that the Government itself was a partner in the sale of arms, 'the most vicious features', he said, 'of all the disclosures'. What would he say today, when it is the Government's major business?

The Neutrality Act of 1936, enacted by both Houses almost unanimously, provided for mandatory arms embargo on belligerents. President Roosevelt could not obtain discretionary power to distinguish between aggressor and victim because the legislators believed this would involve us in alien quarrels. When Europe at last took up arms against Hitler, isolationist sentiment, as expressed in the 'America First' movement, was such that the draft enacted for one year in 1940 was only renewed in 1941 by a single vote. If not for the Japanese strike at Pearl Harbor and the strange stupidity of Hitler's declaration of war on the US, who knows how long American entry might have waited, and with what consequences?

The Age of Insecurity

The military powers and attitudes developed by America during World War II need no retelling here. Our creation of the atomic bomb marks the beginning of a new military age, and the advent of the intercontinental ballistic missile at the end of the 1950s has ended isolation forever, as a practical possibility if not as an emotion. Every American now knows we can be hit, and killed in millions, if not invaded, and none can cling any longer to a dream of immunity. The question before us is how will the attitudes formed over the last two centuries operate on American performance in the trials ahead?

The first point to consider is who are Americans, and how relevant to them is their adopted country's past experience? We are, as everyone knows, a collection of immigrants from many origins. We are all foreign stock, but how lately? At the time of the Revolution we were largely homogeneous and native-born, with about 80 per cent originating in the United Kingdom. Beginning about 1830, the influx of Irish, Germans and Scandinavians came, followed at the end of the century and continuing into the next by the wave of Italians, Slavs and Jews. Altogether, a net total of 11.5 million foreign-born entered the US population in the first quarter of the twentieth century.

Restrictions and quotas enacted in 1924 cut back the flow drastically. Since World War II, liberalization of the laws has reopened our doors to another eleven million in the last thirty years, with European origin giving way to Hispanics and Asians. At present, the foreign-born plus the first generation of their children represent about 20 per cent of the people in this country. Most are citizens; in 1970 only 2 per cent were not.

Two hundred years ago, Crevecoeur asked his famous question, 'What then is the American, this new man?' He believed such a creature, classless, independent, self-reliant, had indeed been formed by new opportunity and challenge in a new land. In the nineteenth century the favourite image was the melting pot fusing all national identities into a re-shaped American person. Now the demographers and ethnographers are busy rejecting the melting pot and discovering a resurgence of what they call 'ethnicity', which treats the notion of 'assimilation' and 'Americanization' with scorn. They ascribe this phenomenon to a rejection of traditional American values and to cynicism replacing patriotism as a result of Vietnam, Watergate, the problem of the blacks and our other misadventures. The analysis may be valid but not, I think, determining. Those who call policemen 'pigs', who see America as no longer progressive and good but oppressive, immoral, hypocritical, militarist and imperialist are a small minority, but the attitude is not one that policy-makers can entirely disregard.

On the whole, I suspect, the citizens of this country, leaving aside the immigrants of the last ten years, have absorbed the attitudes of the nation from schools, towns, press, surrounding affluence and all the workings of public life without necessarily having experienced them through themselves or their ancestors. You cannot change your grandparents, it has been said, but you can forget them. If ethnicity is on the rise, it is likely to be ephemeral; Americanization is stronger and possibly even deeper.

To determine how these various components of the national experience will affect American attitudes toward war and foreign policy in the next few years is, I think, beyond our powers, if only because attitudes are the creatures of events, and the events that history has in store for us are often surprises. Given the substantial *bloc* of isolationist sentiment that so nearly defeated the draft in 1941, what prediction made at that time would have ventured to foretell the united and purposeful belligerency that was to engage us six months later and carry us through a double war in Europe and Asia? An external event owed to the will and the miscalculation of another people was responsible for that.

In that connection it is worth recalling that three major alterations of the course of history have occurred because of underestimating the American people: by the British in 1776, who assumed that the fractious colonies would never combine in united resistance and that as soldiers the Americans were a 'rabble' who would run in a fight and melt away before the redcoats; by the Germans in 1916 who decided they could risk bringing in America against them by resuming unrestricted submarine warfare because the Americans would not be able to mobilize, train and transport to Europe sufficient troops in time to affect the outcome; and finally by the Japanese delusion of 1941 that the United States would be so panicked by the smashing of the capital ships of her Pacific Fleet that she would be persuaded to sit out further hostilities, leaving Japan a free hand to achieve her empire in Asia.

I cite these as examples of the frailty of pre-judgements, not as a suggestion that Americans will necessarily defy expectations in the same way again. In fact I rather think they may not. We no longer have the fresh spirit of 1776, nor the uncomplicated beliefs of 1917, and only chance can tell if history will offer us again an opponent's delusions equal to those of 1941.

Meanwhile, in the peculiar crisis of the new military age – the age of insecurity – America has already lost one of its three principles, having gone from unpreparedness to over-preparedness, at least mentally, and staggering under the weight of overkill.

War is now a problem of avoidance – or should be. Military studies deal with force-employment, hard-targeting, weapons-technology and with strategies that shift from massive retaliation to flexible response to mutual assured destruction to theatre nuclear deployment, or whatever it is this year – in short to the means and methods of waging war – whereas, if survival is the goal, our study should be how to gain our ends without shooting. If all the skills and energies now invested in weapons and strategies were diverted to working out a reasonable basis for detente and perhaps co-existence, we might in fact find one.

Military power is now greater than ever but less useful; it can destroy but it cannot gain objectives, as Americans have painfully learned in the last generation. Stalemate in Korea, fiasco at the Bay of Pigs, defeat in Vietnam, impotence in Iran and incompetence in the hostage rescue mission is not a record to persuade us of the effectiveness of military power as an instrument of policy. (Except for the bungling of the rescue mission, I do not blame the military for this record so much as policy, but that is another controversy.) Military means could not hold Indochina nor Algeria for France. What has it gained the Soviet Union in Afghanistan? What can it do with regard to oil, the overhanging black threat of the decade ahead? There seems to be no military analyst who believes we could successfully seize and effectively run a Middle Eastern oil field. To the layman, the oil problem seems relatively simple, requiring only a solid front among the importing nations. That takes not guns but common sense, which seems not to be the world's *métier* for the present. 'Where wisdom is called for', said Herodotus well over two thousand years ago, 'force is of little use'.

Can it be that military power is verging on the obsolete, and that all the discussion rising around us recently of nuclear war as feasible is a last gasp of war professionals who conceive of no other option? I am well aware that the problem is seen as a confrontation between two hostile super-powers, but I am not prepared to believe that security lies in an endless race for superiority that can never be either reliable or lasting.

Uncertain Popular Support
Security does not depend upon arsenals but upon political and economic strength, on trade, alliances, friends and enemies, balance of power and, above all, on the internal health of the nation. Is it security for America to have technical marvels of weaponry in the hands of armed forces drawn from High School dropouts and functional illiterates? Or to have the automobile industry, once king of American enterprise, managed by dimwits? Is it security to have a decrepit educational system, drug addicts in grammar schools, arson in the cities, a frustrated black underclass which feels it has no stake in our society? Is it security to have half the population so alienated from its government that it does not bother to vote?

Security in the end depends on the will of the people to fight in defence of their institutions, and that depends on the degree to which they value them.

While this may seem far removed from targets and tactics, strategists must take into account, I believe, as regards the United States' role in the 1980s, the public and its perceptions. One should not forget the Mormon's resistance to MX deployment in Utah and Nevada. While they cannot be accused of being soft on Communism, the Mormons have no desire to be a primary target, and I think that this sentiment may be extrapolated. Americans for the first time feel for their safety. This is a new element on a general scale in our history, and we cannot be sure of its effect. At the same time, Americans want to feel strong again after the frustrations and humiliations of recent years, and for that reason may be ready, as the Reagan Administration assumes, to support increased military spending. Although indications point that way, a swing could occur. 'No nukes' sentiment seems to be rising and making itself heard from many parts of the country, as it definitely is abroad.

As regards issues of power in this disturbed time, the public, a not very rational quantity, is hard to predict. Americans are susceptible to scare propaganda and respond easily to the 'red menace', but, while they fear the spread of Communism, they fear the bombs more; that is to say, they do not want to be obliterated. Whether this will translate itself into pressure for common sense in foreign policy is an open question.

A second factor in the public attitude is disbelief. Given lies and cover-ups and various shenanigans at all levels in recent years from the White House to the press, Americans are now less inclined to accept official gospel on faith. Floating El Salvador as a red menace to our security has had all the success of an iron balloon. Reports and figures on Soviet superiority by pressure groups and vested interests and lobbies of one kind or another merely serve to confuse. We are told one day that the Soviets have 1,500 naval units to our 700 or some such ratio, and on the next, that this may be true, in the words of a Brookings analyst, 'if you count everything you can float in your bathtub', and that in fact the ratio is the reverse if judged by tonnage. We get the same kind of contradictions on warheads and missiles and fighter-plane capabilities and target-accuracy and tanks and every other kind of measurement. Since none of it is remotely comprehensible to the layman, he believes neither pro nor con and will respond, I suspect, like the Mormons, to his nearest interests.

One thing that can still be counted on is resistance to the Draft. Personally, I think this is regrettable. I believe a citizen's army with *no* preferential deferments is not only the only just system but ultimately the only sound defence, and re-enactment of the Draft the only way we will be taken seriously by the antagonist and – if we believe national defence is so urgent – by ourselves. Fearing political disaster, Washington will not put a toe in that water, preferring to pour our resources into a mindless proliferation of and dependence on materiel. No doubt by this means we can even the balance and probably draw ahead for a few weeks, but that will not have advanced us a single step towards achieving a *modus vivendi* – a way of living, not dying – for the 1980s.

A final factor is speculative. I think Americans would like to feel moral again, which is not to say that morality has always characterized our actions in the past, but the image generally prevailed. Doubt of our virtue has succeeded in the last fifteen years, which may lead to some resistance to the use of military power for purposes other than self-defence. That, too, is an open question.

I cannot foretell what effect these public attitudes may have; they are not susceptible to being run through a computer. My impression is that armaments and their combat potential in the nuclear age have become so complex and dangerous, and relations of states so uncertain, that the war professionals and policy-makers do not really know *what* to do. It may be left to the public, that frail reed, to prevent them, as Lloyd George said of the nations in 1914, from 'backing their machine over the precipice'. I would not count on that either.

Congress and the Making of US Security Policies

WILLIAM BADER

God help the American People if Congress starts legislating military strategy
Senator Richard Russell

'Last night we did the dirty deed. We assassinated liberty under the pretext of aiding a belligerent in the war'. Thus was the crusty and embittered 'High priest of isolationism', Senator Hiram Johnson's welcome of the passage of H.R. 1776, the 'Lend-Lease' Bill which vested the President with sweeping powers to make or procure *any defense article for the government of any country whose defense the President deems vital to the defense of the United States* and to transfer any such article to any such government. The bruising Congressional battle of February and March 1941 which brought forth the Lend-Lease package was more rationally and certainly prophetically described by Senator Arthur Vandenberg:

Unfortunately our national course is rather definitely established by the passage of H.R. 1776 and from now on we shall be very much at the mercy of unfolding events. Of course these events can be tremendously affected by the decision of the President under broad discretionary powers which are now vested in the White House. But Congress itself will have very little more to say about these decisions . . . in a word, we now find ourselves in the precarious position of trying to stop ourselves half-way down Niagara Falls.

How little or how much Congress has to say about 'these decisions' is the centre-piece of a long-standing dispute between the Executive Branch and the Congress as to who shall be involved in important national security decisions, when they should be involved, and how. With all due deference to the special genius of the framers of the Constitution, Madison and his colleagues created not 'an effective check to the Dog of War by transferring the power of letting him loose from . . . those who are to spend to those who are to pay', but an open invitation to the Executive Branch and the Congress to struggle for primacy in the formulation of foreign and national security policy.

The controversy is as old as the Constitution. From the Versailles Treaty to the Panama Canal, from Neutrality Legislation to the 'War Powers Resolution', Congress has specifically asserted its prerogatives and fought Executive power in the national security area. But, for all the moments of resistance, there were long periods of unfettered willingness to go along with presidential initiatives in the international security areas. In the contemporary period, this view prevailed from the late 1940s until the middle of the 1960s and was strongly marked by the 1950 commitment of American forces to the Korean War without congressional authority and the lightly given blank cheque of the South-east Asia Resolution of 1964.

The dramatic change in congressional attitude from acquiescence to agitation, from faith to scepticism that began in the early 1960s would take full flight in the years 1968 to 1978 – during a 'Congressional Spring' – a brief and fragile post-war American experiment in checking the powers and prerogatives of the President and fundamentally questioning the role of American power in the world.

The reasons for this change in atmosphere include: the frustration and bitterness of the Vietnam war; the weakening if not the collapse of the notion of a unified Communist challenge, which shattered the need to keep all controversy over national security policy behind closed doors; and the emergence of a simple truth that when Congress began to look at its collective face in the mirror it finally decided it really was not doing its job and should re-define its role.

There are three dominant and interrelated themes that condition and guide the actions of those Congressmen and Senators who have expressed dissatisfaction with Congress' role in the making of American national security policy. The first is historically recurrent concern over the erosion of legislature authority and the accompanying growth of the Executive Branch. Second, there is the burgeoning congressional disposition to bring the military budget under the same painful scrutiny that has been applied to the budgets of civilian agencies. Third, the temptation and tendency of Congress – most recently and dramatically illustrated by the Senate Armed Services Committee – to use the authorization process to exercise an increasing amount of Congressional influence over formulation and execution of national security policy. This Paper, while not ignoring the historic or sometimes near historical clamour over constitutional prerogatives, will concentrate on the last two themes – the growing congressional disposition to scrutinize and even shape the military budget through the authorization process – and the increasing willingness of congressional committees, through a combination of the authorization process and hearings, to bring Senator Russell's uncomfortable fantasy to reality: Congress legislating military strategy.

The congressional reaction to the assault on prerogatives that was seen during the 1950s is certainly an oft-told story. The 'Congressional Spring' referred to here was a period of political passion, and in its unfolding left a durable – possibly irreversible – legislative legacy. The thesis of this Paper is that this legacy, when combined with changes in congressional committee structure and technique, will come to frustrate the new President as he attempts to control and drive American foreign and national defence policies in the manner that he has done so successfully in the economic sphere. To this point in his Administration – the early summer of 1981 – President Reagan has yet to be seriously challenged from the Congress in the management of foreign and national defence policy. What will be argued here is that when and if that challenge comes, the Congress is well equipped with both an array of legislative restraints and committee skills and techniques to be able to confront him in a far more effective way than we have seen in the domestic sector.

From 'Congressional Spring' to 'Sorcerer's Apprentice'

Whether in the late 1960s or in today's world, Congress can affect foreign and national security policy in three basic ways: as cheerleader for executive initiatives as was the case from 1959 until 1965 when the 'cheer' was usually a stirring joint or concurrent resolution giving Presidential blank cheques from Lebanon to the Gulf of Tonkin; as educator and crucible for change as was Senator Fulbright's approach during the Vietnam period; or thirdly (especially since Vietnam) by legislative intervention, incentives, impediments, or barriers that in their accumulation tend not only to 'seek out waste and corruption' but to condition if not to shape the course of American national security policy.

From roughly 1969 to the Russian invasion of Afghanistan, the Congress indulged in a fitful, often incoherent, but cumulatively impressive effort employing legislative restriction and restraint to define a more assertive role for Congress in shaping national security policy. Consider the record from 1970 to 1979 – and the list is selective:

- The Cooper–Church Amendment: 'None of the funds appropriated by this Act shall be used to finance the introduction of American ground combat troops into Laos or Thailand';
- 'War Powers Resolution': to 'ensure that the *collective judgment* (emphasis added) of both the Congress and the President will apply to the introduction of the United States Armed Forces into hostilities, or into situations where imminent involvement in hostilities is clearly indicated by the circumstances, and to the continued use of such forces in hostilities or in such situations';
- The Jackson Amendment to the resolution of approval of the SALT II Interim Agreement instructing the Executive Branch not to conclude a new strategic arms agreement which did not provide for numerical equality;
- Section 116 and 502B of the Foreign Assis-

15

tance Act which calls for suspension of aid if there is a 'consistent pattern of gross violations of internationally recognized human rights';

– The amendment of Senator Dick Clark, then chairman of the Foreign Relations Commitee's African Subcommittee, to the International Security Assistance and Arms Export Control Act of 1976 which in effect banned covert assistance to anti-Marxist guerrillas in Angola;

– Section 669 of the Foreign Assistance Act (The Symington Amendment) cuts off aid to a country determined to be on the threshold of building or acquiring nuclear weapons. The Glenn Amendment to the same Act is also important. When the Administration first wanted to give economic/military assistance to Pakistan after the Afghanistan invasion, it was the Symington Amendment which caused the most problems because of the extremely stringent provisions for presidential waiver;

– The Hughes–Ryan Amendment (Section 662) to the Foreign Assistance Act which brought notification and vague Congressional concurrence to covert actions for the first time;

– The Congressional prerogative under Section 36(b) of the Arms Export Control Act of 1976 to disapprove – i.e. block – by concurrent resolution *or threat* of such a resolution an arms sale or transfer of nuclear materials. Examples are: the F-15 sale to Saudi Arabia and the follow-on Administration hopes for an enhancement package; and, most recently, AWACS for Saudi Arabia;

– Section 130 of the 1978 Nuclear Proliferation Act which provided the basis for the nearly successful effort to block the transfer of nuclear fuel to the Indian reactor at Tarapur;

– The Jackson–Vanik Amendment to the Trade Act of 1974 which linked most favoured nation (MFN) treatment and export credits to Soviet emigration;

– The Jackson–Nunn Amendment requiring European allies to offset US balance of payment deficits or face American troop withdrawal;

– The embargo of arms transfers to Turkey in order to force concessions on Cyprus.

The key differences in these Congressional actions, as contrasted with earlier ones, is the growing extent to which Congress seeks to prescribe the *details* of policy and of implementation, and increasingly to retain for itself the power to block or veto Executive Branch actions not in conformity with congressional interpretation of policy.

As the Panama Canal Treaty debate stimulated the Senate to write its own handbook on 'creative' ratification (and as practised with respect to SALT II, raised serious questions whether any Administration can push through the Senate an important controversial national security treaty), so did the 1970s give the Congress a virtually unlimited field of legislative fire that has brought to the White House grounds and its new tenant an impressive array of legislative land mines and barbed wire – much of which he has yet to discover.

It can certainly be argued – or profoundly hoped for – that this fabric of restraints, restrictions and reports can be torn apart. Laws are made to be repealed or modified beyond the original architect's recognition.

There is as yet no important indication that the Republican/'conservative'-controlled Senate is in the mood to undo the handiwork of those departed – however unlamented by contemporary standards – Fulbrights, Gores, Symingtons, Coopers, Javitses and Mansfields.

Review of Military Spending Policy
A far less dramatic result of the 'Congressional Spring' of the 1970s was the demand (and emergence of the procedural machinery to translate that demand into influence) for greater legislative impact upon government policies and expenditures in the field of defence.

The 'text' is ambiguous enough: the Constitution gives Congress no guidance in choosing the forms of control over military spending. Article I, Section 8 simply confers upon Congress the responsibility to 'raise and support armies . . . to provide and maintain a navy . . .' and 'to make rules for government and regulations of the land and naval forces'.

Although Congress first delineated its specific responsibility for overseeing the military budget with the Legislative Reorganization Act of 1946, the mandate of the standing

16

committees was simply to 'exercise *continuous watchfulness* of the execution (of any laws) by the administrative agencies . . .' – and each standing committee was given the magnificent total of 4 professional and 6 clerical staff to assist in this 'continuous watchfulness'. In addition – and probably to the occasional relief of the 'staffers' of the period from 1946 to 1961 – most spending for military personnel and operations was permanently authorized, or in the comfortable statutory condition of 'uncontrollable'. During these years, the process created its own stereotypes which – and rightly so – found their way into the literature of defence policy: the House Appropriations Committee, as the 'defender of the public purse'; the Senate, as the wise and judicial board of appeal. Preoccupied with waste and 'logrolling', self-deprived of coherent procedures to deal with the unco-ordinated decisions and unrelated actions of several committees in each House, the Congress lacked the authority and political capacity to bring together the diverse and often conflicting interests involved in the making of defence policy.

This is not to say that the 'military oversight' role was not well and usefully played during the 1950s and early 1960s. The Preparedness Investigating Subcommittee of the Senate Armed Services Committee, the Subcommittee on National Security and International Operations of the Senate Governmental Affairs Committee, the Subcommittee on Military Applications of the Joint Committee on Atomic Energy, and the Subcommittee for Special Investigations of the House all held impressive hearings on government contracting, waste, overruns and corruption – from the TFX (F-111) fighter-bomber, to *Atlas* ICBM, *Nike* and *Bomarc/Nike Hercules* surface-to-air missile contracts, and to close ties between military contracting firms and the Pentagon. But today's Congress has the Government Accounting Office (GAO) with its some 5,000 employees; and a very different appetite – to *manage*, not to 'oversee'.

Through the progressive imposition of annual authorizations and the burgeoning of congressional staffs armed with powerful tools of access to information unheard of twenty years ago, the Congress – particularly the Senate Armed Services Committee – has laid the organizational and procedural groundwork over the decade of the 1970s not only to influence but to determine ('direct') what new major weapons systems the United States will have at its command in the years to come, and further, to venture into substantive policy and planning.

In the arena of national defence there was a brilliant gloss during the 'Congressional Spring' – and a hard, durable reality. The gloss was the vainglorious effort of Senate liberals to 'reform' defence policy, discipline the defence budget, and eliminate weapon systems thought inimical to arms-control negotiations. As Senator Culver, a former Marine, put it in sounding the battle cry of the mid-1970s: 'nothing causes more ambiguity in foreign policy than a defense structure that is artificially high, redundant, or unnecessarily provocative'.

The line of attack was not directed at weaving a fabric of legal restraints and procedural prohibitions, as was the case in foreign policy arenas, but was a direct assault on aggregate defence spending and specific systems. The defence amendments called for aggregate cuts in defence spending – 3, 5, or 10% of a specific number of billions of dollars. The systems under attack included the likes of ABM, the B-1 bomber, and nuclear-powered aircraft carriers.

The hard, durable reality is that authorizing committees in the 1970s learned the system of how to shape and mould the Defense Budget. The paradox was that for the majority of that decade, buffeted by conflicting public signals on whether more or less defence was mandated, the Congress chose or acquiesced in 'less', including those vintage southern Democrats – such as Senator John Stennis – whose instinct was to look for presidential leadership and guidance on defence policy.

Therefore, while the specific system deletions and aggregate cuts proposed by the Senate liberals usually failed, the fact remains that in every fiscal year in the 1970s, the Senate voted to cut the defence budget offered by the President. By way of illustration, and using the Procurement and RDT&E (Research, Development, Testing and Evaluation) Titles in the defence budget, some 67% of the Senate and House Armed Services Committee actions by budget title in the 1960s were either in conformity with the Executive request or represented an increase in that request; while in the 1970s there was a dramatic change – only 24% of requests were agreed to or increased. Moreover, with respect to the longstanding contention that Congressional changes are in the 'marginal' category (less than 5%) there has also been a major change: for example, reductions of greater than 5% account for some 25% of total Procurement and RDT&E category changes for the period 1960 to 1969 – and that climbs to 70% for the period 1970 to 1980. These are only illustrations; the evidence is rich that the Congress in the 1970s, through the authorizing committees, learned to bring attention to the military budget in a way that was intense, meaningful and comprehensive.[1] And when 'less' became 'more' – much more – beginning in 1979, the techniques and intensity would remain.

The force behind this Congressional surge that outlasted the 'Congressional Spring', particularly in the Senate Armed Services Committee, derives from a number of factors. Military budgets are divided into several authorization titles. The four most critical are: procurement; RDT & E operations and maintenance (O&M); and personnel. Prior to 1961, there was no annual authorization of any part of the defence budget. Gradually, and almost unnoticed, the two Armed Services Committees began to reach for the authorizing power.

This was seen first in the 'procurement' budget beginning in FY 1962 – representing some 27% of defence expenditures. Then, RDT&E was added in 1968 with another 10%. This addition, when coupled with procurement, goes right to the heart of national defence policy with the combined impact on present and future weapons systems. In FY 1972, manpower was also added – another 30%. With the addition of O & M in the FY 1982 budget, the Armed Services authorizing committees now manage 98% of the defence budget.

Much has been made of the expanded, in fact exploding, size of Congresional staff, now over 20,000, as opposed to 500 in 1947. But staff that is technically expert, politically sure-footed, and cognizant that the one true measure of success on Capitol Hill is the ability to draw up legislation that will win on the floor, is essential to the analysis and translation of multi-billion dollar defence requests into enacted legislation. This growing role and importance of Staff also raises Congressional expertise and confidence in dealing with the *details* of policy and implementation – already cited as a key difference between the Congressional actions of 1968–1975 and those of an earlier period.

The intensity of inquiry and inquest has matched the use of staff. As the Department of Defense sees it from the vantage point of its Congressional liaison staff of 227:

	1964	1979	% of Increase
Witnesses who appeared	630	2,268	260%
Hours they testified	650	1,459	124%
Pages of justification	7,189	17,457	143%

As for the Committees, the increase in witnesses, pages of testimony, and the volume of reports has been equally staggering. As an example, the Senate Armed Services Committee hearing on military procurement involved 27 witnesses and 603 pages of testimony in 1961 and 409 witnesses and 5,921 pages of testimony in 1973.

In addition, witness the astonishing access of the authorizing committees to information and documentation that was long thought to be privileged and proprietary. It is even fair to say that certain individuals in Congress are better informed, have deeper access to documentation and personalities, and possess a more impressive array of security clearances than any counterpart in the Administration.

The practical effect of this development has been to reinforce and strengthen the Congress' *ability* to reach even more deeply into the military procurement authorization legislation and to shape critical defence policy decisions. Over the past few years we have seen the Congressional impact on a number of specific systems: *Phalanx* naval defence system, *Cheyenne* attack helicopter, ELF (extreme low frequency communication system), the Main Battle Tank (MBT), and the much publicized *Condor* (a navy-developed glide bomb), to cite a few examples.

The recent legislative cycle for the 1982 defence authorization bill shows the same attention to procurement detail:

- Both Committees rejected the $1 billion requested for a 10th *Trident* submarine;
- Both added more than $300 million to build a new amphibious landing ship;
- The House terminated the NAVSTAR Global Positioning System (GPS);
- The Senate denied and the House panel approved the request for $364 million to reactivate the carrier *Oriskany*.

These changes were certainly modest in scope and unacrimonious in the 'doing' when compared with both panels' deep-seated disagreements with President Carter's defence budgets; and, indeed, both Senate and House Committees warmly embraced President Reagan's approach of bringing the country the largest defence authorization bill in history. But there was one small procedural straw in the authorization wind that may be a portent of a Congress that will use its enhanced skills and organization to imprint its mark on military planning and strategy.

The House Committee on Armed Services recommended, and the House sustained in legislation, the following recommendations:

The committee recommends specific authorization of the $1.942 billion requested for the Long Range Combat Aircraft for procurement of the B-1 bomber, as well as the $302 million requested for research and development for the Long Range Combat Aircraft. Concurrent with the full-scale B-1 development, the Secretary of Defense is directed to continue ongoing research and development of an advanced technology bomber. The committee recommendation provides a mechanism for later transferring B-1 monies to the advanced technology bomber, if the President so recommends and the Congress concurs within a 60–day period.

The requirement that funds be spent only on a B-1 version unless the President recommends another advanced technology bomber that must also be agreed to by concurrent resolution

within 60 days might have died in the House–Senate Conferences, but the intention of shaping the role and mission of US strategic forces was clear enough. When Senator Tower moves in 1982 beyond shaping the overall size of the defence budget to addressing the character of the threat to national security when making budget decisions, as this author believes he will, then the line between fashioning a more rational and cost-effective allocation of defence resources on the one hand, and military planning and strategy on the other, will be blurred, perhaps irreversibly.

Prospects
The national stakes are enormous as Congress' authorizing Committees move not only to examine and shape the largest defence budget in the history of this country but, as argued here, to venture into substantive policy and planning. As it is now designed, the Department of Defense authorization bill for FY 1982 is the first year of a $1.5 trillion five-year programme, in which we are likely to see defence spending go from $146 billion in 1980 to $374 billion in FY 1986. Over these five years the portion of the Federal budget assigned to national defence will grow from 23 to 33%.

Against this challenge, and in the face of a peculiarly volatile political climate where personal eccentricity often defies political and party discipline, the first question is whether the authorizing Committees will succeed in the critical test of drawing up of legislation that will win on the floor. Second, will the defence authorizing Committees be able and willing to start 'legislating military strategy', as this Paper argues the Senate Armed Services Committee is already organized and perhaps driven to do as a result of costs of weapons and their consequences for foreign policy?

And, finally, given the almost total blurring of defence and foreign policies in today's international 'back alleys', will the legislative legacies of the 'Congressional Spring' not only slow President Reagan's efforts to assert US power abroad but bring a strong element of unpredictability into America's security relations with the rest of the world?

With a 9–8 Republican committee majority in the Senate of the 97th Congress, a reorganized subcommittee structure along 'functional lines', total command of the appropriation titles, and a national consensus for 'more ' spending, Senator Tower is strongly positioned to dominate both the Senate and the Conference proceedings. He was so successful during the 1981 debate in 'rolling' the competition that Defense Appropriations Subcommittee Chairman Ted Stevens accused Senator Tower of reducing the Appropriations Panel to a rubber stamp for the Armed Services Committee: 'If it keeps up, I am going to suggest that the Armed Services Committee go to conference with the House Appropriations Committee on defence'.

On the question of 'legislating military strategy', there is a major challenge before the Senate Armed Services Committee that will caution the Committee if it decides to move (as I believe it will): the emergence in the Senate of a 'new right' in the area of military planning and strategy.

With respect to the conservative tide, if Senator Tower is not inclined through his Committee to examine the character of the external threat and explore theories of how to handle nuclear weapons, he may be forced to do so by the energetic and aggressive Western Conservatives who cater to the thesis that strategic nuclear defence systems shall be given greater emphasis. A veritable 'no-name' coalition of conservative Senators – Harrison 'Jack' Schmitt (R-NM), Malcolm Wallop (R-WY), Pete V. Domenici (R-NM) among the most prominent – are pushing hard for space laser programmes, which include satellite-based anti-missile systems, as well as for ABM defences for land-based MX ICBM. Clearly the cumulative effect of such measures, if eventually approved, would radically change US strategic policy which now presumes the overwhelming dominance of the strategic offence.

In the years past, when a Schmitt or Wallop Amendment was brought to Senate floor, the Cloak Room door would open almost majestically and the towering figure of Senator Russell would emerge to still the troubled parliamentary waters, and to chide any deviant who indulged in 'strategic' chatter. Those days are gone as Committee skills, access and organization have paradoxically come into conflict with a Congressional individualism that sometimes borders on the eccentric. Senator John Tower can speak with an authority beyond that of all his predecessors but he will clearly have difficulty controlling the Senate's new individualism.

As for the legislative legacies of the 'Congressional Spring', removal or major modification of those restraints *appears* to be a major objective of the Reagan Administration. Once the International Security and Development Cooperative Act of 1981 comes to the floor, we will have a better sense of whether the Administration will permit or encourage amendments designed to begin the dismantling of the legislative restrictions of the 1970s. Perhaps in anticipation of such a challenge, the Foreign Relations Committee has artfully tailored the 'form' of this year's bill without seriously touching the principle – i.e. granting a national security waiver on prohibitions to Pakistan; lifting the prohibitions on assistance to Argentina; and repealing, under stringent conditions, the restrictions on covert operations to Angola.

Whatever the nature of the challenge, it appears unlikely that the fabric of legislative restraints of the 1970s will be torn. If this proves to be the case, the 'Congressional Spring' will provide an enduring legacy; and that legacy will continually restrain (and frustrate) the new President as he attempts to guide American foreign policy.

Another legacy of the 'Congressional Spring' may prove to be an erosion of confidence among friends and adversaries that the United States will meet commitments made by the President on behalf of the country. Senator Jacob Javits used to say that great nations do not bluff; great nations also do not enter into agreements to deliver nuclear fuel to Indian reactors, or deliver arms to Egypt, Turkey, or Saudi Arabia, only to have these commitments snatched away at the last hour by a hostile Congress. At issue is America's predictability – and reliability – as a great power.

In every test case thus far of a threatened Congressional 'veto' of a specific national security decision, the President – often with enormous effort and no little cost – has beaten back Congressional interference, as we have seen most recently in the case of AWACS for Saudi Arabia. Nevertheless, the means and the machinery for asserting such 'vetoes' remain in place, and will come repeatedly to distract the

President and bring into question the reliability of the United States.

Time and experience will tell whether this new Congressional engagement is truly 'irreversible' or simply the latest swing in the long-standing rivalry between the President and the Congress for predominance in defence and national security policy. The marriage of Congressional control of military spending with defence policy and planning is probably unavoidable. Unlike early periods in American history, the *character* of weaponry, especially but not solely nuclear, has a direct impact on foreign policy and the priorities the nation sets for itself. The immense costs of weapons, the inability to have everything, and the persistence of the present international situation impose the need for choices and for priorities. Only when Congress can relate the choices and priorities to an understood policy can it make decisions rationally. The legislative legacies and the organizational and procedural skills acquired in the 1970s are now firmly in place. We will see if the wisdom will be there as the Congress moves to assert these powers and use these skills.

NOTES

[1] See Robert L. Bledsoe and Roger Handbert, 'Changing Times: Congress and Defense' in *Armed Forces and Society*, Vol. 6, Spring 1980, pp. 415–429; R. L. Bledsoe, 'Congress and Defense: The Role of the House and Senate Armed Services Committee', presented at the Annual Meeting of the Southwest Political Science Association, Dallas, Texas, March 1981; see also Edward J. Laurance, 'The Changing Role of Congress in Defense Policy-Making', *Journal of Conflict Resolution*, Vol. 20, No.2, June 1976.

Domestic Factors in US Defense Policy

PHILIP ODEEN

Most of us who are concerned about defence and security issues focus our attention on questions of strategy, force requirements, cost-effectiveness, and comparative US/Soviet capabilities. We often ignore the powerful economic and political factors that play important and often dominant roles in decisions on security policy, the size of the defence budget, and the nature of major programmes. This Paper examines these factors and suggests a number of issues that US defence decision-makers should consider in formulating long-term plans.

The Paper discusses five areas that may influence the shape of our defence and security effort over the next five years. They are:

- Macro-economic considerations (i.e., the possible effects of defence spending on GNP growth and inflation);
- Federal budget and fiscal policies and their implications for defence spending;
- Internal Defense Budget issues that complicate Administration efforts to live within its fiscal guidelines;
- Underlying public opinion trends that affect defence and foreign policy;
- The shift in population and its effect on voting patterns and thus on Congressional support for activist security policies and strong military forces.

The Economy
The share of the economy currently devoted to national defence is near the post-World War II low. During FY 81, about 5.5% of the GNP will be devoted to the Defense Budget. This burden is well below the level of the 1950s and 1960s when it ranged from 7% to 10%. The post-war peak of 13% was reached during the Korean War, and during the US involvement in Vietnam it approached 10%.

The ambitious programme proposed by the Reagan Administration will raise the level to 6.5–7% of the GNP by the mid-1980s, only 1% or 1.5% above the current level. Even if the President's goals for economic growth are not achieved, the percentage is unlikely to exceed 7.5%. Thus the overall impact of the Defense Budget on the economy will continue to be far less than during most years since World War II.

Moreover the planned increase from 5.5% to 6.5% or 7% over four or five years is far from unprecedented in magnitude. For example:

- During the Korean Conflict, the percentage increased from 5% to 13% in three years;
- During the Vietnam War, it increased from 7% to 9.5% over a similar time span (and was accomplished without broad public support for the war).

From a strictly economic viewpoint, therefore, it is difficult to argue that the US economy cannot sustain such an increase. This 1.5% increase over three years would absorb only about one-eighth of the increase in GNP over that period, and, given the planned cutback in non-defence programmes, total Federal programmes will actually constitute a smaller share of the economy in 1984 than they do today.

While the economic ramifications of this growth of defence spending may be minor, the politics may not be benign. The Defense Budget increases will come at the expense of other Federal programmes having large and powerful constituencies. Moreover, cuts will almost certainly have to be made in the so-called 'safety net' programmes, which make the potential political problems even more severe. These issues are discussed in more detail later.

Some economists have raised a different issue. They claim that because of the nature of defence spending and the size of the increase, the results will be more inflation and larger federal deficits. These charges have received wide attention in the press.[1] Commentators often cite as evidence the US experience during the Vietnam conflict.

Most economists, however, view these forecasts, and in particular the Vietnam analogy, with considerable scepticism.[2] Macroeconomic conditions are almost certainly going to be different during the 1980s. In addition to a slower growth of defence spending, already noted above, other important factors will differ:

- The economy was essentially at full employment in 1965 as the Vietnam war began. In contrast, there is considerable slack today and the same is true of productive capacity in most sectors.
- Real Federal spending increased at about 10% a year in the late 1960s as the 'New Society' came into being: this contrasts with an estimated 1% a year for the next few years. In short, the fiscal stimulus will be negligible.
- Monetary growth was especially rapid during the late 1960s (exceeding the rate of inflation). The opposite is likely to be the case for the next few years, given President Reagan's and the Federal Reserve's policies.

The net result of these factors is that defence spending is unlikely to be a significant factor in the inflationary picture; other considerations will dominate.

The Federal Budget and Fiscal Policy
The implications for the Defense Budget of the Federal Government's budget outlook are less clear and probably more ominous than economic circumstances. President Reagan is committed to a balanced budget by 1984 (an election year). Although there is a broad support for greater defence spending, Congressional sentiment for reaching a balanced budget by the mid-1980s is also strong. Thus the Department of Defense (DOD) is almost certainly going to have to operate within the limits of a fiscal policy intended to reduce deficits each year and achieve a balanced budget for FY 84.

The currently planned expansion of defence spending is starting at a time when Federal deficits are at near record levels (an estimated $55–60 billion in FY 81). In the past, when defence spending increases began, budgets were in balance; moreover, inflation was minimal and the economy was experiencing strong growth, which generated added tax revenue. None of these conditions exists today.

An equally important difference is that taxes were well below current levels as a percentage of GNP and modest tax increases were a realistic prospect. Today, tax cuts are universally expected. Indeed, Congress passed a record tax cut during 1981 that will reduce taxes each year for three years and, starting in 1985, index taxes to offset inflation. As a result, the only increases in Federal revenues that will be available to fund growing defence programmes will result from the overall growth of the economy. (Historically, about 20% of the GNP has flowed to Federal Government in the form of taxes. Thus, if the GNP grows by 5% in a year, about 1% will be available to support Federal programmes).

The Reagan Administration has taken on an unusually difficult fiscal policy challenge. Taxes have been cut sharply, defence spending has increased, non-defence programmes have been slashed, and further cuts are promised. The President has sketched a broad plan to accomplish his objectives and in a few months has made considerable progress:

- The tax reduction plan is in place, albeit modified and somewhat changed from his original proposal;
- The FY 81 and FY 82 Defense Budgets have been increased by 4% and 11% respectively, and future planning is based on an assumption of 7% real growth in funds;
- Non-defence programmes have been pruned severely in many cases, yielding outlay savings of $46 billion in FY 82 (roughly 9% of total non-defence spending);

Nonetheless, many uncertainties remain. If a balanced budget is to be reached in FY 84, four things must occur: the defence programme must be held to the levels projected by the President; the economy must grow rapidly in order to generate higher revenue despite lower tax rates; Congress must approve a number of revenue-producing tax reforms; and further deep cuts in non-defence spending must be identified and accepted by a less-than-enthusiastic Congress.

None of these four key steps is certain. But the latter action, further non-defence budget reductions, is likely to be most difficult. In fact, as this Paper was being written, the $25 billion in FY 84 budget cuts proposed by the President in September 1981 was very much in doubt. And a substantial number of yet 'unidentified' cuts remain to be found in Reagan's fiscal planning, and sold to a sceptical Congress. According to the Administration's September 1981 projections, the additional cuts must total $23 billion by FY 84, as Table 1 shows.

Table 1: Reagan Fiscal Programme
($ billion)

	FY 81	FY 82	FY 83	FY 84
Projected Revenue	606	666	714	771
Defence Outlays	160	186	220	248
Non-Defence Outlays	503	523	529	546
Total Outlays	**663**	**709**	**749**	**794**
Deficit or				
Required Cuts	(57)	(43)	(54)	(23)

Cutting $23 billion in FY 84 from a non-defence spending total of $546 billion (an 8% cut) may seem achievable, but as Table 2 shows, the most likely targets for reductions are the large and politically potent transfer payment programmes (social security, unemployment benefits, food stamps, Medicare, etc.)

Table 2: Projected FY 84 Non-Defence Spending
($ billion)

Interest Debt	84
Transfers to Individuals	366
State/Local Grants	43
All Other	53
Total	**546**

Since interest payments are unavoidable, the $23 billion reduction must be made in the remaining $460 billion. The 'All Other' category (i.e., energy, agriculture, environment, and civil service salaries) as well as grants to state and local agencies have already been cut sharply and more cuts will be difficult. Moreover, even a further reduction of 20% in these areas would not generate the needed savings. Thus, the Administration will have little choice but

to cut transfer payments, including social security, if it continues its planned defence build-up.

Failure to achieve the non-defence savings, however, is only one of the risks for the planned defence build-up. Slower-than-expected economic growth would generate less revenue and would increase spending for programmes such as unemployment compensation above projected levels. Furthermore, if interest rates continue to run at rates well above the rates forecast earlier this year, the projected interest costs for FY 84 would climb higher yet and thereby reduce the funds available for defence.

The Reagan economic forecast is for real growth at about 4.5% a year for FY 82 to FY 84. Most of the standard econometric models project somewhat lower growth rates in the 3.5% to 3.7% range. A mere percentage point difference in President Reagan's figure (still yielding a respectable 3.5% growth rate) would reduce the GNP by $95 billion in FY 84 and Federal revenues by nearly $20 billion. Plainly, economic performance is a critical variable in the Reagan Administration's fiscal policy. The revenue shortfall could well be greater if Congress refuses to approve the various revenue-raising measures proposed by the President in September 1981.

Moreover, the Administration projects FY 84 interest spending at $68 billion, close to projected expenditures for this year even though the debt will be at least $100 billion higher by 1984. If interest rates persist at higher than forecast rates into FY 82 – which is virtually certain – FY 84 interest costs will be higher than planned (given the three and a half year average maturity of the debt). The magnitude of the underestimate depends on how long the higher rate persists, but the shortfall could well amount to $10 billion or more.

The combined effect of these factors may well cause a major dilemma for the Reagan Administration in FY 84 and beyond. If they are to achieve a balanced budget in FY 84, the Administration must make further substantial budget cuts. The magnitude is almost certainly going to be greater than the $23 billion forecast in September 1981. As shown in Table 3, the additional cuts will probably need to total $50 billion or more. Whether the problem turns out to be this severe, only time will tell. But it would certainly take a fortuitous set of circumstances to occur for the Reagan forecast to come true.

All these considerations of the Federal Budget and fiscal policy have powerful implications for defence policy and planning. Unless the President backs away from his commitment to a balanced budget, the Department of Defense may well be forced to reduce its spending below the Administration's currently planned levels, especially if the economy grows more slowly than expected or the necessary non-defence reductions are not fully realized. For example, the one percent shortfall in projected growth discussed above could reduce the real growth in the FY 84 Defense Budget to zero. Failure to achieve the non-defence budget cuts would have the same impact.

Table 3: Required FY 84 Budget Cuts
($ billion)

	Outlays
Reagan September Programme	23
Higher Interest Costs	5–10
Slower Economic Growth	15–20
Rejection of New Revenue Measures	10
Total	**53–63**

It is far too early to make any firm forecasts of the extent to which the Defense Department will be faced with these problems. And if complications develop, the Administration has options (i.e. tax increases, further non-defence budget cuts, and deficit spending) for avoiding the need to scale down its planned defence spending. But the practicability of these options is at least subject to question.

The next time these issues will have to be addressed will most likely be in the summer of 1982. When the Reagan Administration begins to develop its FY 84 budget, the strength of the expected economic recovery should be apparent, as should the outlook for interest rates. Moreover, the fate of the present round of budget cuts (submitted to Congress in September of 1981) will be decided.

The Defense Budget
The defence programme used for the Administration's expenditure forecast is still only partly defined. At the time of writing, President Reagan's initial five-year programme review was still underway. Indeed, given the range of issues facing the DOD leadership, it is unlikely that the programme will be fully decided until late 1981, and many issues are likely to be postponed until the 1982 decision cycle. As a result, the ability of the Defense Department to achieve the ambitious planned programme within the projected spending limits is still uncertain.

In fact, senior DOD spokesmen have already stated that real growth of 9% a year appears to be needed to carry out the Reagan programme, a level well above the 7% initially approved by the President.

The Defense Department faces an unprecedented range of difficult issues in its initial five-year programme review. In addition to resolving the challenges of new strategic systems – MX, B-1, and ABM – it must develop a sensible multi-year ship-building programme, manage a menu of costly new Army weapons, and cope with a range of contentious manpower issues such as how to retain skilled and experienced personnel (which is a far tougher problem than the more publicized questions of how to attract enough volunteers in the absence of conscription).

Many observers doubt the ability of a new and largely untested defence team to address these issues conclusively in the few months available during their first programme review cycle. If the planned 7% real growth in DOD funds fails to materialize, the problems and strains will increase exponentially. The implications of this pessimistic outlook are discussed below in three parts: investment in new equipment, operating costs, and planning for possible cutbacks.

Investment in New Equipment
A massive equipment modernization effort has been launched in order to make up for ten years or more of inadequate investment funding. This programme has several components:

– An increase in production rates to more efficient levels for some existing procurement

programmes (F-14, F-15, and F-16 aircraft and M-1 tanks);
- Initial production of controversial systems such as the F-18 and AV-8B aircraft and the IFV (infantry fighting vehicle);
- An unprecedented naval ship modernization aimed at rebuilding the fleet to around 600 ships by 1990;
- The modernization and upgrading of America's strategic deterrent, including the B-1 Bomber, the MX missile, a much improved C³I, and increased Research and Development funding for the *Trident* II missile, 'Stealth' bomber technology and ABM systems.

As a result, procurement funding has increased much more rapidly than the budget as a whole (the FY 82 procurement budget was up 42% over FY 81). Setting aside disputes about the need for this equipment, the new commitments greatly limit the flexibility of defence planners, making it extremely difficult to cut spending later if changing fiscal policy would require it. Only a small portion of equipment investment funds are actually spent in the year that Congress authorizes them. Most spending actually occurs one, two or even more years later. Congress gives DOD authority to obligate the government, which is done by letting contracts. The funds are not spent until work is complete, often several years later in the case of major weapons. The spending profiles of the three investment accounts are shown in Table 4.

Table 4: Spending Patterns
(% of Budget Authority)

	Years: 1	2	3	4 onwards
Procurement	12	37	30	21
Research & Development	56	36	6	2
Military Construction	8	36	30	26

As Table 4 shows, the budget authority granted by Congress in Year 1 would heavily influence spending in Years 2 and 3. Conversely, deep cuts in the procurement or construction authorizations in Year 1 would do little to ease outlay pressures in that same year. The actual problem could be even more nettlesome

because ship construction proceeds very slowly and is likely to be the largest component of the expanded procurement effort. The ship construction outlay profile is shown in Table 5.

Table 5: Ship Construction Outlay
(% Budget Authority)

Years:	1	2	3	4	5	6	7
	2	15	18	18	18	18	11

Operating Costs
Funds will be required to add manpower for a 600-ship Navy, for two more Army divisions, for more airlift and tactical aircraft, and for expanded logistics and training. Assuming the extra personnel can be recruited and retained, manpower costs will increase sharply, even if conscription were resumed; funds will also be needed to support and operate these forces. In addition, plans to improve readiness mean more dollars for training and operations as well as for ammunition and spare parts.

Planning for Possible Cutbacks
Should it prove necessary to slow the planned build-up, for example, from the Administration's goal of 7% real growth down to 3% or 4%, the effects could be very disruptive and wasteful. If FY 84 monies are $10 to $15 billion less than now planned, DOD's options will be surprisingly limited. Even deep cuts in equipment investments (45% of the total Defense Budget) would generate only limited outlay savings, unless entire programmes are cancelled in order to cease production of equipment authorized in prior years. Similarly, military and civilian personnel (50% of the total budget) cannot easily be cut back. The only way to make significant personnel savings is to reduce force levels or the support that sustains combat readiness. Given these restrictions on flexibility, the required savings would probably be made by the following actions:

- Cutting R&D for new weapons and especially for more advanced technology;
- Stretching out purchase of major weapons, and thus buying fewer weapons while increasing the cost of each item;

- Cutting readiness by reducing training, flight operations, and ship operations;
- Cutting sustained combat capability by slowing the build-up of essential war stocks (ammunition and spares);
- Limiting military pay increases which would weaken recruiting and retention and lower manpower quality.

By FY 84 the Defense Department may face even more severe difficulties than those caused by the $10 billion to $15 billion shortfall suggested above, depending on the success of the Administration's fiscal and economic plan. Indeed, the problems may pile up by the mid-1980s, even if the 7% real growth increases should be achieved. There are reasons for such pessimism:

- The costs of new weapons are always underestimated, partly because costs are driven up by unanticipated but inevitable development and production problems;
- Service planners are adept at packing more programmes into the annual budget than they can truly afford in future years, on the theory that cuts may have to be made later, but hopefully in someone else's programme;
- There are relentless pressures to underestimate the rate of spending for programme commitments. The Office of Management and Budget (OMB) tends to focus on outlays and to give less attention to new budget authority; the resultant incentive to understate budget outlays is not surprising. Indeed, the Congressional Budget Office (CBO) projected a $5-billion to $7-billion underestimate of FY 84 outlays based on the programme information provided in the original Reagan defence five-year projections.

In light of these considerations, it seems likely that the Defense Department will have to cope with uncompromising budget pressures in the mid-1980s. The strength of these pressures will depend largely on the success of the Reagan economic recovery programme and the Administration's effort to cut back non-defence spending. These factors will be far more significant in shaping defence policy than changes in security strategy or sophisticated analyses of the threat.

Public Opinion and Security Policy
While economic and budgetary considerations play major roles in shaping security policy, public attitudes also exert considerable influence in policy and spending decisions. The 'Vietnam trauma' was certainly a factor in framing the Nixon Doctrine and establishing the Defense Budgets in the early 1970s. And it is no coincidence that President Carter's decision to increase defence spending in 1978 closely followed a major shift in public attitudes on this question. Congressional views mirror shifts in the thinking of the public on major issues even more closely.

Public Opinion and Foreign Policy Issues
Recent sharp alterations in US policies in such areas as arms control, relations with the Soviet Union, and the rise of military force are deeply rooted in public attitudes that changed markedly during the late 1970s. While these changes took place gradually, the hostage episode in Iran crystallized many of the public's concerns about the role of the US in the world, the state of our military forces, and the ability of President Carter to provide the leadership needed in the 1970s.

In February 1980, 44% of the respondents in a Gallup Poll rated international and foreign policy problems as the most important ones faced by the US, the highest such response since 1972 at a time of an acute phase of the South-east Asia conflict. Inflation ranked second with 39%, and energy was a distant third at 12%. This was a dramatic shift from a poll just five months earlier (October 1979, prior to the hostage seizure), when only 6% saw international or foreign policy problems as the most pressing.

The Yankelovich article in *Foreign Affairs* earlier this year documented a major coalescing of public attitudes in 1980 that were significant to Reagan's landslide victory. It summarized the American public's view as follows:

By the end of 1980, a series of events had shaken us out of our soul-searching and into a new, outward-looking state of mind. The public had grown skeptical of detente and distressed by American impotence in countering the December 1979 Soviet invasion of Afghanistan. It felt bullied by OPEC, humiliated by the Ayatollah Khomeini, tricked by Castro, out-traded by Japan and out-gunned by the Russians. By the time of the 1980 presidential election, fearing that America was losing control over its foreign affairs, voters were more than ready to exorcise the ghost of Vietnam and replace it with a new posture of American assertiveness.

Americans have become surprisingly explicit about how the United States should seek to regain control of its destiny, and in the context of the disquieting realities of the 1980s, these ideas create a new, different and complex foreign policy mandate for the Reagan Presidency. The national pride has been deeply wounded; Americans are fiercely determined to restore our honor and respect abroad. This outlook makes it easy for the Reagan Administration to win support for bold assertive initiatives, but much more difficult to shape a consensus behind policies that involve compromise, subtlety, patience, restrained gestures, prior consultation with allies, and the deft geopolitical manoeuvering that is required when one is no longer the world's preeminent locus of military and economic power.[3]

While 1980 was the culmination of many developments leading to a more hawkish public attitude, these changes were evident some years earlier. A 1976 *Foreign Policy* article pointed to these changes, and in particular to a deepening disillusionment with US–Soviet relations and a mounting concern for the threat of war.[4] Public opinion polls also reflected these shifts. A CBS–*New York Times* Poll in early 1978 found that over half of the US public believed that the US should 'get tough' with the USSR. And, as will be discussed later, attitudes on defence spending were changing rapidly too. The most complete assessment of these new views is contained in a publication of the Chicago Council on Foreign Relations in early 1980, *American Public Opinion and US Foreign Policy, 1979.*

Public Opinion and Defence Spending Issues
Public attitudes to defence spending shifted dramatically during the 1970s. An April 1981 Harris Poll found that 63% of the public supported increased defence spending, even if it

Table 6: Defence Spending Attitudes

	1960	1969	1976	1980
Too Much	18%	52%	36%	14%
About Right	45	31	32	24
Too Little	21	8	22	49

meant sacrifice elsewhere. Public views on the defence spending issue are well documented, since Gallup has asked this question many times during the past 20 years. Changing attitudes are summarized in Table 6.

The shift in attitude from 1969 to 1980 is especially striking, with 49% believing that too little was being spent compared to 8% eleven years earlier. While Republicans were more concerned about this issue, support for more spending was bipartisan; according to the February 1980 Gallup Poll, 45% of Democrats also agreed that more spending was needed.

Not surprisingly, there is a clear correlation between public attitudes on the issue and the funds appropriated by Congress. The chart below plots public support for more spending and the budget authority provided by Congress. The budget authority lags about 2 years to reflect the time it takes for attitudes to affect the budget process.

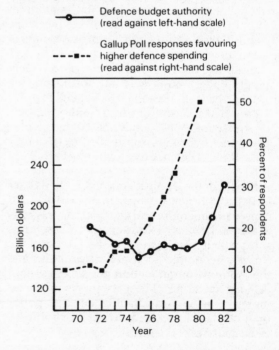

28

The Volatility of Public Attitudes

Despite evidence that the public supports a more aggressive foreign policy and greater attention to military defence, there is indication that these views may be volatile. For example:

- In September 1980, 19% of the respondents in a Harris Poll felt that keeping the US strong was the top priority task of the government. This proportion dropped to 8% in May 1981, only eight months later;
- A recent Harris Poll showed a drop in the Public's favourable rating of Reagan's handling of foreign policy, from 54% in February to 48% in July, with 47% giving him an unfavourable rating;
- The public support for an active US role in world affairs dropped from 71% in 1956 to 66% in 1974 and only 59% in 1978;
- Despite growing suspicion of the USSR polls repeatedly show solid support for arms control.

The neutralist movement in Europe will not necessarily spread to the US, but the evidence above indicates conflicting views on the part of many Americans. This could lead to a wavering of public support as circumstances change. Among the developments that could erode the current supportive attitude of the public are:

- Seeming mismanagement of the defence programme – major cost overruns, erratic stops and starts of major programmes, or open controversy within DOD over an important element of the Reagan programme (e.g. MX);
- Failure by our allies to support our expanded effort, either through repeated failure to meet NATO commitments or by lack of support for major foreign policy initiatives.
- Major domestic problems that could be blamed on the cuts in domestic programmes (urban riots or serious financial problems among state and local governments) or continued deficits and inflation.

The recent organization of a Congressional Caucus composed of Democratic and Republican members of the House and Senate Armed Services and Appropriations Committees is an early sign of problems. Their goal is to force the Administration to give more attention to defence economies and hard choices, in order to prevent a public backlash which, they fear, will develop when the real impact of the non-defence budget cuts are felt.

To avoid problems of this type will take some combination of luck and leadership as well as good management. So far President Reagan has exhibited leadership, and luck has been on his side, but he has three more difficult years to sustain this.

Population Shifts and the Political Process

Changes in public opinion will be reinforced by the shift in population toward the Sunbelt, and in particular by the continued flight of people from the cities to the suburbs and more recently to small cities and towns. The result is a shift in political power from Democratic strongholds to more conservative areas that normally vote Republican. It also portends greater Congressional support for defence spending and a 'tougher' foreign policy.

The major gaining and losing States in the recent Congressional reapportionment are shown below. The conservative Sunbelt region is the big winner, while industrialized Democratic areas in the East and Midwest lost heavily.

Winners

Florida	+4 Seats
Texas	+3 Seats
California	+2 Seats
Arizona	+1 Seat
Colorado	+1 Seat
Nevada	+1 Seat
New Mexico	+1 Seat
Oregon	+1 Seat
Tennessee	+1 Seat
Utah	+1 Seat
Washington	+1 Seat

Losers

New York	−5 Seats
Pennsylvania	−2 Seats
Ohio	−2 Seats
Illinois	−2 Seats
South Dakota	−1 Seat
Indiana	−1 Seat
Massachusetts	−1 Seat
Michigan	−1 Seat
Missouri	−1 Seat
New Jersey	−1 Seat

The implication of these population moves is shown more starkly when the specific Congressional districts that gained or lost significant population are examined. The 25 Congressional districts gaining the most population from 1970 to 1980 elected Representatives who are almost entirely white, male and conservative. Nearly half (10) are Democrats, but all of them are from the South or West. The losing districts by contrast are all Democratic and contain 11 of the 16 black members of Congress. All but one are from the North or Midwest. These shifts have a number of implications, but not the least is much greater support for the security policies advocated by President Reagan.

Conclusions

The shift in population and the resulting shift in political power from the urban North to the Sunbelt should reinforce the more militant foreign policy of the Reagan Administration. Moreover, President Reagan's national security policies are consistent with major shifts in public opinion that have occurred over the past ten years. Support for more defence spending is at a post-World War II high and there is persuasive evidence that the public supports a tougher line with the Soviet Union and more activist policies in other parts of the world.

Nonetheless, public attitudes are volatile, and events could well undermine the support President Reagan is now receiving. The greatest threat and the one most difficult to manage is public reaction as domestic programme cuts take full effect in 1982. A backlash is possible and should be considered in the Administration's planning. Among the steps they can take to minimize this risk are:

– Careful, tough-minded management of defence programmes. Embarrassing cost-overruns or bitter internal battles over major programmes could undercut public confidence. A sense that the funds are wisely used and difficult choices wisely made is essential;
– Continued pressure on America's allies in Western Europe as well as Japan to increase their defence effort and be reasonably supportive of the Administration's foreign

policy. Lack of co-operation could well cause disillusionment and a sharp drop in support for NATO improvements and other programmes perceived as mainly benefiting America's Allies.

Even if public and Congressional support for the defence effort is sustained, economic and budgetary realities may exert considerable pressure on the Defense Budget component of Reagan's security policy. If the Administration is to achieve a balanced budget by FY 84 and augment defence spending by 7% real growth a year, further deep cuts in non-defence spending must be made. OMB estimates that the needed reductions will amount to $23 billion in FY 84. However, if the economy grows more slowly than forecast and interest rates remain higher than Administration projections, the FY 84 budget problem will be far more severe than the President contemplates. All these factors raise doubts that the planned rapid increase in defence spending will prove feasible. The most immediate challenge the Administration faces is to construct its FY 83 Budget (submitted to Congress in January 1982). It must include further deep cuts in domestic programmes and there seems no way that changes in social security can be avoided much longer. Postponing such cuts until after the 1982 Congressional mid-term election will reduce substantially the savings possible in FY 84, thus forcing the President to forgo his hoped-for balanced budget or to cut back defence spending.

If the projected military spending increases are not fully realized, DOD will be faced with serious planning and budgetary challenges. The investment programmes already underway limit DOD's flexibility to cut outlays in FY 83 and FY 84. Moreover, planned force expansions will generate major increases in operating costs that cannot be trimmed in the short run without severe impact on readiness or risking the ability of the services to attract and retain the numbers and quality of military personnel they need. Some actions taken now can reduce the impact of future reductions in planned spending. For example:

– Large weapons programmes should be staggered rather than funded concurrently. This will require hard choices in setting priorities, but is essential. Current problems result in part from fifteen years of having funds diverted to Vietnam or budgets held without growth. It will take a long period, five to ten years, to correct these differences. They cannot be solved in a brief span of time;

– Any funds freed by this approach should be used to accelerate programmes that can be modulated quickly as more or less funds become available. Examples include war reserves, improving our industrial readiness, and catching-up on deferred maintenance;

– Greater attention should be given to efficiency in solving manpower problems. Most problems can be solved in various ways. For example, a costly (multi-billion dollar) GI Education Bill is being considered to improve recruiting and retention. There may well be other, less expensive (i.e. more efficient) ways to accomplish this same goal such as bonuses, better housing, or added in-house technical training opportunites.

Planning for the contingency that the Administration may not be able fully to deliver its 7% real growth commitment can reduce the dislocations and potential wasting of funds. Some object to such planning on the grounds that it makes the cuts more likely. But, given the clear desire of the Administration to strengthen the American defence posture, the risk is minimal and planning clearly prudent.

NOTES

[1] For example, see MIT Economist Lester Thurow's article in *The New York Times*, 31 May 1981, p. F-3.
[2] Citibank *Monthly Economic Newsletter*, July 1981, p.12, or William Nordhaus, 'No Great Threat from Military Spending', *The New York Times*, 17 May 1981, p. F-3.

[3] Daniel Yankelovich and Larry Kaagan, 'Assertive America', *Foreign Affairs*, 'America and the World', 1980, Vol. 59, No. 3, pp. 696–713.
[4] William Watt and Lloyd Free, 'Nationalism Not Isolationism', *Foreign Policy*, Fall, 1976, pp. 3–26.

US Strategic Nuclear Forces

JAN LODAL

For nearly two decades, the nuclear forces of the United States have remained unchanged in their basic structure. A 'triad' of land-based intercontinental ballistic missiles (ICBM), submarine-launched ballistic nuclear missiles (SLBM) and heavy bombers has formed the backbone of the central strategic nuclear force, while a wide variety of nuclear systems have been deployed in Europe, Asia and at sea. These latter systems, the 'theatre' and 'tactical' systems, include nuclear artillery shells, short-range missiles such as *Lance*, longer-range missiles such as the *Pershing*, nuclear bombs on tactical aircraft, atomic demolition munitions, nuclear torpedoes, and nuclear air defence weapons. The US maintained at one time 7,000 of these 'non-central' weapons in Europe alone but 1,000 were withdrawn in 1980.

One major change has occurred throughout the last two decades – the deployment of multiple independently-targetable re-entry vehicles (MIRV) on US missiles. This technology has permitted the placing of several warheads on a single missile, significantly increasing the military capability of each missile. Yet even this technology has changed neither the structure nor the basic size of the US central strategic force. It is frequently forgotten that, by the mid-1950s, the US had deployed on her bomber force alone almost as many weapons as exist in the central strategic forces today. Since the number of bombs in the force has been steadily reduced as MIRV have been deployed on missiles, the overall destructive capacity of the force has remained roughly constant for 25 years. Only the character and the nature of the weapons have changed.

The 1980s will see a significant change from the last two decades. Land-based ICBM will be modernized, a new strategic bomber will be deployed, and air-launched cruise missiles, which do not even exist today, will form a major component of the force. The predominant sea-based force will be the *Trident* submarine and its associated longer-range missiles. In Europe, the *Pershing* II and ground-launched cruise missiles will be deployed. Finally, the operational accuracy of land-based missiles will reach the levels long predicted, opening up a much wider range of possible military options by permitting these weapons to attack hardened Soviet military targets.

While the general outlines of these changes are clear, some of the specific deployment decisions have yet to be made, although President Reagan has announced the decision to procure 100 B-1 bomber variants and 100 MX missiles, the latter to be deployed at least initially in existing silos. But even these decisions will not necessarily remain firm. Considerable engineering development and Congressional debate remain before the new systems are deployed, and changes in technology or economics could force revisions to original programmes, as they have done so often in the past. Furthermore, while the basic changes I have outlined will be made in one form or another, leading to a significant alteration in the character of US nuclear forces, many systems will remain in place. In particular, the issue of vulnerability – the growing vulnerability of US nuclear forces to Soviet attack – will continue to underlie much of the strategic debate of the 1980s. Two other key programmatic questions also remain to be dealt with; the possible deployment of anti-missile defences (ABM), and the need for a major restructuring of command, control, communication and intelligence (C^3I) systems associated with nuclear forces.

In the following sections, I discuss these three technical issues, as well as two closely related but much broader issues – the proper role of nuclear forces in the overall defence posture of the United States and NATO, and the place of nuclear arms-control agreements in protecting our security.

Ballistic Missile Defence

Perhaps the most explosive issue of the 1980s will be whether or not the United States should deploy an ABM defence. The United States all but abandoned her ABM programme following the 1972 SALT I Agreement which limited ABM to no more than 100 interceptors, all located at a single site. The Treaty also prohibited mobile ABM, ABM in space, and ABM based on entirely new technologies.

Deployment of an ABM would require either modifying or abrogating the 1972 Treaty. Since this Treaty stands as the only major arms-control agreement of the decade still in force, such a step would clearly have major political repercussions.

But ABM are controversial for other reasons as well. Many experts question whether any ABM could be effective enough to justify its immense cost, despite major improvements in ABM technology over the last decade. Others question whether an ABM, especially if it were designed to defend American cities and population, might actually destabilize the strategic balance.

These arguments have been made frequently and widely, so I will not elaborate on them here. Rather, I would like to emphasize a different aspect of the ABM debate – one which I believe will take on increasing importance in the coming years.

Since the mid-1960s, few have argued the feasibility of defending US cities against an all-out Soviet attack. When Secretary of Defense Robert McNamara announced President Johnson's decision to deploy a limited ABM defence in 1967, the rationale was to intercept accidental launches by 'third countries', i.e. from China. This rationale did not sit well with Congress, especially since the Chinese did not develop a capability to attack the United States, US–Chinese relations began to thaw, and there were technical problems with the proposed ABM system. As a result, President Nixon reorientated the emphasis of the ABM system towards defence of US ICBM sites, giving up almost completely the defence of American cities.

Even today, the mission most commonly cited for a new ABM system is to defend US strategic forces, and more specifically, to defend land-based missiles. If the nation were subsequently to return to the basing system approved by President Carter, in which the MX missile was to be deployed in multiple protect-ive shelters (MPS), a mobile ABM with its interceptor and radar also hidden in the shelters would theoretically provide an extremely effective way to protect the missile, even against a full-scale Soviet attack. It is less obvious that an ABM defence would be able to protect adequately any missiles in silos. Cost-exchange ratios immediately look less attractive.

Yet ABM could potentially serve another purpose altogether – one which I believe will attract increasing interest within the Reagan Administration. Even though an all-out Soviet attack could overwhelm *any* ABM system which might be deployed in the next decade (or probably in this century), even a partial defence of US cities could be useful to a President contemplating the limited use of nuclear weapons in response to a successful Soviet conventional attack against our Allies. By creating a second nuclear 'firebreak', a limited defence of US cities would significantly increase the credibility of a US threat to use nuclear weapons first against Soviet forces, either in Europe, the Persian Gulf, or elsewhere. Such a defence could intercept all Soviet 'demonstration' or limited retaliatory attacks against US territory, forcing Soviet leaders to respond to a US first use of nuclear weapons either by stopping their invasion or by increasing the scale of their retaliatory attack enough to defeat the US defence. Since a larger attack would increase the risk of escalation to all-out war, such a move would be more difficult for a Soviet leader to make.

Advocates of 'nuclear warfighting' strategies for the United States have long insisted that ABM must be a major component in such a strategy. As the US and her Allies face an increasing number of Soviet conventional challenges throughout the world – many in locations which are difficult to defend with conventional forces – demands will grow for more reliance on the use of nuclear weapons to defend Western interests. Such demands will almost certainly lead to a re-examination of the potential role of ABM defences of US cities. This argument, when added to the ever-present calls to use ABM to protect US ICBM, almost certainly guarantees a major debate concerning ABM during the 1980s.

A debate over ABM will in turn further stimulate an emerging debate over the proper role of nuclear forces in the overall security policy of the West – an issue which I discuss below. Moreover, reconsideration of city-oriented ABM will generate considerable argument within the NATO Alliance by reopening the question of 'coupling' and the quality of America's commitment to avoid a nuclear war confined only to Europe.

Command and Control

In addition to ABM, C³I components of US nuclear forces are also likely to be a major issue in the 1980s. Concern about the adequacy of US C³I systems stems from several factors. First, the Soviet forces which threaten US land-based missiles also threaten the C³I system. Few individuals question the capability of the United States to launch a retaliatory attack against an all-out Soviet strike on US territory, but many question the ability of the C³I system to survive a direct attack for more than a few minutes or hours. As a result, the chance of a spasmodic all-out nuclear war erupting is greater than it need be. Some even raise the possibility that the C³I system might break down altogether in the face of attack, leading to a complete failure to respond. This breakdown could be either technical or human. US leaders, faced with all-or-nothing choices, might find themselves unable to order an attack on Soviet cities for fear that this would lead to al-most certain Soviet retaliation in kind, if US cities had been largely spared up to that point.

A second concern is related to the European Theatre, where the command system takes on even more significance. NATO has long relied on the threat of first use of nuclear weapons, should conventional defences fail to deter Soviet conventional attack. Yet unclassified sources state that the present NATO command system would require at least two days to trans-mit nuclear release authority to a NATO field commander, once such authority had been requested. Some believe that even this timeframe is optimistic. Thus it is not clear that NATO's present command system permits a rapid enough response to thwart a Soviet invasion.

The intelligence component of the C³I systems should not be underemphasized. In Europe, the use of long-range weapons (such as the *Pershing* II now under development) to attack rear echelon concentrations of troops

and supplies has been advocated as a way of significantly improving NATO's capability to defend against a Soviet invasion. However, such attacks require accurate and extremely timely information on the location of the units to be targeted. Present systems are unlikely to provide adequate information. Likewise, un-less much improved strategic intelligence is made available, the use of strategic nuclear forces in a European conflict must be limited to targeting fixed sites.

In summary, the C³I system will receive increasing attention, not only because improvements must be made to keep it survivable enough to ensure retaliation against all-out attack, but perhaps more significantly because major improvements will have to be made if the West is to rely more heavily on nuclear warfighting capabilities for its defence. As with ABM, it is this interaction of the C³I system with a nuclear warfighting strategy that will most dramatically thrust the issue forward.

Vulnerability

To a large extent, the impending deployment of new ICBM, bomber and cruise missile forces is a response to the growing vulnerability of US nuclear forces to Soviet counterforce attack. For a period, it seemed possible that arms-control measures could help assure the survivability of these forces, but this hope was disappointed by the experience of SALT II.

The growing vulnerability of America's nuclear forces to Soviet attack is an issue which cuts across virtually all others. The two major issues I have discussed above, ABM and C³I, stem at least partially from concern with vulnerability. The most obvious use of ABM is to reduce the vulnerability of America's forces to attack, and it is also the vulnerability to attack that leads to calls to spend as much as $25 billion to improve the C³I system.

For the last two decades, it has been widely assumed that mounting an effective military campaign against the enemy's nuclear forces was simply impossible for both sides. Now, however, dramatic improvements in the accuracy of missile systems (both ballistic and cruise), when combined with a major increase in the number of weapons available to each side have led to the technological possibility that many systems which previously were beyond contemplation of effective attack are now potentially vulnerable.

These changes in technology and deployment have brought about much of the anxiety associated with current US nuclear forces. If the United States' land-based forces had remained invulnerable to attack, if her command system was secure, and if she had no real hope of being able to mount effective attacks against Soviet nuclear military targets, then there would be little rationale for many of the weapons programmes currently advocated and little need to move away from the systems which have served the US well for the last two decades.

It is important to note three technological facts concerning the vulnerability of nuclear forces. First, the achievement of highly accurate nuclear delivery systems by both the United States and the Soviet Union is inevitable. Technology is now available to develop missiles with accuracies of 200 metres and better. Many of the uncertainties regarding ballistic missile accuracy have been resolved by a decade of satellite mapping of the earth's gravitational fields and the increasing sophistication of modern computer simulations. Cruise missile guidance systems are also the product of modern computer technology; ground contour matching can now be done with relatively small and inexpensive computer systems.

The second technological fact is that there remains no way for either side to have a high degree of confidence that an attack against any one component of the enemy's force will be fully successful. Some missiles will miss their targets because of reliability failures, even if they are as accurate as predicted, and the side being attacked may launch some missiles on warning to prevent their destruction. Bomber defences are never likely to be fully effective, and pre-launch attacks against bomber bases require a high degree of co-ordination to catch all aircraft before they are airborne.

The third technological fact is that there are no foreseeable systems which threaten the invulnerability of submarine-based missiles while the submarines are at sea. At least two decades would be required to develop and deploy a system which could effectively locate submarines to within a radius of about 20 miles – the radius necessary to attack them with

nuclear weapons. But even if the submarines were located, launching a co-ordinated surprise attack against all submarines simultaneously would represent an additional major technical challenge.

Unfortunately, these technological facts imply no clear policy conclusion. The increased ability to mount successful counter-military capabilities, combined with NATO's present strategy of threatening the first use of nuclear weapons to bolster a failing conventional defence, leads to powerful arguments in favour of the United States developing nuclear counterforce capabilities, but the technical impossibility of mounting a fully effective counterforce attack undercuts much of the rationale for proceeding with counterforce weapons.

The other side of the vulnerability question relates to the vulnerability of human beings, the structures in which they live and work, and to nuclear weapons effects. The fact that new weapons increase this vulnerability makes the possible use of nuclear weapons in any circumstances less desirable and less likely, at the same time as technology opens up the possibility of effective counter-military nuclear options.

The tension between increased weapons vulnerability on the one hand and increased population vulnerability on the other will drive much of the nuclear debate throughout the 1980s. The increased vulnerability of Soviet weapons pushes the development of US counterforce weapons, and the increased vulnerability of US weapons pushes the development of new systems which are more survivable. Yet new force deployments increase the overall vulnerability of populations and societies, rekindling anti-nuclear sentiments and undercutting domestic political support in the western democracies for nuclear weapons programmes.

The Role of Nuclear Forces
The cumulative effect of Soviet deployments, changes in technology, and international politics are very likely to lead to new US ICBM, new bombers, and new long-range theatre nuclear forces in the 1980s and to re-open questions about ABM and C^{3}I. In turn, public debate will discuss a more fundamental issue – the role

35

nuclear weapons *ought* to play in the security policies of the West.

In the 1950s, the US relied almost exclusively upon nuclear weapons for her defence through her strategy of 'massive retaliation'. By the 1960s, the Soviet Union had developed a basic nuclear force of her own. In response, the US reduced her reliance on nuclear defence and changed her policy to one of 'flexible response'. In 1967, NATO officially adopted a flexible response strategy (MC 14/3).

Flexible response is a compromise strategy which straddles the US belief that first use of nuclear weapons would be close to suicidal in the face of Soviet nuclear capabilities, and the European belief that any war in Europe would quickly become nuclear. The strategy requires that the USSR believes that the US will in fact use her nuclear weapons if faced with no alternative but defeat, no matter how much such use might risk her own destruction.

This strategy, which incorporates a large amount of uncertainty and some simple bluff, left everyone reasonably satisfied so long as America's nuclear forces remained *superior* to those of the Soviet Union and so long as NATO's conventional forces could probably blunt a Soviet conventional attack without relying on nuclear weapons. However, throughout the 1970s the Soviet Union engaged in a major build-up of her conventional forces in Europe and brought her nuclear forces up to parity with the United States. Furthermore she developed the capability to fight with conventional forces outside Europe, leading to greater challenges for the West's conventional defences.

This Soviet build-up has led to serious questions about the credibility of the flexible response strategy. Yet, moving away from the current strategy forces one to face the dilemma of either choosing to rely more heavily on nuclear forces for our defence or undertaking a build-up in conventional defences.

Unfortunately, there is no simple solution to this dilemma. The dramatic growth of Soviet conventional forces, including her new ability to project these forces outside the Eurasian land mass, puts a serious strain on Western non-nuclear defences. To mount an effective counter to the new Soviet deployments will be extremely expensive for the West, requiring perhaps a doubling of arms budgets, a return to

the draft in the United States, and lengthened periods of conscript service in Europe. These are bitter pills.

The alternative – more emphasis on nuclear defence – is a bitter pill as well. A nuclear defence against conventional Soviet attack necessitates a credible Western threat to use nuclear weapons first. Such credibility is not easy to obtain, largely because the Soviet Union has now deployed effective and diversified nuclear forces of her own, comparable to those of the West. These forces would permit her to respond in kind to any US nuclear attack, so that the advantage obtained by the initial nuclear strike would be likely to be ephemeral. At worst, the escalation would proceed uncontrolled, leading to the holocaust neither side wants. Although it is this possibility of escalation and holocaust that undercuts the credibility of our threat to use nuclear weapons first, it is the same possibility that forms the basis for our deterrence of a Soviet pre-emptive nuclear strike or indeed of any aggressive move in Europe. This is a fundamental paradox that simply cannot be overcome.

Nor would a nuclear defence be inexpensive. An effective nuclear war-fighting capability would certainly require the deployment of active ABM and air defences in the United States, and perhaps even active defences in Europe. The C³I system would also require massive investments to ensure enduring survivability. These costs, which could be many tens or even several hundreds of billions of dollars, would be over and above those associated with supplying the necessary offensive nuclear weapons.

The West could simply fail to respond to the Soviet arms build-up, hoping that the Soviet Union will be deterred from hostile action by the simple uncertainty associated with the ever present possibility of holocaust. Alternatively, some mix of relatively inexpensive superficial measures could be undertaken to demonstrate 'resolve', but these solutions are unlikely to be satisfactory to any of the governments involved.

Another alternative is arms control, which many have seen as a solution that is in the mutual interest of both the Soviet Union and the United States. Arms-control efforts to date have proved painful and divisive, but they offer at least some possibility for reducing the risk of nuclear war.

Arms Control

Throughout the 1970s, arms control played a major role in determining US nuclear force structures. Many in both Europe and the United States continue to hope that this role will continue.

It is important to be clear about the origins of the current difficulties faced by arms control. In my view, these difficulties go back to 1973 when the Soviet Union began deploying the SS-19 ICBM as a replacement for her 'light' SS-11 land-based missiles. In SALT I, the US accepted a five-year freeze on the number of Soviet and American missile launchers on the assumption that a variety of collateral agreements ensured that Soviet modernization would not represent a dramatic break with past deployments. But the SS-19, while technically a 'light' missile under the terms of SALT I, carries six megaton-size warheads and was nearly three times the size of the SS-11 it replaced. Simultaneously, the USSR developed an effective MIRVed 'heavy' ICBM, the SS-18, to replace her heavy SS-9. Moreover these new weapons were more accurate and were deployed more rapidly than expected.

This rapid, unexpected and major build-up in the Soviet offensive land-based missile force began the process of undercutting US domestic support for the SALT Treaty. The build-up was seen as clearly inconsistent with the spirit of SALT I, if not its letter. Moreover, from a military standpoint, the new weapons represented a serious threat to the US land-based *Minuteman* ICBM force. For over six years the US attempted to negotiate limits on MIRVed land-based missiles which would control this threat to America's retaliatory capacity. These negotiations were only marginally successful – resulting in the unratified SALT II Treaty.

I recite this history in order to emphasize that disappointment with the arms-control process is not a new phenomenon; it began almost immediately after the completion of the SALT I Agreements. An extraordinary number of approaches have been attempted in the intervening period to find a common ground between the two sides. So far, there has been no success.

Given the non-ratification of SALT II, a new approach is essential if there is to be progress, yet any approach to arms control is clearly inconsistent with a major increase in the nuclear warfighting capabilities of the United States. Thus, the underlying issue of the proper role of nuclear weapons must be resolved before progress in arms control can be made. This is as true with regard to theatre weapons as it is for central strategic weapons.

As I have argued earlier, an increase in warfighting capabilities would at some point require major modification (or possibly even abandonment) of the one arms-control treaty still officially in force – the ABM Treaty of 1972. I simply see no compatibility between arms control and a nuclear warfighting strategy.

But a full-fledged nuclear warfighting strategy has not yet been adopted by the United States, although it has strong advocates within the Reagan Administration. In its absence, there are arms-control approaches which might be successful.

The Reagan Administration has indicated that it favours an approach of negotiating deep cuts in the size of the two nations' central strategic arsenals and long-range theatre nuclear forces, but I find it difficult to conceive of circumstances in which deep cuts could be negotiated. First, there are serious strategic and military questions concerning the benefits to nuclear stability of deep cuts. A war which involved only half the weapons on each side would be no less destructive to mankind than one which involved all the existing weapons, and the force cuts themselves might actually tempt pre-emption in a crisis. Second, defining a mechanism for how the cuts would be taken that would be equitable and verifiable is a major and probably impossible task.

It is my personal belief that the most promising approach for arms control is to set aside detailed limits on specific weapons systems, moving instead to a simple aggregate ceiling on the total number of nuclear warheads contained in the combined central strategic forces and long-range theatre forces of each side. The main advantage of this approach is that it eliminates a variety of arguments, such as how to classify the *Backfire* bomber, how to weigh one weapon system versus another, and what types of modernization to permit each side to under-

37

take. Furthermore, the current and projected numbers of warheads are approximately equal for the two sides, with the Soviet Union's larger number of long-range theatre warheads offsetting the US's larger number of central strategic warheads. Many of the Soviet weapons have higher yield than comparable US weapons, but in an age of under 200-metre missile accuracies, these differences in yield are almost completely immaterial.

Without some positive approach to arms control in the 1980s, the US will have major problems in convincing her European Allies of the wisdom of her nuclear policy. Thus, despite the Reagan Administration's initial coolness toward arms control and its appointment of a bevy of critics in almost all positions of responsibility for arms-control policy, political realities, combined with the economic, strategic and technical difficulties of engaging in an unrestrained strategic offensive arms race, are pushing the Administration towards increased efforts to reach agreements with the Soviet Union. Nevertheless, the last nine years of failed efforts cannot lead one to be optimistic about the chance of successful arms-control agreements in the 1980s.

Conclusions

The 1980s will be a period of some uncertainty for US nuclear forces. The deployment of a new manned bomber eventually to replace the aging B-52, a large cruise missile force, the *Trident* submarine, and a new land-based missile system to supplement or replace the *Minuteman* have all been announced. Yet the basic role of nuclear weapons in US strategy will be increasingly questioned, with strong advocates for both positions: on the one hand even more reliance on nuclear weapons for our security and on the other greater emphasis on conventional defence.

Much of the uncertainty concerning the future direction of US nuclear forces is inherent in the scope of the problem itself. There are an extraordinarily large number of factors which a US President must consider in making any decision concerning nuclear deployments. In addition to questions of overall strategy and doctrine, he must evaluate the technological and industrial capabilities available to produce a particular system. Perceptions of the nature

and extent of the Soviet threat often differ, as well as evaluations of the importance of a particular threat. Domestic politics must also be considered (witness the strong reaction against the MX), along with Allied preferences and the internal politics of the NATO Allies. Existing treaties and agreements set limits on what can be done. Finally, nuclear forces must compete for funds with other defence programmes and non-defence needs, forcing painful budgetary trade-offs.

The President must not only have factual information on each consideration but he must also have in mind a particular weighting of the relative importance of each factor, since no alternative will be favourable with regard to all considerations. Something always has to give way – sometimes Allied preferences, sometimes domestic politics, sometimes strategy, and sometimes budgets. The result of this process is that the US nuclear force posture at the end of this decade is likely to have been determined as much by a complicated process of political and bureaucratic trade-offs as it is by any clear rational policy. This is not inherently bad; it is simply a fact of life.

Thus, one can offer only the most tentative speculations concerning the shape of US nuclear forces a decade from now. My own view is that the US nuclear forces will be modernized and enhanced more or less as announced, but no move will be made to increase their fundamental role in Western defence. To do so would require a move to much greater emphasis on nuclear warfighting capabilities, and nuclear warfighting is, quite simply, fraught with too many risks and uncertainties to be an attractive strategy. Furthermore, abandonment of the ABM Treaty and the deployment of nationwide ABM defences, which are essential components of any possible nuclear warfighting strategy, are pills simply too bitter (and expensive) to swallow. Thus, we will probably see the cruise missiles and *Pershing* IIs eventually deployed in Europe, we will see 100 or so new bombers, a small land-based complement to the *Minuteman* (perhaps 100 MX), the *Trident* submarine with the D-5 missile, and some improvements in C³I capabilities, but no ABM and no massive increase in offensive force levels. It is not at all clear what the eventual basing mode for the

MX will be. Arms control may play a limited role in modifying the competition in strategic and long-range theatre nuclear arms, but major reductions of force levels are unlikely.

I reiterate that this is at best tentative speculation. Major differences from this scenario are possible. But if my speculations turn out not to be accurate, the real question for the 1980s will not be the future of the nuclear forces, but rather the future of the West's conventional defences. As the credibility of a nuclear response to a Soviet conventional attack continues to erode, the West will face little choice but to increase its conventional defences if it is to match expanding Soviet power. Only a major change in the political relations between the United States and the Soviet Union could reverse this trend – an unlikely event during this decade.

US Conventional Forces

THOMAS R. WHEELOCK

Because of Soviet–American strategic parity, the burden of deterring Soviet military action during the 1980s will fall increasingly upon American and European conventional forces in Europe and upon American forces elsewhere. This statement summarizes an important argument being heard in the West at present.[1] It implies, of course, that the United States, along with her allies, should improve and possibly build up land, air and sea forces to defend the West's interests against a growing Soviet military threat.

In thinking about how to improve the non-nuclear forces of the United States, a certain conventional wisdom, instead of informed debate, unfortunately dominates public perceptions. The elements of this conventional wisdom are as follows:

- *The Military Balance.* Because of the Soviet military build-up and American neglect of its conventional forces during the 1970s, the military balance has eroded to the point where NATO defences are inadequate especially against a surprise attack, the Persian Gulf is particularly vulnerable to Soviet military occupation, and the Soviet Navy is dangerously close to threatening Western control of the seas.
- *The American Defence Build-up.* In response to the Soviet build-up, the United States will have to increase her active duty forces to meet a global Soviet threat and add more of the traditional kinds of weapons – large aircraft carriers, sophisticated fighters and heavy tanks – the high costs of which may be staggering.
- *The All-Volunteer Force.* The United States must return to the Draft now to solve her manpower problems, and in any event will have to revive selective service by the mid-1980s to man increased forces.

Several consequences could result from these attitudes. American and Allied publics might suffer a crisis of confidence in their ability to resist Soviet provocations, some 'doves' might argue that there is no way that the United States could make the necessary conventional force improvements at acceptable social and economic costs, and some 'hawks' might give top priority to attaining an elusive strategic nuclear superiority.

Table 1: US General Purpose Forces

Land Forces:	
Army Divisions:	
Active	16
Reserve	8
Marine Corps Divisions:	
Active	3
Reserve	1
Tactical Air Forces:	
Air Force Wings:	
Active (Full Strength Equivalent)	26(24)
Reserve	12
Marine Corps Wing:	
Active	3
Reserve	1
Navy Attack Wings:	
Active	12
Reserve	2
Naval Forces:	
Active Fleet	429
Carriers	13

SOURCE: Harold Brown, *DOD Annual Report FY 1982* (Washington DC: USGPO)

In the hope of avoiding such outcomes, this analysis seeks to prepare the groundwork for informed public debate on conventional forces in the 1980s by looking at the problems and prospects for these forces. (See above for US forces.) It asks whether the military balance is

Table 2: Warsaw Pact/NATO Central Front Peacetime Ground-Force Personnel and Divisions

	NATO[a]	Warsaw Pact[b]
Military Personnel (millions)	1.045 – 1.096	1.124 – 1.216
Divisions	22 – 32	26 – 50

SOURCES: Derived from John M. Collins, *US–Soviet Military Balance, 1960–1980*, (New York: McGraw Hill Publications, 1980); *The Military Balance, 1980–81*, (London: IISS, 1980); Robert Lucas Fischer, *Defending the Central Front: The Balance of Forces*, Adelphi Paper No.127, (London: IISS, 1976); Congressional Budget Office, *Assessing the NATO/Warsaw Pact Military Balance*, (Washington DC: USGPO, December 1977).

NOTES: [a] The NATO low estimates include only active NATO divisions deployed in West Germany, exclude all reserves, West German territorial forces, French divisions, and Belgian and Dutch forces. The high estimates include active-duty German territorial forces, three French divisions normally deployed in Germany, and two Belgian and three Dutch divisions normally stationed in their respective home countries but designated for forward defence lines in West Germany.

[b] The Warsaw Pact low personnel estimate includes all of its Category II and III divisions at their peacetime strength; the high estimate counts them at full strength. The low division estimate includes all Warsaw Pact Category I divisions in East Germany. The high estimate includes all Category I divisions deployed in Poland, East Germany and Czechoslovakia. In addition, there are two Soviet Category I divisions in the Western Soviet Union that could quickly deploy to East Europe.

so one-sided, the remedies for improving American forces so straightforward, and the demise of the all-volunteer force so near at hand as the conventional wisdom suggests. armed with answers to these questions, the analysis also offers some suggestions for American conventional forces in the 1980s.

Assessing the Balance: Capabilities and Commitments

What is the balance of conventional forces and what shortfalls does the United States face in meeting her commitments in the 1980s? How well can American and Allied forces accomplish their missions against Soviet forces or other threats?[2]

Central Europe

NATO forces are outnumbered by those of the Warsaw Pact in almost every comparison of capability – personnel, most types of weaponry, and fighting units. (See Tables 2 and 3.)

Table 3: Warsaw Pact/NATO Central Front Ground-Force Equipment

Category	Pact: NATO[a]
Medium and Heavy Tanks	2.5:1
Artillery and Multiple Rocket Launchers	2.4:1
Armoured Personnel Carriers and Fighting Vehicles	2.4:1
Anti-tank Guided Missile Launchers	1:2
Helicopters	1:1.8

SOURCE: Department of Defense, *FY 81 Defense, Research & Evaluation Annual Report*, p.11–27.
[a]Equipment in combat units or stored in Central Europe. Excludes French forces.

NATO's purpose, however, is to deter Warsaw Pact attack, and so it does not need, nor has it ever intended, to match Warsaw Pact forces.

In contemplating the prospects for a successful conventional attack, Soviet leaders are unlikely to be confident that they could prevail quickly either from a 'standing-start' surprise attack or after completing their mobilization. To the extent that the Soviet Union might see an advantage, it would occur about ten to fourteen days after Pact troops begin mobilizing and as the first American reinforcements arrive. Then Soviet leaders might decide that, if they were not initially successful and a conventional war were prolonged, the costs and risks would be prohibitive given the destructive power of modern conventional weapons and the ever-present risk of escalation to nuclear war. Also, the Soviet Union would have to worry that the armies of her East European Allies might not be reliable or that political trouble might start in Eastern Europe which would require Soviet troops to perfom occupation duty.

NATO can take little comfort, however, from the uncertainties that the Warsaw Pact would face, for the West would still have some real military and political problems in defending itself. The Warsaw Pact's steady build-up in the last two decades has led to slightly higher levels of ground forces and the fielding of equipment qualitatively equal, if not superior, to NATO forces. NATO's advantage in tactical air capabilities remains but with a lower margin. Warsaw Pact units are designed to fight in contaminated chemical/nuclear environments whereas NATO forces on the whole lack sufficient protective equipment or an adequate chemical retaliatory deterrent. NATO's major problems would be political, however. Would the Alliance collectively agree to mobilize in the event of a Soviet build-up? And would France join her Allies quickly enough?

Contrary to recent concern, the more serious problem for NATO is not the threat from the 'standing-start' surprise attack, but an attack after a short mobilization period. Warsaw Pact forces would hold a higher advantage in combat power over NATO two weeks after mobilization (at least 2:1 in combat personnel) than is the case with forces currently deployed in East Germany (1:1). The Soviet forces may also achieve tactical surprise more easily during a mobilization period, when NATO would become used to seeing large and frequent troop movements that could be explained away, than if NATO detected a sudden upsurge in preparations and movement from routine positions. Finally, whereas political decisions to respond to an actual Soviet attack would be virtually automatic, NATO leaders might tend to defer difficult mobilization decisions during a Soviet build-up when Soviet intentions were ambiguous and when some Western leaders might hope that abstention from NATO mobilization would defuse the crisis.

Persian Gulf

Judging the outcomes of possible Soviet-American conflict in the Persian Gulf area is fraught with uncertainty. Key variables are the amount of warning time the United States would have and the role of American friends and Allies in permitting overflights, granting access to bases or facilities en route or in the area, and helping to fight the Soviet Union.

Another important factor is geography. The fact that the Soviet Union is adjacent to the area and the United States is thousands of miles away favours the USSR. Nevertheless the Soviet Union would have a difficult time moving troops into Iran because of the mountainous terrain. She would also have difficulty in mounting and sustaining a large-scale offensive because of the topography and dry climate of the area. Forces available for both sides are shown below.

Bearing these uncertainties in mind and assuming that the United States does not also face a simultaneous crisis in Europe, the balance in the Persian Gulf appears to be as follows: it seems certains that the USSR would dominate conflict near her border with Iran by using her land and air forces, and that the United States could prevail in the southern part of the Persian Gulf by using her carrier-based air power. At the head of the Persian Gulf, near Iranian oil fields, the Soviet forces would face considerable problems in bringing ground forces to bear but may be able to do so more quickly than the United States for the next few years. However, the US would have the advantage in tactical air power if land bases were available. The speed and cost of a Soviet attack would be largely determined by Iranian resistance, the reaction of local states, and by American air power. The immediate outcome of conflict near the Iranian oil fields would be uncertain but in a prolonged conflict, if the USSR was able and willing to commit additional forces from other theatres and the war remained conventional, the Soviet Union would probably prevail.

Naval Balance

The navies of the United States and her Allies have more and better warships and remain more capable than the Soviet Navy in absolute terms. However, the naval missions of American and Allied forces in controlling the seas are far more demanding than Soviet missions (generally to deny that control). Thus, Western naval forces require a margin of superiority. The Soviet naval build-up, however, has made increasingly uncertain the ability of Western navies to perform some of their missions in a timely manner and at acceptable costs.

During a general war with the Soviet Union, Western navies would have two important missions: protecting the sea lines of communication and helping to defend NATO's flanks and Japan. The West should be able to protect the sea lanes to Europe, Japan and the Persian Gulf. How quickly this could be done and at what cost would depend on whether the Soviet Union used the bulk of her attack submarines to defend the Soviet homeland and strategic missile-firing submarines or to challenge Western convoys.

Forces Available for Persian Gulf Contingencies

US	USSR
Naval Forces:	*Naval Forces*:

Naval Forces:
  2 Carrier battle groups on station in the Indian Ocean (16 surface combatants) with some 110 fighter and attack aircraft.

Air Force Units:
  AWACS early warning and air defence control aircraft on station in Saudi Arabia.
  1 Tactical air wing stationed in Europe (about 70 combat aircraft) with support equipment available in 24 hours.
  B-52 bomber strikes from bases in Spain or Guam within a few days.
  4 US-based tactical air wings and support equipment available in about 10 days.

Ground Forces:
  2 light infantry battalions (one army airborne battalion from Italy and one Marine amphibious battalion in Indian Ocean) in 24 hours.
  1 Marine amphibious brigade (about 12,000 men and 40 attack aircraft) in 7 days using prepositioned equipment stored on commercial ships at Diego Garcia.
  1 Airborne brigade (about 5,000 men) within 7 days and the entire division (16,500 men) in about 14 days.
  1 Pacific-based Marine amphibious brigade (about 12,000 men and 40 attack aircraft) in 21 days in amphibious ships.
  1 Airmobile division (about 18,000 men) in 4 weeks.
  1 Mechanized infantry division (about 18,500 men) by ship in about 6 weeks.

Naval Forces:
  Indian Ocean flotilla (8 surface combatants).
Air Forces:
  2 Tactical air armies (combined total of over 600 combat aircraft). (These aircraft could not conduct operations from Soviet bases against targets in southern Iran or much of Iraq).
  Backfire and *Badger* medium range bombers that could attack a wide range of Persian Gulf land targets and naval forces in the Indian Ocean.

Ground Forces:
  2 Airborne divisions (about 7,000 men each); six other airborne divisions could be available on short notice from other military districts in the Soviet Union. These are Category I units with a high state of readiness and have 75–100% of their authorized personnel.
  21 Motorized rifle divisions (authorized strength 14,000 each). These are Category II and III units which have a lower state of readiness, are manned at 10–50% of their troop authorization, and have older equipment than the Category I divisions generally found deployed against NATO and China.
  1 Tank division (about 11,000 men) of Category II or III status.
  KGB border guards of several thousand men equipped with armoured vehicles. These units would secure the rear of an attacking force.

SOURCES: US: Carnegie Panel on US Security and the Future of Arms Control, *Challenges for US National Security – Assessing the Balance: Defense Spending and Conventional Forces*, (Washington DC: Carnegie Endowment for International Peace, 1981).

SOURCE: *The Military Balance 1980–1981*, (London: IISS, 1980).
Except where noted, ground and air forces come from the southern military districts of the Soviet Union: North Caucasus, Trans–Caucasus and Turkestan.

Defence of NATO's Northern Flank would be difficult because this area is close to the heart of Soviet naval and land-based air power. Defence of the Eastern Mediterranean is becoming both more important for the West strategically and more difficult militarily. Keeping the sea lanes open to Turkey is important in order to be able to threaten any Soviet advance through Iran. At the same time, the United States has sent one of two carriers normally deployed in the Mediterranean to the Indian Ocean to help protect Western interests there. The Soviet Union would have difficulty in launching successful assaults to secure the

Japanese straits. However, the Soviet Pacific fleet is improving while the US Navy has also drawn on Pacific forces to reinforce the Indian Ocean.

The US Navy by itself could conduct other missions to place the Soviet Navy on the defensive and thereby limit its ability to interdict Western sea lanes. It could mount anti-submarine warfare operations against Soviet strategic submarines. The US Navy has extensive capabilities against Soviet strategic submarines in the open ocean, and the Soviet Navy could not even be confident of protecting from US attack its submarines deployed in defended areas near its homeland. The US could also conduct carrier-based air strikes against naval and air bases on Soviet territory. However, US aircraft carriers would come under heavy attack if they moved near enough to the Soviet Union to conduct such air strikes and would have great difficulty surviving in these waters, let alone being able to conduct effective air strikes against hardened Soviet targets.

In addition, the US Navy must be able to project force by air strikes or amphibious assaults in the Third World. At present, most third-world nations could offer little resistance. Soviet naval forces could seriously challenge US force projection operations only in those regions covered by land-based Soviet strike aircraft. In other areas, the Soviet Union is now better able to interpose her navy between her third-world clients and US fleets as a deterrent to US intervention.

Problems and Trends

Contrary to popular perceptions, the conventional military balance does not therefore overwhelmingly favour the Soviet Union. Instead, there is ambiguity about which side would prevail in areas vital to the West. On the one hand, the Soviet Union would not have high confidence in being able to win if she were to challenge American and Allied interests in Europe, East Asia, the Persian Gulf, or on the seas. Only in border areas such as Northern Iran would the USSR have a preponderance of military power. On the other hand, the United States would not have the high confidence that she wants in being able to defend her interests without resorting at some early point to nuclear weapons.

The United States faces three major problems in order to gain greater confidence in her military posture during the 1980s. First, US strategic air and sealift forces do not have enough capacity to send all the requisite forces within the desired time to either Europe or the Persian Gulf. For NATO, the US is improving her rapid reinforcement capabilities by pre-positioning in Europe additional sets of equipment for Army divisions (POMCUS), thereby reducing the burden on her airlift requirements.[3] For Persian Gulf contingencies, the United States is also moving to preposition equipment and supplies in friendly countries and at the island of Diego Garcia. The shortfall in lift capacity would be worse if the United States had to send forces to both theatres at the same time.[4]

Second, the United States lacks sufficient ground and tactical air forces to engage the Soviet Union's forces simultaneously in both Europe and the Persian Gulf. Most units of the Rapid Deployment Force designated for Persian Gulf contingencies are also earmarked as reinforcements for NATO. US forces would need an additional 2 to 4 divisions and six tactical air wings to make up the difference.

Finally, the United States faces a major shortfall in meeting her naval commitments in three oceans. At the same time, the growing Soviet naval build-up poses the prospect of greater risks for the US and Allied navies in being able to accomplish wartime missions such as safeguarding sea lanes and protecting NATO flanks and Japan.

American forces face other problems as well: retaining mid-career leaders and skilled manpower; operating fully ready forces; and being able to conduct sustained operations. The United States will have to solve these problems first by raising pay, by purchasing spare parts, and by building up stockpiles of ammunition and equipment before giving priority to additional new forces.

America's problems in meeting possible Soviet threats will multiply during the 1980s if past and present trends in the military balance are not reversed as the Reagan defence programme is trying to do. CIA estimates of Soviet procurement costs show steady, real increases in recent years for land, air and naval forces.[5] The CIA also estimates that Soviet investment spending, which covers the costs of procuring plants and facilities as well as new weapons, will continue to increase steadily over the next few years.[6] Finally, and most importantly, Soviet production of new weapons far outpaces that of the United States and her NATO Allies. Soviet annual tank production exceeds that of the United States by 3 to 1 and that of NATO as a whole by over 2 to 1; other armoured vehicles by 2.2 to 1 and 1.8 to 1 respectively; and jet aircraft by 2 to 1 and 1.3 to 1 respectively.[7]

In short, the United States faces major problems in the military balance, but the Soviet Union also faces problems and is not likely to conclude with high confidence that she could prevail in areas of vital interest to the West. This assessment is no reason for complacency, however, because trends in the current balance favour the Soviet Union, and the United States will face a larger gap between her capabilities and her commitments in the 1980s unless she finances increased military programmes over a sustained period of time.

American Strategy and Forces
Narrowing the gap between capabilities and commitments in the 1980s will depend largely on decisions about strategy, and on the size and composition of land and naval forces. Contrary again to popular perceptions, however, simply adding more active forces and more of the same weaponry may not be the only or best solution for American defence needs.

Strategy and Ground/Air Forces
Strategy: What range of possible Soviet provocations should the United States plan to meet? During the 1970s the United States prepared to fight a war in Europe while simultaneously containing a minor conflict elsewhere, the so-called '1½-war' strategy. However, the Soviet invasion of Afghanistan coupled with increased dependence of the West on Persian Gulf oil has prompted debate over the need to also meet a Soviet threat to the Persian Gulf.

One view holds that a Soviet military threat to the Persian Gulf is unlikely because the USSR would face high political and economic costs in occupying Iran and very considerable military difficulties in launching large-scale operations through Iran to the Persian Gulf. Increasing the American military presence in the region would only exacerbate the more

likely regional and internal threats to Western oil interests. Thus the United States does not need military capabilities in the Persian Gulf area beyond an over-the-horizon naval presence.

On the other hand, advocates of building up American capabilities for the Persian Gulf threats argue that even if the Soviet threat is unlikely, the consequences of a Soviet move into the Persian Gulf would be so harmful to Western interests that the United States needs to do more to guard against this worst case. Also the balance of US–Soviet military power in the region has an important bearing on the perceptions and policies of Persian Gulf leaders. Influenced by these arguments, the Carter Administration created the Rapid Deployment Force – largely from NATO reinforcements – to fight in the Persian Gulf.

Most American defence experts now say that the United States must be able to fight the Soviet Union simultaneously in Europe and the Persian Gulf as well as to defend South Korea from an attack from the North. This is a '2-war' strategy – one war in Europe, and a half war in the Persian Gulf and another in Korea. War in Europe would not be likely to occur without Soviet pressure on Western oil supplies in the Middle East. A Soviet move into the Persian Gulf would certainly raise tension in Europe, perhaps leading to the mobilization of troops and ultimately to the outbreak of war there.

Finally, there is the global or 'war-widening' strategy that seems to be evolving as official American policy. On top of the 2-war requirements, US forces must be able to strike at vital Soviet interests in areas where American forces have military superiority. In this view, the United States should deter the Soviet Union from moving towards the Persian Gulf, where Soviet forces would have many advantages, by posing the risk that the United States would not only try to defend the oil fields but would also impose costs on Soviet positions in other regions. Some likely targets might be the Soviet Indian Ocean squadron, Soviet fleets worldwide, the Soviet brigade in Cuba, and the client regime in South Yemen.

There are several questions to be asked about this 'war-widening' strategy. To the extent that the West has vital interests in access to oil and Moscow has less important interests in South Yemen or Cuba, is the US threat a meaningful one? Would the Soviet Union care much about losing Cuba, given her possible net gain in acquiring leverage over Western economies? Would American operations against Soviet interests around the world detract from military capabilities needed to stem a Soviet advance through Iran or in Europe? Are the benefits of possibly deterring the USSR in this fashion worth the risks of a war spreading beyond control? The questions are apt even if no ready answers are available.

Land, Air and Mobility Forces: Next the US has to decide how many and what kind of new forces to add. These answers, in turn, depend on judgments about how much risk is acceptable, how much warning time is defined as adequate, and what flexibility is necessary.

First and most obviously, the United States can add more active forces. The Defense Department appears to be headed in this direction according to reports that specify force goals for the mid-1980s of another 2 active Army divisions, 6 Air Force tactical air wings, 150 ships, and increased air and sealift capability. Further reports say that the number of new troops on active duty could reach 200,000, a 10% increase over present manpower levels. Arguments for increasing active duty forces depend in part upon judgments that warning for a Soviet attack into Iran is likely to be short (less than a few weeks), that more, well-trained active forces reduce the risk that the Soviet Union could win in Europe and the Persian Gulf simultaneously, and that more forces would be available for meeting third-world contingencies.

Against these considerations, there are the costs involved. Can the United States really acquire the additional equipment and manpower within the projected 7% real increase in defence spending at the same time as current forces are being made more ready and modernized? Or would there be consequent penalties for the readiness and modernization of existing forces? What are the implications for reviving the Draft if enough manpower cannot be raised within economic constraints? Some of these questions are discussed below but there is certainly room for honest doubt.

Alternatively, there is the view that the shortfall in capability can be met within the present force structure by redeploying some forces, and by improving US reserves and fast sealift capabilities.[8] This proposal assumes more than a month of warning of a Soviet attack into Iran. Previous Soviet military operations into Czechoslovakia and Afghanistan involved several weeks of observable preparations. With longer warning, American forces would have less need for forward bases, pre-positioned equipment, or strategic airlift and could rely instead upon fast sealift and mobilization of US reserves. This proposal would bolster US capabilities for a two-front conflict by reassigning two Marine amphibious brigades to the Indian Ocean from the Mediterranean and the Pacific and by modernizing four reserve divisions (3 Army and 1 Marine), 15 Air Force reserve squadrons, and the Marine Corps reserve air wing. The reserve units, it is argued, could be made ready to deploy a month after mobilization.

The benefits of this approach – more efficient use of present military manpower and less cost than active force expansion – must be weighed against the drawbacks. First, there is a risk in counting upon a sufficient lengthy warning time. Soviet intentions can be ambiguous, and during a long period of Soviet mobilization and manoeuvres, it would be difficult for any Western leader to summon and sustain the political support to activate tens of thousands of reservists. Then there is the risk that reserve forces could not meet the deployment goals nor be sufficiently combat-ready to enter battle. Finally, this solution takes away reserves earmarked for a long war in Europe, weakens the US commitment to NATO, and raises problems with US Allies.

New Types of Forces: Should the United States continue to purchase expensive and sophisticated equipment for her forces? A non-traditionalist argument suggests 'No'.[9] This view opposes the regular approach to planning – designing ground forces to fight the most demanding conflict with the expectation that they will be able to meet any lesser threats. The main criticism is that forces designed and procured for a European land war are not flexible or mobile enough to meet the more likely but unpredictable challenges elsewhere. 'Heavy' Army divisions with 60-ton tanks and a great deal of outsize equipment[10] are dependent, moreover, upon forward-basing and prepositioning of equipment if they are to move quickly to critical areas. However, bases and prepositioning in the Third World have political costs and are vulnerable to changes in policy of foreign governments. The United States could build up her strategic air and sealift, but this alternative is even more expensive.

Instead, the non-traditionalists argue that American military strategy in the Third World must rely upon interventionary forces centred around Marine units and aircraft carriers that can forcibly seize sea ports and nearby airfields, upon rapid airlift capability to bring in reinforcing *light* Army divisions, and fast sealift capability to support military operations thereafter. Such a strategy requires mobile and flexible forces with light tanks and artillery, less sophisticated tactical aircraft, more capable amphibious ships, and smaller aircraft carriers with V/STOL (vertical/short take off and landing) aircraft.

In this view, the United States will find it too expensive to develop different sets of forces – a heavy force for Europe and a light force for third-world contingencies. Moreover, bureaucratic politics and the services' preference for traditional forces would ensure that the necessary technologies for light forces would be neglected in the budgetary process. The United States, it is argued, should instead develop dual-capable forces, able to meet European contingencies with less armour protection and sophistication and better able to react to other crises than current forces.

Many observers would find much merit in this critique of American force planning, but questions arise about the proposed solution. Designing equipment for both high- and low-threat areas runs the risk of falling between two stools, adequate for neither set of circumstances. Moreover, there is the potential problem of incurring political costs in Europe, as today's problems of weapons standardization may multiply, and there may be questions about the combat effectiveness of the reconfigured NATO forces. It is at least encouraging that the Army is testing several new technologies for lighter and more combat-effective equipment and may scale back plans for equipping new 'heavy' divisions in the future.

Naval Strategy and Forces
Strategy and Missions: The debate on naval strategy centres on the choice between a forward defensive and an offensive strategy. Current NATO naval planning seeks to establish sea control by mounting a defence in depth along a series of anti-submarine barriers from Norway's North Cape to the Greenland-Iceland-United Kingdom (GIUK) gap and by conducting open-ocean, anti-submarine warfare (ASW) operations. The US Navy would also bottle up other Soviet fleets by closing exits from the Baltic Sea, Black Sea and Sea of Okhotsk.

The offensive strategy advocated by several high-level Defense Department officials seeks instead to ensure sea control by giving the Navy the controversial mission of attacking Soviet bases and fleets in home waters – such as military bases on the Kola Peninsula. With current forces, the US Navy would have great difficulty controlling the seas near Soviet territory, defending against barrages of missile attacks, penetrating Soviet air defences, and destroying hardened military targets. Again, questions arise. Would such attacks compel the Soviet Navy to use its forces for defence of the homeland and thereby prevent Soviet warships from conducting offensive missions? Would not the Soviet Union retaliate against US aircraft carriers with tactical nuclear weapons? Would the Soviet Union view an American attack using nuclear warheads as being essentially the same as an attack by US central strategic forces? Could not long-range cruise missiles, probably launched from submarines, be more capable of performing this mission?

There are also questions regarding other missions, such as controlling the Eastern Mediterranean and defending Norway, in view of greater Soviet naval capabilities in those areas. The purpose of controlling the Eastern Mediterranean is not controversial, but there is concern about the best means to this end. In the face of the Soviet *Backfire* bomber threat to US naval forces in this area and the demand for US ships in other areas, could more US and Allied land-based aircraft adequately substitute for carrier-based aircraft in the Mediterranean?

What would be the political costs of permanently reducing the US naval presence?

Some naval analysts question the wisdom of relying on naval forces to defend Norway. As many as four aircraft carrier task forces might be required to perform this mission, but it is not certain that carriers could survive in the high-threat environment near Norway. Is a carrier-based defence of this area worth the risk of losing important naval forces that could be used elsewhere? Could not additional land-based aircraft and combat troops, perhaps based in Norway during a crisis, substitute for naval forces to some degree? How would readjusting our defence posture in this area affect US relations with Scandinavian countries? Again, the fact that these questions can be legitimately raised tends to cast doubts on the concept.

The US Navy in the Indian Ocean: It has been suggested that the carrier task forces on 'temporary' duty in the Indian Ocean since 1979 should be assigned permanently to the area. Such a deployment would certainly lower the chance of being able to defeat Soviet fleets in the Mediterranean Sea and the Western Pacific, at least in the near term.

Unfortunately, there is no quick solution to this problem. There simply are not enough carrier task forces to meet old and new commitments. It would take many years and over $30 billion to add three more carrier battle groups for the Navy to meet its three-ocean commitments. As noted above, an alternative might be to build up US and Allied land-based air capability in the Mediterranean and the Western Pacific as a substitute for naval-based air power. To avoid this becoming a major political issue, it would have to be made clear that there was no overall loss in capability, and it would probably be necessary to deploy some carriers periodically in the Mediterranean and Western Pacific.

Naval Force Structure: The US decision on which naval missions to perform and how to handle a three-ocean commitment will in turn determine the size of the Navy. Building up the Navy to the size necessary to deploy in three oceans and in wartime to attack Soviet bases would require large increases in ship-building programmes and budgets. As a major step in

this direction, the Navy is reported to have recommended a new five-year ship-building and aircraft procurement programme leading to a 600-ship Navy of 15 carrier battle groups at a constant dollar (FY 82) cost of $120 billion. It is not clear that this costly proposal to perform better a wide range of naval missions is also the best way to increase US security overall. Some of the resources going to highly capable but expensive ships might be spent more profitably on greater numbers of less capable ships or on the Army and Air Force.

The Composition of the US Navy: The debate over the composition of the Navy centres on whether to rely on large aircraft carriers and accompanying escort ships or move toward greater numbers of smaller, faster ships armed with cruise missiles and V/STOL aircraft. Critics contend that the present Navy risks placing too many eggs in one basket. Today, the bulk of US naval offensive power is contained in 13 large carriers, the huge cost of which prevents the Navy from buying them in large numbers. In an age of satellite-based detection systems, long-range/high-speed cruise missiles, and nuclear warheads, all surface combatants are vulnerable to enemy attack. The Soviet Union can concentrate her resources on destroying the 2 to 4 carriers operating together in a particular ocean area. The loss of even a few carriers would seriously reduce US naval capabilities. The military rationale for building a larger fleet of less capable ships is to spread the US Navy's offensive capabilities.

The Navy counters by saying that large carriers are more cost-effective than smaller ships and that they can carry more and better aircraft and greater stocks of weapons and supplies. Moreover, large carriers are able to carry the heavy armour protection lacking in small carriers, and thus would be more survivable even if hit by several conventional warheads.

If the thrust of the reformers' arguments is correct, there is still the question of turning the new technologies into operational systems. Substantial commitments of research, development and procurement funds would be needed. To go all the way would mean curtailing now the current naval building programmes, and accelerating instead the development of new technologies prior to building more ships. There may be a middle road of modestly improving present naval forces while at the same time beginning to develop new technologies for future forces.

Manpower Constraints

In bridging the gap between capabilities and commitments, the US may face a major problem in attracting sufficient recruits of desired quality to man a larger all-volunteer force (AVF).[11]

Discussion of the AVF must focus on the Services' demand for manpower and the market's supply. The Services' demand for recruits is about 300,000 to 500,000 young men and women each year to maintain the active force of 2.1 million and the Selected Reserve of about 850,000. The Services seek a general level of quality among these enlistees by trying to recruit a large percentage of high school graduates and by limiting the fraction of enlistees who score 'below average' in mental tests. The Services' recruiting goals also depend upon the attrition rate among first-term soldiers, re-enlistment rates, and the number of Defense Department civilian employees who can fill military positions, for example at depot repair facilities. The Services can certainly affect recruiting goals at the margin by changing other manpower policies and can make up a recruiting shortfall at the cost of accepting lower-quality enlistees. On the supply side, the quantity and quality of prospective recruits will depend upon military pay relative to civilian wages, youth unemployment rates, recruiting budgets and national attitudes.

At present, the major problems of the AVF boil down to issues of 'quality' in the active forces and 'quantity' in the reserves. The main criticism against the AVF has been that the Services are meeting recruiting goals at the expense of accepting too many 'below-average' enlistees. As a result, the argument runs, the Services incur problems in maintaining force readiness. A second problem is that the AVF reserves are not getting enough new recruits. The Selected Reserve at 877,000 personnel is slightly above its authorized strength, but is 17% short of wartime mobilization requirements of about 1,000,000. In the Individual Ready Reserve (IRR) there is a shortfall of at least 200,000 and perhaps up to 400,000 of wartime requirements, principally for the Army.[12] The Services also face problems in retaining mid-career leaders and skilled specialists. This latter problem, however, is more a matter of pay comparability and quality of life than a direct result of an all-volunteer force.

Another criticism of the AVF has been that it is not representative of American society. About 22% of enlisted personnel in all services and over 30% in the Army are black, as compared to 13% of the population, and whites entering the Army tend to have poor education and are from the lower income groups. Thus critics say that the poor and minorities will bear disproportionate costs of the next war.

Setting aside arguments about the socioeconomic composition of the AVF, most manpower analysts maintain that major shortcomings in the active forces – quality and retention – could be resolved with increased pay and selected bonuses, and that the Selected Reserve could better meet its wartime strength with higher compensation incentives. The fact is that the AVF experiment during the 1970s was purchased 'on the cheap'. Military pay comparability to civilian wages fell by 15% from the base period of 1972 until the pay rise of 1980. Recruiting budgets were not adequately funded until recent years.

The large IRR shortfall, however, cannot be made up with pay increases. The problem is simply that, because of longer enlistments and fewer recruits entering active service, there are now not enough trained soldiers leaving active duty to fill the IRR. Indeed, there have been proposals for a draft limited to the IRR only.

The main alternative to the AVF is a return to selective service. Here the argument for returning to the Draft must demonstrate that the AVF cannot solve its manpower problems within acceptable costs, that the Draft *can* solve them, and that the advantages of a conscripted force outweigh the political and economic costs to society. Regarding the first point, the evidence is not conclusive, but figures from the first half of 1981 indicate that increased real wages for the military (from the October 1980 pay increase) have helped the services to meet recruiting goals, largely with high school graduates, and to exceed re-enlistment quotas. With respect to the second point, the Services might need only a relatively small number of draftees to make up recruiting shortfalls. Thus, the Draft may not raise the quality or change the socio-economic composition of the armed forces.[13] It can be argued that this marginal gain in quantity and quality is not worth the political problems in restoring the Draft, and a public perception that a few unlucky draftees are paying unfair costs. It is even doubtful whether the Draft would save much money. It would only save about $370 million according to one estimate – if the present force was maintained and the draftees were paid current military wages. Other estimates indicate that costs might even rise under the Draft because of greater turnover and larger training needs.[14] In other words, the pay of all first-term soldiers would have to be cut in order for the Draft to save large sums of money, and this could only be done if the services were no longer to rely on voluntary enlistments to fill the majority of manpower requirements.

In contrast to current arguments about the quality of the AVF, future debate will turn on the issue of quantity. The question that must be asked is whether the AVF can field an even larger active force – perhaps 200,000 more – at acceptable cost from a steadily declining manpower base. The number of newly eligible male recruits (18 year olds) will fall 15% from 2.1 million in 1980 to 1.8 million in the mid-1980s, and a full 25% to 1.6 million in the early 1990s.

The answer is not clear and much depends upon how the Defense Department is able to control some key variables. On the demand side, recruiting goals can be held down if more civilian workers are hired, if more first-term soldiers serve out their initial enlistment, and if more first-term soldiers re-enlist. On the supply side, the number of prospective enlistees will again depend upon pay comparability and inducements such as bonuses and education programmes. The Army, the prime beneficiary of a revived Draft, maintains that the services can expand the AVF despite the smaller manpower pool in the mid-1980s.[15] The key would be to increase retention, for this would immediately lead to a lower recruiting requirement. To do this, Congress must provide pay comparability, permit the services to target pay incentives where needed, and pass a new GI Bill of educational benefits that would cost about $1.5 billion the first year and about $5 billion annually in later years.

Thus, in expanding her forces, the United States may not necessarily face a shortfall in volunteers to man the forces, again contrary to conventional wisdom. Nevertheless, although prospective costs have not been detailed, they are likely to involve several billions of dollars.

Conclusions

If conventional wisdom exaggerates the Soviet position in the military balance, simplifies American choices for building up its forces and overstates the need to abandon the AVF, what does this analysis then suggest?

First, a more realistic assessment of the balance would make American leaders and the public more confident in conducting US foreign policy and acting to defend vital interests. Paying too much attention to one's own problems without considering those of the other side could lead to self-deterrence – failing to protect American interests when necessary because of an undue fear of losing a conflict with Soviet forces. Also, the Soviet Union could gain undeserved political dividends if America's friends and Allies were to perceive a crisis of confidence in the United States and begin shifting their policies as a result. While not overstating its military problems *vis-à-vis* the Soviet Union, the American public must nevertheless recognize that a shortfall between commitments and capabilities exists now and will only become worse unless a sustained effort is made to remedy present shortcomings.

Second, the United States should add to her conventional military capabilities after ensuring that present forces are modernized, fully manned, and made ready for combat. In deciding how to fill the gaps in capabilities, however, the Administration faces a richer menu of choice than simply adding more active units and traditional kinds of weapons, as conventional wisdom would suggest. The nation's economic difficulties and public pressure to reduce Federal deficits mean that no Administration can afford to do all things at once in rebuilding its defences and that the US must set limits and priorities among missions and forces. The following suggestions blend several ideas discussed above, but do tilt in the direction of acquiring more forces employing on-the-shelf technologies to meet the current shortfall in commitments, rather than waiting for new technologies to become available in a few years time. At the same time, research and development should proceed on promising technologies for future deployment. The following incorporate the main suggestions. America should:

- Adopt a two-war strategy. Being able to meet simultaneous threats in Europe and the Persian Gulf is a prudent strategy given the dependence of the West on Persian Gulf oil. Going beyond that to a global or war-widening strategy has uncertain benefits for deterring the Soviet Union, risks dissipating US military strength, and is more costly.
- Prepare and plan for meeting third-world contingencies. An exclusive American focus on the direct Soviet military threat risks not thinking about the more likely forms of Soviet aggression using third-world proxy forces and exploiting internal unrest. In these cases, the US military must find ways to assist the armed forces of friendly third-world states with command and control networks, logistics lines, air defence radar coverage, including AWACS, and other forms of support not involving combat units. The firepower of US naval and air forces must be available to support third-world forces if needed. US military assistance and arms transfer programmes can be useful to particular countries and lessen the need for deploying American forces nearby.
- Build up strategic air and sealift forces as top priority. Moving current forces in time to Europe and the Persian Gulf makes better sense than acquiring more forces that would get there too late or not at all, and would not involve the political problems of pre-positioning equipment abroad.
- Acquire additional light, mobile divisions equipped with anti-tank guided missiles, tank-killing helicopters, and light armoured vehicles. The Soviet Union is more likely to be deterred from direct military action in the Persian Gulf and the Third World by the certain prospect of facing several Army and Marine divisions that could get to a trouble spot quickly and aggressively, and thereby pose risks of direct super-power confrontation, than by heavy divisions that would have difficulty deploying in time. Reserve armoured divisions could be modernized to serve as reinforcements for these light divisions. American leaders also would have flexibility with light forces to meet unpredictable third-world threats. US ground forces in Europe would remain – as now – heavy divisions.
- Maintain a forward-defence naval strategy. Attacking Soviet military bases, as an offensive strategy requires, does not appear to be necessary for the Navy to accomplish its major sea control and power projection missions. Moreover, the high risks of operating near Soviet home waters and the cost of acquiring the requisite high-quality ships are likely to outweigh any military advantages that could be gained.
- Build more ships to perform current missions against a growing Soviet threat and undertake three-ocean deployments. Consideration must also be given to the possibility of substituting land-based aircraft for some of the carriers' responsibilities in the Mediterranean and perhaps in the Pacific.

Third, it would be prudent to continue the AVF, with pay comparability restored, to see whether volunteers can fill manpower requirements in the 1980s. By doing this, American leaders would avoid a potentially divisive political fight that could undermine the present national consensus for rebuilding American defences. If the AVF faltered, the need for a Draft would be more evident. If the AVF met its requirements, this approach at least would move the debate away from the technical issues of quantity and quality to the real political question that in the end will determine the future of the AVF. Does the United States really want a fighting force that is socially and economically representative of the country? No other justification is likely to overcome the strong opposition that a proposed return to the Draft would encounter.

NOTES

[1] See Jan Lodal, 'US Strategic Nuclear Forces', pp. 32–39.

[2] The conclusions on the military balance are derived from the recently published study by the staff of the Carnegie Endowment Panel on US Security and the Future of Arms Control, *Challenges for US National Security – Assessing the Balance: Defense Spending and Conventional Forces* (Washington DC: Carnegie Endowment for International Peace, 1981).

[3] By 1983, six US-based divisions could deploy to Europe within ten days, more than doubling US combat forces in Germany and eliminating much of the Soviet advantage in combat power that would come after a short period of mobilization.

[4] US mobility forces (sea and airlift) would not meet one half of the desired lift requirement for the first 30 days of reinforcing NATO and sending troops to the Persian Gulf, according to a recent Defense Department study. Even with forces programmed for the mid-1980s, the United States will not have sufficient strategic lift capacity for reinforcing Europe and the Persian Gulf simultaneously. See Patrick Oster, 'US Ability to Move War Gear Lags', *Chicago Sun-Times*, 28 June 1981; and *Armed Forces Journal*, May 1981.

[5] Central Intelligence Agency, *Comparison of US Outlays Against Estimated Cost of Soviet Activities* (Washington DC: CIA Publications, National Foreign Assessment Centre, 1979).

[6] Central Intelligence Agency, *Soviet and US Defense Activities, 1971–80: A Dollar Cost Comparison* (Washington DC: CIA Publications, National Foreign Assessment Centre, 1981).

[7] US Senate, Committee on Armed Services, *Hearings on Department of Defense Authorization for FY 1982* (Washington DC: USGPO, 1981), p. 548.

[8] William W. Kaufmann, 'The Defense Budget' in Joseph Peckman *et al*, *Setting National Priorities – The 1982 Budget* (Washington DC: The Brookings Institution, 1981).

[9] Stansfield Turner, 'Toward a New Defense Strategy', *The New York Times Magazine*, 10 May, 1981.

[10] 'Outsize' cargo consists of equipment, such as tanks and self-propelled artillery, that are too large for military transport aircraft, except the C-5A. The new Army mechanized division of the 1980s will have 60% more outsize cargo than now, thereby compounding present problems in transporting these units. One C-5A transport can carry over 100 tons, but one M-1 tank weighs 60 tons.

[11] The AVF consists of active duty and Selected Reserve units as well as individual replacements from the Individual Ready Reserve (IRR). The Selected Reserve, to include the National Guard, comprises trained combat units and most of the Army's support units. The IRR is a pool of previously trained manpower which must provide individual fillers and replacements for active and reserve units between the time of initial mobilization and several months later when trained draftees begin entering the forces.

[12] The range of estimated shortfall is due to different assumptions about how many IRR replacements report for duty, what the mismatch may be between skills and positions, and what casualty rates may be. See Robert L. Goldich, 'Recruiting, Retention, and Quality in the All Volunteer Force', *CRS Report No. 81-106F* (Washington DC: Congressional Research Service, 1981).

[13] Kenneth J. Coffey, 'If the Draft is Restored: Uncertainties, Not Solutions', in William J. Taylor *et al*, *Defense Manpower Planning: Issues for the 1980s* (New York: Pergamon Press, 1981).

[14] Robert L. Goldich, 'Military Manpower and the All Volunteer Force', *Congressional Research Service Issue Brief IB77032* (Washington DC: Library of Congress, 1981), p. 7.

[15] Interview with Lt-Gen. Robert Yerks, Army Deputy Chief of Staff Personnel, *Army Times*, 3 August 1981.

The International Context for US Security

HENRY KISSINGER

There are many complexities ahead of us on both sides of the Atlantic with respect to the area of national security. Of course, no-one has ever lived in a golden age; it was always a previous period. But when one thinks back to the 1940s and 1950s and maybe through the middle of the 1960s, I am struck by the fact that there was a substantial consensus about the general direction in which we were supposed to go. Moreover, there was some mutual reinforcement between groups like the IISS and those in governments, not in the sense that the intellectual community always agreed with what people in the government did – in fact they very frequently disagreed – but it was within a matrix of assumptions which permitted a dialogue that in the long run could only be helpful. I have the impression that in almost every country represented at this IISS Conference and in the national security community in general, these shared assumptions have substantially broken down. Thus, while it is perfectly possible to have debates about individual policies, what seems to be lacking is criteria for what we are trying to do and what reasonable goals might be.

The Structure of Politics

Let me therefore address some of the issues as they now seem to me to be emerging. I think the most fundamental one in all our countries, and the one that is least susceptible to intellectual analysis, is the fact that the structure of politics is in a process of change. The relationship of men to events is being substantially transformed in almost all democracies. The effort of getting elected is so irrelevant to the process of government, it takes so much of the energies of potential candidates, it tends to select from candidates those with qualifications that are not necessarily related to what has to be done when they are in office, that this in itself is an obstacle to conceptual thinking. Candidates must devote years of their lives focusing on how to get on the evening news, not

on what they will do when they get into office. I suspect that there is not a difference in kind, only a difference in degree, with other societies. So the intellectual backdrop becomes more important than ever, or else the problems of statesmanship become harder and harder to solve.

And the most difficult problem of all is to take a society from where it is, from what it is familiar with, to a future in which it has never been. How to bridge the gap between the familiar, which in a revolutionary period can be highly misleading, and that which is only conjectural, is perhaps more anguishing than ever in our time. It is complicated by the fact that the machinery of all of our governments – and certainly the machinery of American government – has become so complex that servicing it turns into an objective of its own. It grows increasingly difficult to disentangle departmental or agency self-will from the national interest. Or, what is more realistic, they tend to be identified. If one traces the evolution of debates on weapons decisions in the United States – and I suspect this must happen in other countries as well – it would be interesting to determine at what point bureaucratic calculation and at what point strategic calculation were dominant and to what extent they merged. I can think of any number of improvements of weapons systems during my period of office that were rejected because the services wanted to keep open the option of something entirely new and were afraid of precluding themselves from the entirely new by agreeing to improvements of what existed. The amusing thing is that the end result of the process was usually that they got neither the improvement of what existed, nor the entirely new.

What is even more significant is that, in these discussions, there was no sense of a strategy that would give one criteria on which to act. This resulted from many factors, of which Vietnam, compounded by Watergate, was the

53

most important. There has been a collapse or, at the least, weakening of the kind of intellectual consensus, of the type of dialogue from which outside groups could act as a reservoir of reflection and as the supplier of some criteria.

And so we find ourselves in a position in the United States – and in this respect, I repeat, I think this is a problem of the modern democratic state – that almost any new Administration acts as if the fundamental American objectives were never permanently settled, as if one could start over and over and over again. I am not saying this is a criticism of the current Administration, for I substantially agree with the direction it is taking, but as a description of the contemporary scene.

Essentially I agree with the strengthening of American defence and I agree with the general attitude that it reflects. But if asked to what strategy that increased defence expenditure is allied, what it is we should be aiming for in a specific way, I have to tell you honestly that I have difficulty in finding an answer. And if I have difficulty, as somebody who more or less has studied the problem for a long time, what will the general informed opinion be? I suspect many of us at this Conference are in substantially the same dilemma.

The Strategic Environment

We have been talking for over twenty years about the change in the strategic environment. When I first started talking about change, as Albert Wohlstetter and others pointed out, I was premature – or, as others have put it less kindly, I did not know what I was talking about. But whether there was strategic parity in the 1950s, or 1960s, or 1970s – and no matter how you measure strategic power or what the significance of strategic superiority is – the fact is that we have all known for twenty-five years that the growth of strategic nuclear stockpiles on both sides was bound to create a fundamentally new strategic, political, psychological and moral situation. Whether a leader will ever feel confident enough with esoteric weapons that have never been tested in combat conditions to launch a first strike, and whether the significance of the vulnerability of one facet of our strategic forces achieves a decisive advantage or not, are subjects of endless controversy. But everybody who has thought about the problem

has substantially agreed upon one fundamental fact: once the United States lost its strategic superiority, the overall relationships in the world would inevitably change. Whether we are inferior, whether we are now liable to be subjected to a first strike, belongs to another debate. But the mere fact that a plausible first-strike counterforce capability has been lost, or is being lost, has created new conditions. How then will the defence of other areas be conducted?

One of the weird aspects of the current debate about theatre nuclear forces (TNF) is that Europe insists that she cannot submit herself to the devastation of nuclear war on her territory, and that therefore the pristine, true strategic doctrine is one that exposes the United States to the devastation of her own territory for people who will not run that risk in the defence of themselves. When I say that it is not possible for the indefinite future to rely on strategic nuclear weapons for the defence of NATO, I am accused of undermining American credibility, or of confirming only what has been going on for twenty years anyway. Yet every European familiar with the debate in his own country must know that the same inhibitions that he is facing cannot fail to exist in the United States. While of course we can get away with avoiding the issue for ten years or twenty years, the growth of pacifism, which I think is a better description of what is happening than the growth of neutralism, is a reflection of a sense of impotence, a sense that there are no reasonable alternatives.

All of this is familiar. We have been debating, talking about it for twenty years so it is not even worth spending too much time on the subject except to say that we have known strategic parity was approaching and we have not done anything significant about it. We are increasing defence budgets by some agreed percentage at regular intervals, which rarely has the quality of translating itself into forces and never into a qualitative change in the military dispositions or into a change in the strategic concept.

The Weakness of Analysis

So we are left with the problems of no longer being able to implement the strategy of the 1950s, of having a mish-mash of forces in

NATO (for what, it is difficult to say), and of having six American divisions on a continent that rejects local defence but no American divisions in the area in which we rely on local defence. We may be lucky: the USSR has her own problems; there may never be a challenge that the US cannot cope with. But I would have to say again that we have no intellectual rationale for current NATO strategy, that we have all failed to some extent, and that you have every right to include me in this catalogue of criticism. I can tell you that I did ask the question (I am not saying this as an excuse), but it is one of the symptoms of modern government that you do not always get answers to your questions in a time span that is relevant to decision-making.

One of the problems is that, in the 1960s and 1970s, the intellectual community split into at least three groups: a group that rejected the very concept of defence or strategy; a group that identified strategy with arms control; and a group that identified strategy with whatever new weapons could be built. There is no point in discussing here the anti-defence group in this forum. It sems to me that all subsequent debates among defence intellectuals have been affected by the debates between the other two groups. The paradox has been that it was the liberal community that on the whole developed the most blood-thirsty strategies. Contrary to their natural proclivities, they would attempt to reduce strategy to an engineering problem; they argue that if you can kill a stated number of individual people and destroy a given amount of industrial capacity, you have achieved deterrence. Almost any new weapon system that has come along has been opposed by the liberal community on two grounds: first, that existing weapons were in any case adequate to do the job and, second, that, if they were not, some marvellous weapon was coming along fifteen years from now that made it unwise, uneconomical and provocative to build the available weapon systems. The conservative group on the other hand saw virtue in the accumulation of arms, usually only in the strategic field, unrelated to any manner in which they could be used.

The end result is that we are facing the danger of strategies which, if they work, involve horrendous consequences. It is not therefore irrational for pacifism to develop. We all know that the real problem is regional defence; yet this country has a volunteer army that everybody realizes cannot possibly meet these necessities. And all European countries are reducing their terms of service.

Nevertheless in America we are at least, it seems to me, now trying to become serious. Whether or not one agrees with every conclusion drawn by the Administration, there is a greater consensus in America now than there has been in fifteen years, which it is in the interest of our friends to preserve. The basic direction seems to me to be valid. Yet the breakdown in our domestic debate that I have described, which is now being healed to some extent, is accompanied by a growing breakdown in discussions with Europe.

Traditionally an alliance was an aspect of a balance of power; it had some common perception of a common threat, and shared some theory of how you were going to deal with this threat. Moreover, there was a shared assumption that you needed the accumulation of power represented by various allies in order to meet that threat more effectively. It is rare that alliances which are perceived simply as unilateral guarantees work indefinitely without demoralization on both sides. In the past, alliances usually broke down either when the threat seemed to become so overwhelming that the alliance was no longer seen as a protection, or when the threat was felt to have lost its menace so that alliance was no longer perceived to be necessary. It is a distinguishing feature of the Atlantic Alliance at the current period that both of these tendencies are occurring simultaneously: there is either an absence of belief in a particular threat or, if the threat is admitted, its menace is considered to be so overwhelming that it cannot be dealt with by Alliance procedures.

When one adds to the disagreement on strategy, which is endemic in our community, disagreement on East-West relations, disagreement on third-world relations, and insistence that the Alliance applies only to those areas which are contained in its legal definition, you have a recipe for impotence. It is as if, when a crisis occurs, a President of the United States must turn first to his legal adviser and collect a group of lawyers to determine exactly what the text of the document says. If there is no perception of common interests and of means to deal with them, how can the Alliance continue? How can it not lead to crisis unless we are lucky and our opponents disintegrate?

Everybody agrees that the Persian Gulf is vital to everybody's interests in the Alliance; yet everybody also argues that membership in the Alliance implies no obligation for security in the Persian Gulf or for Afghanistan or for any other area you may name, and that therefore it is possible to pursue totally separate and sometimes contradictory policies. Leaving aside what is right on the merits of any one of these issues, I do not believe it will be possible for the indefinite future to maintain present deployments which cannot be explained either in terms of a strategy on the ground for the defence of Europe or in terms of a global strategy for the defence of what is called 'The Free World'.

East-West Relations

In this connection, let me make a few observations about East-West relations. I have the impression that the debate in the United States about what came to be called 'detente' was characterized by two broad schools which, as with all broad schools, represent an over-simplification. There was what may be called the 'psychiatric school' that dealt with the Soviet Union by the precepts of personal relations. This school believed that fundamentally the Soviet Union reacts to the American threat, that therefore reassurance is the answer and negotiations the mechanism. Then there was the 'theological school' that saw relations with the Soviet Union as an aspect of a general ideological liturgy and resisted any contamination represented by the implication of compromise inherent in negotiation. This school concentrated on pointing out the benefits to the USSR of any agreement that might be made, as if the USSR would ever make an agreement in which she had no benefits. The real problem is whether one can balance the benefits to the US against the benefits to the USSR. To believe that one can negotiate a series of agreements of unilateral benefit to the US is a nostalgia which reality will not permit.

The same division occurs between Europe and America. One reads constantly about European pressures for negotiation and about the 'over-militarization' of American foreign policy. I can hardly be accused of being an apologist for this Administration but I would nevertheless like to raise the question: negotiation about what? What is it that we are trying to achieve? What is the purpose of it? I favoured detente in the 1970s and I favour detente in the 1980s if it can be properly defined. My definition of detente is that, in a world of two nuclear super-powers, one cannot conduct foreign policy by the maxims of the era of conventional weapons; statesmen have a responsibility to their publics to demonstrate to them that they are trying to come to grips with the nuclear problem. I do not think we can maintain the domestic cohesion of our societies if there should be a series of crises in which we have not demonstrated a serious effort at an alternative. We will not be able to keep our Alliance together unless this problem that preoccupies mankind is dealt with. Yet I do not believe that we can deal with these problems by abstract emotional assertions about negotiations which are never reduced to concrete programmes. The argument that detente led to a period of American weakness is a very convenient argument; it enables both conservatives and liberals to avoid the responsibility for some of their great causes; what happened in Vietnam and Watergate is swept under the rug; symptom becomes confused with cause. An America that went through Vietnam and Watergate was bound to experience a period of uncertainty; nor will a 'tough' Administration be able to avoid negotiating, as is in fact constantly asserted by its representatives. Our problem is not whether we should negotiate with the Soviet Union but whether we can negotiate with her without illusion on the basis of some concrete ideas of a world towards which we ought to be heading.

After every crisis – after Czechoslovakia, after Afghanistan – there is always the fear that this is the beginning of a general Soviet military assault. Instead it always presages a new Soviet peace offensive and it always leads to the same debate in all the NATO countries as if the initial provocation had never occurred. Fifteen months after the Soviet invasion of Afghanistan, every retaliatory measure that was taken has been dismantled and the major price the

Soviet Union has paid for her invasion is what the people of Afghanistan, without much help from the US, are exacting from her. We now see a crisis in Poland, and it has become a shibboleth that there will be very serious consequences if the Soviet Union goes into Poland. But have we answered the following questions? In the trade embargo that everybody seems to be talking about, are we going to apply it only to new business or also to existing orders? And if we apply it only to new orders, does it really mean anything? Do we apply it to all of Eastern Europe or only to the Soviet Union? If we apply it to all of Eastern Europe, do we also apply it to East Germany? And if we have no answers to these questions, which have now been before us for over a year (and I doubt whether we do), how serious is our policy going to be?

I have believed in linkage, both domestic and international. Domestic in the sense that it has always seemed a pity that we do away with many weapon systems as a result of budgetary decisions without ever offering them in arms-control negotiations. I believe in international linkage because I think that there is a relationship between events in different parts of the world and because one has to be careful not to let the process of negotiations become a safety valve for expansionism rather than a means of improving objective conditions. Of course, one can have a merry old time proving that if you link everything to everything, nothing will ever happen. It is a marvellous form of intellectual pyrotechnics. But the art of policy-making is to know how to make distinctions and the art in linkage is to know which events are related to each other. It cannot be sensible, for example, that we all announce great embargoes and then sell grain and butter to the East and that the Europeans build pipelines. It cannot be sensible that we maintain no relationship whatever between our economic policies and our political policies, not to speak of our strategic policies. It is certainly rational to debate to what extent trade should be related to other issues and what circumstances should be linked to which other circumstances, but one cannot and should not deal with each event separately.

Nor do I want to leave the impression that I believe that the Soviet Union is some mythical super-power carrying out devilish long-range plans in every category. The paradox is that the Soviet Union has great military strength and enormous political and sociological weaknesses. It is a system of government that has no legitimate means of succession. Not only do our experts not know who is going to replace Brezhnev, but Brezhnev probably does not know who is going to replace him. He may know who is going to replace him immediately but not in the longer term, and in any structural sense that is an inherent weakness. The economy is obviously not working, and all Communist countries, without exception, face the problem of what to do with the Communist Party in a developed state. The Party is not needed for government and it is not needed for economy. Under the socialist system you have the kind of absurdity that appeared in the Soviet press three years ago: the system operated on the basis of a tractor factory that was never built and they fired a Minister because he reported the existence of a refinery that did not exist. When you can lose track of factories and refineries, your system is not likely to be the wave of the future. Yet it presents us with a massive problem when enormous military strength co-exists with the necessity of fundamental domestic reforms. We should be concerned lest there be a temptation to try to clean up the external environment before dealing with the domestic one, or to deal with China before it becomes a kind of Japan. Those seem to me to be the dangers of the Soviet system, much more than a Hitler-like plan of world domination pursued with a specific timetable. There is a general attempt to expand influence but I do not believe there is a precise timetable.

Theatre Nuclear Negotiations
So we face an adversary that is both strong and weak and with the confusion within our systems that I have described. This is a situation crystallized for me by the TNF negotiations. Now for some weird reason the TNF negotiations have become in many countries the test of allied cohesion and of East-West relations. Whether that decision should ever have been taken is another matter. The argument is made that these weapons are designed to enable the United States to fight a nuclear war in Europe without destroying the US. Of

course, it is not self-evident to me that it helps Europe greatly if we are are all destroyed together, but I will put that aside. I would rather argue that on a purely technical analysis, the one thing these weapons do *not* do is enable the United States to escape unscathed. In fact these weapons guarantee that, if there is a war in Europe, it will couple the American nuclear defence to European nuclear defence. If we wanted to confine destruction to Europe, America should not change her present nuclear deployment in Europe. It is not, after all, as if these weapons *introduce* nuclear strategy to Europe. In my view, the reason for the inherent coupling is that, if the Soviet Union herself, and especially Soviet weapons, is attacked from Europe in response to a Soviet move against Europe, she cannot possibly permit the United States to stay undamaged and permit the entire United States' retaliatory force to remain unscathed while the whole nuclear strategy plays itself out in Europe.

But let me turn to the argument over TNF negotiations. In historical retrospect, it is not clear to me how we came to make a test case of a negotiation in which the Soviet Union has already deployed hundreds of weapons and we have not deployed one. A conglomerate of motives have involved the United States in this negotiation. Some are for TNF negotiations because they want to deploy weapons; others are for TNF negotiations as a means *not* to deploy weapons; some are for TNF negotiations as a link to SALT; and some are for TNF negotiations as a means of forestalling a negotiation on SALT. Finally there are those who are for TNF negotiations just because they like negotiations. I would defy anyone to give me a number between zero and 572 that would give us a criterion by which we can tell whether we are making progress or not. Moreover, what happens to the SS-20s that are affected? Do they get moved into Siberia? How was it possible that the absurd Brezhnev proposal – that they would stop deployment in Europe but not, presumably, in Asia if we stopped deployment – could be treated as a serious proposition?

Everybody knows America is getting into these negotiations primarily because it was thought that she could not otherwise hold Europe together or to the decision to moder-

nize. If you negotiate on a subject in which you cannot define what it is you want, you are in trouble. I have intellectual difficulty with TNF negotiations not related to SALT and I believe it would be dangerous for the US to repeat in SALT what happened in TNF, namely to be dragged kicking and screaming into a negotiation that she does not dominate. I have paid my price for SALT and I do not feel that I need to be the cutting edge of this particular debate, but I would like to make a number of general propositions.

Strategic Arms Negotiations
We are now in the strange situation that SALT II, an agreement that is described as flawed and that we are not ratifying, is being observed. For a period of time that is perfectly understandable, to enable a new Administration to make its decision, but it cannot be a permanent state of affairs lest we inherit the worst of every course. We will either have to ratify it or explicitly to drop it, or at least to agree formally on some limits that we are going to observe. If one looks at the debate last year, three arguments prevailed: *Backfire*, heavy missiles and the Protocol. The Protocol is being taken care of by time; the other two seem soluble problems. I decline to express a view on whether it is better to try to fix these problems now or go straight into SALT III, as the Administration has committed itself to do.

I do, however, want to express a view on one particular issue which has become an article of faith in the debate, unchallenged by the intellectual community, that what is wrong with previous SALT Agreements is that they ratified existing building programmes and that they did not lead to reductions. The argument is that the key to the solution ought to be a SALT that brings about major reductions. I have never seen that challenged and I do not know enough to challenge it but I do think a serious study should be made as to what the implications would be at each stage of conceivable reductions. After all, the overwhelming problem of our period in the strategic field is the disproportion betweeen warheads and delivery vehicles. That disproportion does not change at some levels of reduction. Indeed, you can make the case that, at some levels of reduction, if you reduce the number of delivery vehicles without reducing the proportion of incoming warheads in relation to the delivery vehicles, you actually increase the vulnerability of the delivery vehicles. I suspect but I do not know that, if you study this, you will find a curve if you plot vulnerability against reducing number that vulnerability increases for a while before it drops. I think it important to know at what point and to what level you reduce your vulnerability by reductions. And even if successful, reductions will finally return us to our starting point. Assuming that reductions stabilize the strategic environment – not an easy assignment – the problem of regional defence will re-emerge in more acute form; because stability means strategic war has lost its purpose.

The Third World

I am interested in the phenomenon in which the salvation of Western Democracies – their sense of identity, as it were – is thought to depend on *rapport* with the Third World. I favour an intensive dialogue with the Third World but I would question whether that part of the world most in search of identity can help us much with our own identity. But this is not the question I want to ask. I want to ask this: what recommendation about political structure should one tell the leader of a semi-feudal country emerging into modernization? We have debated the impact of certain Western policies on the stability of governments in various parts of the world, and we have debated whether arms sales have contributed to destabilization or whether there were other factors. Whatever the answers, the *process* of modernization has been a major contributory factor tending towards destabilization. Because these societies are feudal and because traditional obligations are broken down in the process of modernization, political insecurity and instability are almost inevitable. Nor are political insecurity and instability always and generally led by what we in the West or some in the West would consider the most progressive forces. But I have no answer to the question I pose. Supposing somebody in Saudi Arabia suddenly asked: 'I'd like to avoid what has happened elsewhere as a result of modernization; can you help us?' What advice would you give him? As I have said, I think we have no answer yet that I am familiar with.

Conclusions

I have pointed out some of my concerns. I want to make clear that I believe that, if one analyses what the Marxists call 'objective factors' on both sides of the dividing line, and the necessities of those parts of the world that do not consider themselves part of this struggle, there is absolutely no reason why we should not be the more relevant part of the world and why we should not be able to solve our own problems. We have torn ourselves apart for a long period. Whether you like the manifestations or not, there is in the United States an attempt now to come to terms with reality. What I believe the IISS can do is begin again to create the intellectual capital on which some of us drew in the 1960s and which has not in my view been replenished in the last ten to fifteen years.

US Strategic Concerns and Capabilities

LAURENCE MARTIN

From the outside, at least, it occasions no surprise that the United States in engrossed in a debate about the balance between her security concerns and capabilities, for few nations can have seen their conception of national security develop so expansively over such a relatively short historical period. Every state has some capacity to defend its independence and integrity, though this capacity does not always include military means. Where it does, and is sufficient to influence the international equilibrium around it, we are on the way in traditional parlance to a 'Great Power'. When there is scarcely a point on the globe at which the state cannot contemplate exerting influence and when the inclination to do so frequently prevails, we are close to a tolerable definition of a super-power.

As the concept of security expands beyond direct defence of national territory to safeguarding trading interests and even to promoting a congenial diplomatic and ideological milieu, there is increasing room for debate – in such circles as are permitted such luxuries – over the appropriateness of the concerns and their relationship to true national interest. Some concerns arise chiefly – like overseas military bases – to facilitate the pursuit of other concerns, and concern and capability are thus revealed in a complex mutual relationship. Nations acquire 'commitments' which may be embodied in pledges or merely inferred from behaviour and interests; but, as allies and clients often learn to their cost, the substance of a concern or commitment is only truly measurable when the contingency envisaged arises. Circumstances and occasion are vital variables and these can cut either way; Munich stands as the symbol of concerns abandoned in crisis and Korea as that of concerns only discovered when the moment came. This reminds us that one can never be safely dogmatic about concerns and capabilities, that it can never be unarguably clear what provision should be made for contingencies, and that a wise security policy will consequently embody a good deal of flexibility both material and mental.

The pre-war United States of 1939, isolationist and to a large degree securely isolated, enjoyed a vast surplus of potential capability for pursuing what it conceived as its security concerns. After 1945, the effects of the war on American society and economy, in relation to the rest of the world, gave the United States an even more marked ascendancy with which to adopt, after some domestic debate, an extremely extended conception of national security. The Truman Doctrine and the North Atlantic Treaty – only the second treaty of alliance in American history – made some of the implications of this conception explicit, while the Korean War and the collapse of Indochina nourished an Asian extension. Though vast, the tasks were lent some appearance of manageability by the supposed monolithic nature of the Communist Bloc, and by the residue of colonial power possessed by America's new allies, with a corresponding lack of other autonomous actors in Afro-Asia. Soviet power, potentially considerable enough, was for the moment restricted by economic weakness and lack of strategic 'reach', except in Europe, where the Allies of the United States displayed an exceptional degree of political stability and cohesion that made a strategy of generalized deterrence plausible.

Subsequent years have, of course, bred a sense of disillusionment and frustration. Defeat in Vietnam was undoubtedly the most painful and influential episode in this process but other and perhaps more fundamental trends have been at work: the emergence of nuclear multipolarity and a somewhat paradoxical belief in many Western quarters that this makes war and even military policy impracticable, the disappointing results of decolonization so far as stable and congenial regimes are concerned, the increasing independent-mindedness of erstwhile deferential allies, and the distraction of domestic social problems, have all contributed to what Vietnam was thought to demonstrate – a gross overstretch of American commitments and a dangerous imbalance between strategic concerns and capabilities.

The Nixon–Kissinger regime purported to handle this problem with a retreat from positions on the accepted defence perimeter, making continued American participation dependent on the efforts of the threatened extremities, and attempting, in a manner not unreminiscent of Mr McNamara's arrogant belief that the Soviet Union could be educated to adopt American strategic theories, to train the USSR to play 'linkage-politics'. President Carter, though in practice presiding over the beginning of an up-turn in American military effort, gave currency to a much more extravagant rhetoric of retreat from both the traditional goals and methods of containment.

The last two or three years have seen an abrupt reversal of this trend of retrenchment, a trend ratified in President Reagan's election and perhaps most sharply registered by the abortion of President Carter's effort to remove forces from Korea. Realization of the rate at which Soviet defence expenditure has been rising throughout the years of so-called detente, and appreciation of the quantity and quality of armed forces that these efforts have conferred on the Soviet Union, particularly amongst alarmed military specialists, while Angola, Ethiopia, Afghanistan and other episodes did more to arouse public alarm and were wisely believed to signal a new phase in the employment of military force to the extension of Soviet influence. Simultaneously the oil-shock, the Iranian Revolution, and the wars in the Gulf demonstrated other dangers to Western interests to which, with or without a Soviet role, the military balance might be relevant. American voices which had been trying to break through the sliding consensus against concern for the balance suddenly found a hearing, and the Reagan campaign pressed this advantage in a frequently strident tone, a stridency exaggerated as the Carter camp wavered between mounting the 'preparedness' bandwagon and tarring the Republicans with the charge of war mongering.

The result has been to lead American Allies to wait with a probably excessive degree of anxiety to see the practical outcome in United States policy. Legitimately concerned that an excess of defeatism and self-denigration should not be replaced by unreflective activism and provocative rhetoric, the Allies also await with rather less admirable nervousness to see what efforts the new American mood may require of them.

Immunity Against Attack and Beyond

The essential basis for a proper resolution of these uncertainties is consensus on the irreducible security concerns of the United States. Of these concerns, the core must clearly be the immunity of the United States herself from direct military attack. Today the main weight of assuring this immunity falls on strategic nuclear offensive and defensive forces that can be deployed almost entirely in or from the United States herself. The healthy state of this balance is therefore the most vital element in the security concerns of the United States – though for technical reasons it may never again be capable of conferring impenetrable immunity. This strategic balance is also an essential basis for any more extended conception of security policy, for only an adequate strategic deterrent can insure against lesser and more localized military efforts being trumped by nuclear threats.

Of the more extended security interests, traditionally the most unquestioned has been the exclusion of Western Europe and, to a considerably lesser degree, Japan, from hostile embraces. In original post-1945 American security policy, as in the rationale for American entry into both the World Wars that have occurred so far in this century, the integrity of Western Europe was thought to play a vital part in the direct defence of the United States, as both a base for attacks on, and counterattacks by, the United States. This rationale has largely expired as a result of evolution in the technology of strategic weapons, though not wholly so, as debates on submarine warfare or cruise missiles illustrate.

The primary residual case for the United States to regard Europe and Japan as vital interests rests on the desirability of unfettered economic access to such valuable trading partners, and on the more sentimental place of Europe – much less so of Japan – in a preferred

American conception of the global milieu. These positive interests have, of course, their negative side: the importance of denying such assets to the hostile Soviet super-power. This was the idea invoked by John Foster Dulles in 1954, to justify the inclusion of Europe under a retaliatory umbrella: 'its industrial plant represents so nearly the balance of industrial power in the world that an aggressor might feel it was a good gamble to seize it even at the risk of considerable hurt to himself. In this respect, Western Europe is an exception'.[1]

Beyond the inner ring of America's European and North-east Asian concerns lies the so-called 'peripheral' zone of Afro–Asia, with a special appendage in Latin America, geographically nearer and often psychologically more distant. It is in these peripheral areas that most American blood has been spilt in recent years. Once seen as an area in which to close the ring of containment begun in Europe and Japan, in more recent years the periphery has been seen as an area less likely to pose threats requiring or amenable to military solutions. This evolution of thought has been prompted by American defeats, by the diffusion of political and military power to these areas, and by the hope that the Third World would prove as intractable to Soviet as to Western power. Unfortunately, one vital area, the Persian Gulf, defies neglect on any of these counts and is lent vital significance not merely by its general economic importance but also by its particular role in the welfare of Europe and Japan. Indeed those who, like Professor R. W. Tucker in well-known writings, warn of the mortal dangers for America in the Persian Gulf, do so in terms reminiscent of Mr Dulles' argument: Western Europe is *the* vital extended security interest of the United States; all that has changed is the line of approach for Soviet power, once by marching from Eastern Europe, now, indirectly by seizure of Europe's energy supplies in the Gulf.[2]

Both Presidents Carter and Reagan, with rather different degrees of enthusiasm, have acknowledged strategic concerns in all three areas outlined: strategic nuclear defence; Europe and Japan; and the peripheral zones. Both Administrations have common elements in their prescriptions for cure: new strategic systems, including mobile and cruise missiles; continued refurbishment of European defence along the lines of the Long Term Defence Plan and Long Range Theatre Nuclear Force deployment, and a Rapid Deployment Force associated with improved lift and renewed acquisition of overseas basing facilities. Much remains uncertain about how these and kindred lines of development will be pursued in practice. In any form, the cost of the programme is high and its success entails a great deal of appropriate response by allies and third parties to the overall American–Soviet competition. What is clear, therefore, for all the surrounding uncertainty, is that public support, both American and foreign, will be essential over a sustained period. The recent recoil of popular feeling in America toward military preparedness could be dissipated by indiscriminate pursuit of security programmes that are not clearly and consistently based on a plausible strategic rationale; a rationale moreover, that is supportable in terms of the 1980s and not only by the surviving clichés of the early Cold War years. Failing such a rationale, the apathy and disillusionment that all too quickly followed earlier surges of enthusiasm characteristic of post-war American security policy – Korean rearmament, missile gap, counter-insurgency, and so on – may appear in their cyclical way before any real progress has been made.

The Military Unity
The whole topic is one of those familiar in strategic studies, where it is almost impossible to say anything novel that is also sensible. It may be wise, therefore, to begin by repeating some commonplaces that are nonetheless important. In the first place, military force is not the only instrument of security policy. Political and economic measures are available to win and support friends and, less readily, to weaken and punish enemies. Such measures, often less decisive than military action, are also usually less costly in terms of domestic and international politics. In a globally integrated world, where some of the interests at stake concern access to national resources, economic policy may also serve security by reducing or rechannelling dependence.

Politico-economic leverage is admittedly often a slow and uncertain instrument when measured by the criteria familiar to protagonists of military action. In particular, such leverage may only be able to influence general trends; the carrot of trade and technical assistance, so beloved by advocates of tying the Soviet Union to good international behaviour by 'linkage', may have effect, for example, in increasing Soviet inhibitions about possible aggressive courses of action; but, if the Soviet Union were nevertheless to opt for aggression, we must not expect the threat of terminating the same trading relations to turn the carrot into an effective stick. Equally, however, there is much that *military* power cannot do. It seems to be of strictly limited efficacy, for example, in influencing the longer term evolution of politics in third-world countries or preserving access to vulnerable economic facilities. Even if force serves such purposes some of the time for some people in some places, it will not necessarily do so everywhere. Moreover, even where force seems the appropriate instrument, we cannot expect to have enough of it everywhere.

Recovery from the illusion that military force is becoming useless, a prevalent error until recently in Western countries, should not lead to the equally erroneous belief that it can do everything. The United States cannot hope to restore the remarkably favourable equilibrium of the 1950s. There has been an absolute growth in Soviet military power, both quantitative and qualitative, that can never be wholly neutralized by competitive effort. Soviet acquisition of a full range of nuclear weapons, of considerable long-range air and sealift, and of ocean-going naval power, alters the strategic context permanently. The problems of extended American deterrence on behalf of allies are, for instance, radically enhanced by these developments. The leading allies in Europe and Asia have themselves so improved their economic status relative to the United States, that this also fundamentally affects the political context within which they can be expected to evaluate American leadership and within which the American taxpayer will assess his own obligations to the Alliance. A further development that invalidates mere revival of strategic notions of the past is the diffusion of significant military, including a modicum of nuclear, power to countries outside the two main East-West blocs.

For all that has changed, however, there remains much that is familiar in any relatively widely accepted inventory of necessary American concerns and capabilities. Despite some vocal minorities, there is widespread consensus in Western countries that *some* military capability is required at all three levels of strategic concern identified here – strategic nuclear, Europe–Japan, third-world 'periphery' – and that, under present circumstances, only the United States can provide a satisfactory core for the necessary effort. The nature and amount of provision needed remains controversial and the controversy must be approached in the realization that failure to establish a consensus credible to more than a handful of strategic specialists has underlain many of the political failures in past security policy.

Strategic Forces and Concerns
So far as strategic nuclear forces are concerned, there seems to be solid support in the United States for the view that it was an aberration to believe that the nuclear balance was evolving to a stalemate of mutual assured destruction based on counter-city forces employing an only slowly-evolving technology. There is, indeed, now widespread anxiety that even the necessary minimal posture necessary to deter an attack on the United States may be temporarily lost at some time in the near future as the theoretical Soviet capability to destroy a high proportion of American land-based missiles, and the unattractive sequence that would be initiated by any American retaliation with the remaining elements in the Triad, confers what might be called a 'functionally disarming' strike capability on the Soviet Union. This would be all the more alarming if technological trends began to undermine the rest of the Triad.

More generally, those who believe in the importance of 'perceptions', argue that such subtle strategic calculations combine with cruder features of the gross, 'static', strategic balance to weaken American influence and encourage Soviet adventurism. From this perspective, the Soviet Union is achieving 'undeterrence'. While the justification for such beliefs is hard to prove, they are found in places not readily labelled hawkish. Thus a Carnegie

63

Endowment study asserts that it 'is generally agreed that the Soviets have acted with enhanced confidence and that this is at least in part due to strategic force improvements'.[3]

Two elements seem common to both the Reagan and the latter-day Carter approach to this problem. Firstly, the construction of some reinforcement, presumably MX, for the vulnerable ICBM force; secondly, the evolution of a limited strategic option to respond to limited nuclear attacks and, in particular, to bolster extended deterrence.

Comment on this approach might begin by endorsing continual perfection of the essential strategic forces to provide the deterrence against full-scale nuclear attack that is the prerequisite of any free hand at all for resistance to a large strategic nuclear power. This requirement is so fundamental that it should not be unduly hampered by arms control or driven thereby into technological courses that are unreasonably more expensive or less viable than would be needed in the absence of negotiated restrictions. On the other hand, there are occasionally signs that the concept of the Triad has been deified beyond all necessity. The essence of the Triad is not the element of triplication but of vulnerability for the total system. Seeking that invulnerability at all times by reference to the three media of locomotion also hallowed in the traditional organization of the armed services is a principle deserving constant scrutiny.

The question of limited options is more debatable. It is true and important to recognize that any positive uses of nuclear weapons must be limited uses. In particular, if the United States is to continue to extend a deterrent umbrella over her allies so that the entry of a nuclear note into extreme crises is not always to militate against Western interests and fortitude to the same extent as we used, in the palmy days of American nuclear superiority, to believe worked in our favour, some plausible possibility for nuclear action must be retained in American capabilities. The acquisition of appropriate accurate weapons for discriminate action and of capable mechanisms for command and control consequently seems to be wholly justified. Whether the forces for controlled response need to be raised to capacity for large-scale counterforce action – the re-ciprocal for the feared functionally disarming strike – seem much more dubious. In theory the idea that protracted counterforce action would be distinguishable from unrestrained counter-city warfare in its consequences is comprehensible enough. But detailed analysis of what such an encounter would mean in terms of casualties and damage makes one doubt whether such extended counterforce exchanges could reasonably be expected to elicit responses more measured than that designed for assured destruction. Consequently it seems dubious whether such contingencies are ones that statesmen would embrace in practice or taxpayers underwrite in preparation. Admittedly, capabilities which may not seem worthwhile for the added margin of deterrence they are thought to provide, may be sorely missed if deterrence fails. But debate on this issue must recognize that nations never choose to provide themselves with all the security that is theoretically possible, quite apart from the argument that some kinds of defensive preparations stimulate dangerous reciprocal responses from others. Thus while the invulnerability of a large retaliatory force of last resort seems an unarguable priority, and while a moderate capacity for limited strategic nuclear strikes seems essential if the approach to the nuclear threshold is not always to be the point at which American – and consequently allied – nerve cracks, more thorough-going preparations for strategic nuclear 'war fighting' need to be handled sceptically if they are not, among other things, to play into the hands of the root-and-branch nuclear disarmers.

Extending Deterrence

That the United States has a powerful interest in the continued freedom of Western Europe from Soviet domination is another relatively uncontroversial aspect of American security debate. What is at issue is, of course, the level and type of investment the United States should make in furthering her interest. Somewhat similar considerations appear in the United States relationship with Japan. For the past two decades the trend has been for American policy to move away from nuclear solutions, impelled by the growth in Soviet strategic and, latterly, theatre nuclear capability. This trend has exacerbated the problem of providing European defence by conventional means. The relative inability of the Soviet Union to bring conventional military power to bear on Japan has, in that quarter, permitted the retention of a remoter, deterrent posture. In Europe the combination late in the 1970s of decayed nuclear guarantees with a rising perception of Soviet capability has led to the emergence of the Long Term Defence Plan (LTDP) to improve NATO's defensive capacity with particular emphasis on readiness, reinforcement and the exploitation where possible of new technology. Despite the drift of American policy away from first use of nuclear weapons, clearly visible in the thinking behind the LTDP, although for obvious reasons never formally stipulated, Soviet aquisition of a possibly dominant first use theatre nuclear capability of her own has prompted the NATO modernization programme of December 1979, with all its attendant political trauma.[4]

The relatively favourable European response to the LTDP, despite some occasional backsliding, testifies to its appeal as a sound, if unimaginative, response to the sustained Soviet threat. There are, however, substantial reasons to keep it under sceptical review. Leaving aside the obvious possibility that the effort may be incapable of providing an adequate defence, it tends to draw more and more allied resources into the maintenance of forces inflexibly committed to what may not be the most likely scene of East-West confrontation. Clearly it is only a degree of defence in Europe that justifies such an estimate of probabilities, but it remains possible that the clarity of political lines and the unquestioned level of the stakes, combined with the existence of some indigenous European nuclear power, may make Europe a safer place than any other in which to rely on the deterrent aura of nuclear escalation even in the present world of relative strategic parity.

So long as the United States remains allied to Western Europe and the interests of the two are also linked in various other areas of the world, particularly the Persian Gulf, the state of the European balance will be a factor in determining American freedom of action everywhere. Crises outside Europe must therefore be managed without drawing down whatever is regarded as the minimal posture necessary for deterrence or defence – and for Western European confidence in them. If, as is already the case, the United States is to urge Europe – and Japan – to help solve this dilemma by increased efforts of their own, a balance has to be struck between whether this effort is to be one of substitutive provision in Europe for American capabilities diverted elsewhere, or of shared participation in extra-European contingencies.

The whole problem could be approached with more confidence were it not that existing levels of conventional and theatre nuclear defence in Europe were already thought inadequate and required at least the 3% per annum LTDP increases before the extra-European contingencies were taken as seriously as they are now. The competition of the flanks of NATO for ready reinforcement and the close entanglement of the southern flank with Middle Eastern crises only adds to the problem. It seems plausible, therefore, that an attempt to devise new concepts of European defence, perhaps embracing weapons and forces less incompatible with employment in other theatres, employing an ever higher proportion of European conventional forces, possibly of a reservist nature, the whole perhaps more frankly directed at deterrence of war rather than sustained conflict, is the only framework within which military programmes will not founder politically for lack of credibility. The political context in Europe deserves, indeed, the most careful consideration as a growing anti-nuclear movement bedevils nuclear solutions, while scarcely breeding an atmosphere in which the logical alternative of conventional defence and personal military service is likely to find support either.

There is a parallel to the European political debate about military service and effort in the problem of manning American armed forces, upon which the NATO contingency places the heaviest potential burden. Whether the United States can discharge her commitments on the basis of voluntary service is not only a highly technical question but one so enmeshed in American politics and society that outsiders would be wise to be modest in their comment. While manning the forces might be superficially easier with compulsion, it is obvious that such a measure would radically alter the political context of all United States defence policy. This context would also alter every time American forces became involved in operations, particularly actual conflict, and it is hard to predict whether compulsion rather than voluntary service would enhance or diminish the ability of the United States to conduct prolonged low-level combat or to run risks in crises. The arguments that made a largely expeditionary army opt for voluntary service were weighty, and the burden of proof lies on the advocates of change. At the very least, the problem enhances the case for strategies that by the exploitation of technology, the restructuring of forces and the maximization of Europe's own contributions, perhaps by way of territorial reserve functions not practicable for the United States, reduce the need for American troops beyond the important minimum necessary to create the deterrent commitment. Such a course would also conform rather than run counter to the perhaps remote but ultimately inevitable prospect of Western Europe devising a more independent system of security.

Third-World Contingencies
America, Europe and Japan alike have become acutely conscious of their interests in the Third World and of their vulnerability to disruption by instability or by active hostility to the West. Such disruptions may well be promoted by the Soviet Union and recent events have made more plausible the danger of direct domination of third-world areas by Soviet armed forces or their allies. Despite the undoubted role of military force and of Soviet influence in the third-world arena, there are lively fears in Europe and Japan that, on the rebound from the extreme recessiveness that followed Vietnam, the United States may exaggerate both the Soviet dimension to third-world conflicts and the contribution Western military power can make to resolve them.

Many instabilities, it is argued, are more amenable to diplomacy than to force or threats of force, and if instability is averted in this way, opportunties for Soviet intervention will be minimized. Conspicuous military preparation may revive waning fears of Western colonialism just as Angola, Ethiopia, Afghanistan and a growing perception of Soviet militarism have

bred an unprecedented readiness in many third-world countries to perceive the Soviet Union as a threat. The Soviet Union should not be relieved of this opprobrium. Few parts of the Third World are absolutely vital to the West so long as the whole edifice does not slide into hostile hands. In most areas remoteness from Soviet power and the pluralism of local politics makes reversability of any Soviet gains an ever-present possibility.

This is not a justification for complacency or for acceding to Soviet intrusions or local hostility when they can be avoided. Military power seems to be playing an increasing part in Soviet policy towards the Third World and this has important implications for the concept of reversability. The Soviet Union should no more be offered a free run in the Third World than be relieved of the stigma of aggressiveness by excessive American reaction. The balance of capability for American intervention is not unfavourable and Soviet strategic mobility, though much improved, remains inferior to that of the United States. It is the trend that is worrying and this can be reversed by prudent action more likely to win political support on the basis of sober analysis than alarmist rhetoric. It is, indeed, the domestic political consensus rather than the physical capability that has been most lacking in the recent American posture toward the Third World, and this lack has probably rested as much on an inadequate rationale for action as on simple infirmity of purpose.

Superior logistics will not help, of course, if Soviet intervention, perhaps by acting covertly or gradually in response to invitation from local sympathisers, offers no clear-cut opportunity for confrontation. Military intervention must thus be kept firmly within a context of coherent political strategy. Given the autonomy and complexity of modern third-world societies, their own increased military capability and very proper American inhibitions about the role of armed force in relations with weaker states, it would seem wise to regard military power as a lever to reinforce politico-economic action, and by no means as an easy substitute for it. Neither in time, place nor method, should hostile action be able to dictate the form of American response. Had the phrase not been given such a bad start by Mr Dulles –

or, at least, by his critics – 'at times and places of our own choosing' would seem a good motto for Western counter-interventions in the Third World.

There is, of course, one painful exception to the possibilities for a relatively relaxed and selective outlook on third-world contingencies. Western dependence on the oil of the Persian Gulf requires and is certainly receiving very special attention. The loss of Gulf oil for more than a brief period would spell economic catastrophe. Conservation of energy consumption, diversification, both technological and geographical, of sources of energy and the creation of emergency reserves could dramatically cushion the effects of even a medium-term cut-off, but could not eliminate them. The danger being such in economic terms, it is obvious that immense political leverage accrues to anyone with the potential to engineer disruption of the oil flows. So long as Western dependence continues, the proximity of the Gulf to Soviet power will render oil a latent factor in *any* East–West crisis. Nor, of course, should the salience of the oil issue make anyone forget the long-established strategic value of the Middle East as a geo-political fulcrum of three continents.

The two dangers most anticipated in current Western discussions are disruption of supply by reason of local circumstances in the Gulf – whether by the deliberate policy of major suppliers or as the involuntary consequence of conflict, and instability, perhaps fostered by the Soviet Union – or an actual direct incursion by Soviet military forces. Opinions on the likelihood of the latter dire event are mixed but few deny an impressive Soviet capacity to undertake such an operation or the difficulty with which the Western allies could respond.

The balance of distance and capability, which still favours the United States in many parts of the Third World, is decisively adverse in the Gulf. Contiguity of the Soviet Union and the large amount of medium-range airlift with which the Soviet Union was providing herself long before talk of 'global-reach' began, gives her a clear advantage over the remote the United States. The occupation of Afghanistan has improved Soviet overland access, with corresponding advantages for air strike and cover. The Red Army's seven or eight airborne divisions possess formidable firepower and tactical mobility once landed. By comparison, American forces, which are the only Western force worth considering against the Soviet threat, despite the small French and British presence, are remotely based, seriously devoid of strategic lift, and lacking in fighting power when delivered. Designed for long-range strategic mobility, they lack the means of tactical mobility and firepower.

Nowhere more than in South-west Asia is the decay of the former Western base system more marked. The neighbouring Soviet Union has in recent years even acquired superior overflight facilities. Diego Garcia and Ras Banas are far away and security access to the latter is clearly doubtful. The bases and overflight facilities of Turkey are often cited as an American asset, but anxiety about Soviet reaction and doubt as to how seriously they are cherished and hence protected by NATO, makes it doubtful whether the Turks would cooperate in many conceivable circumstances. Political objections surely rule out reliance on Israel for most contingencies and certainly render any prior appearance of preparation to do so unwise.

There is no room here to emulate the myriad strategic analyses of the situation in the Gulf. It suffices to record that they all lead to the conclusion that the United States will be quite incapable of defeating a determined Soviet attack, at least by conventional means, for several years to come. This calculation has led some – Professor Tucker, for example – to advocate explicitly casting such American forces as can be introduced into the Gulf as a trip-wire for tactical nuclear weapons. Adequate deterrence might thereby be established.

Admittedly there would be less need to worry about collateral damage than in Western European scenarios. Having said that, however, one has said virtually all there is to say to encourage faith in such a strategy. Western powers might be less inhibited about nuclear weapons than in Europe, but they would also be less galvanized by the stakes. Gulf oil may be important, but the consequences of seizure by the Soviet Union would be slower and infinitely more ambiguous and debatable than an invasion of Western Europe. Primary reliance on nuclear weapons would scare off the United States' allies as well, no doubt, as raise talk familiar in South-east Asian contingencies of racialism in the design of Western nuclear strategy. But, in any case, the Soviet Union, from SS-20 down, is probably better equipped for a nuclear war in the Gulf area than the United States, and aircraft carriers, for instance, would offer targets even less bedevilled by collateral considerations than Iranian mountain passes. As in all super-power confrontations, the United States does need a theatre nuclear capability in Gulf contingencies to neutralize Soviet threats, but any proposal to make nuclear weapons a centrepiece of American strategy would be seriously divisive without in any way guaranteeing a satisfactory outcome to either peacetime deterrence or an eventual armed conflict.

Considerable, though lesser, doubt attaches to the alternative proposal for 'horizontal escalation'; that is, that the United States should attack Soviet interests elsewhere in the world if the Soviet Union commits aggression in the Gulf. Cuba, Angola and such places figure in many of these notions. Any such gambit would have to contemplate the twin difficulties that no remote Soviet assets compare to the Gulf in value and that in the NATO area, particularly perhaps on the flanks, the Western Alliance offers vulnerable possibilities for similar Soviet countermoves. Talk of horizontal escalation is thus likely to take the 'divisible detente' debate to new degrees of acrimony. Just as Gulf oil will henceforth be a latent worry in any European crisis, so the vulnerability of Europe must figure in calculations about the Gulf.

These are daunting prospects. But they may not, perhaps, be so daunting if the political probabilities are evaluated a little differently. Despite the material factors in its favour, an outright Soviet invasion of a Gulf state would be fraught with risks of several kinds and local instability – in which the Soviet Union can fish and which she may promote – is the more probable danger. Massive Western military preparations might well aggravate local tensions, especially if the strategy for exploiting those preparations is implausible. The first line of Western defence against this is clearly political and economic, while military assistance, for which most of the locals can for-

tunately pay, might enable them to implement modest collective security schemes of their own. If, as a final resort, Western military action is called for, it would be on a much smaller scale than the 'Soviet' scenarios require. The resolve of all the Western powers to take action would be immeasurably increased if they had all taken steps to reduce their vulnerability to medium-term interruptions of Gulf oil supplies.

A massive Soviet attack is, as already acknowledged, a very different proposition, and preparing countermeasures over the next few years of maximum danger seems a virtually impossible task if defined as providing an equivalent on-the-spot countervailing force. It may be, however, that while the United States would very probably lose such a contest if it occurred, there are ways to raise the risks for the USSR to the point at which deterrence of the contingency is substantially enhanced.

Some possible Soviet – or local – operations such as mining or otherwise blocking the Straits, could be measured by available naval and air forces, perhaps with Allied assistance. Even the worst case, a Soviet invasion by land and air, would present serious vulnerabilities to a well-designed interdiction effort by carrier aircraft, conventional B-52s, cruise missiles and other aircraft, all much more readliy inserted into forward friendly bases, than land forces – bases that might be available once Soviet forces were committed and which might have been previously enhanced by peacetime programmes of assistance. Such options could pose extremely forbidding risks for Soviet planners. The value that Turkish bases and air space, situated as they are on the flank of important Soviet routes, would have for such operations is very great. Turkey's membership of NATO and the possible serious consequences which would attend reprisals on her, suggests the great desirability of improving Turkish defences and reviving Turkey's confidence in her allies so as to make her a plausible partner in Middle Eastern operations.

At the same time, there would clearly be value in a capacity to inject rapidly even token American ground forces. In the present situation, a Soviet incursion into the Gulf would involve negligible possibility of encounter with American forces, whereas a direct

American response would, by definition, entail the certainty of meeting the USSR. This puts the hallowed and valuable Cold War rule of avoiding direct super-power collisions, firmly on the Soviet side in the balance of deterrence and counterdeterrence. Soviet strategy shows a predilection for operations in which force can be used to protect *faits accomplis*. A capability for rapidly inserting American forces of even modest scale is the natural counter to this inclination.

Training missions, AWACS facilities and other such devices offer opportunites for some low-key preparation for such a presence. Much modern military technology could facilitate both the interdiction and force-insertion operations. Anything that reduces reliance on prolonged warning or precipitate action should mitigate the consequences of inevitable inhibitions within the decision-making processes of the Western coalition. Crises in the Gulf are likely to lay even more stress on decisiveness and operational skill than on the more commonly assessed aspects of the material balance of forces. Forces capable of mobilization at low political and economic cost may be a better deterrent than more powerful but cumbersome establishments geared to major war.

This is not to argue the merits of inadequacy. It does suggest, however, that improving Western capability in the Gulf and elsewhere is not a matter of 'either-or' to be abandoned in despair if perfection escapes us. Forces inadequate for every conceivable crisis may nevertheless improve the odds and history is full, as potential aggressors know, of apparently weaker forces that prevailed. What is envisaged here for a Gulf contingency might perhaps be described as being a trip-wire strategy. But it would not be a trip-wire primarily for nuclear weapons, although it might come to that. The more realistic and by no means negligible threat at the end of the trip-wire would be the prospect of being at war with the US. This, after all, is what NATO strategy chiefly involves and it is faith in the efficacy of this threat that reconciles Europe to the deferred prospect of *their* trip-wire triggering nuclear weapons.

Conclusions: the Setting of Priorities
An effort to summarize and conclude this external survey of the American debate about security concerns and capabilities should begin by observing that the most encouraging development over the past two or three years has been the emergence of the debate itself and the marked retreat of those who for long both closed their eyes to the expansion of Soviet power and denied that it was in any case very relevant to fundamental American interests. The challenge is to build a more adequate American defence posture on this renewed realism without exceeding the politically determined physical capacity of the United States and her allies to do what is necessary; a task demanding that the requisite rhetoric of exhortation does not expand to the point of implausible counter-productiveness.

Among the practical priorities, the strategic nuclear force comes first and should be fostered without unwarranted expectations of what negotiated arms control can achieve. An assured capability for retaliating against any attack on the United States, including some forms of limited attack, seems necessary both for its own and for appearances' sake. So long as the United States has pretensions to extend deterrent guarantees to others, or even to participate without undue fear of nuclear blackmail in the conventional defence of others, a capacity for initiating limited strategic nuclear action also seems desirable along the lines indicated by the 'Schlesinger-PD59' evolution of doctrine. To go beyond that, and begin to flesh out every scenario that the idea of 'warfighting' might suggest, would be premature without a realistic review of practical possibilities for distinguishing such strategies from assured destruction.

Familiar though the priority is, the case for keeping the security of Western Europe next on the American list of strategic commitments seems as sound as ever. Even the currently absorbing debate about the Gulf derives its chief justification from its importance for Europe. As Secretaries of Defense feel compelled to remind Congress periodically, the Western Europeans provide a large proportion of their own defence: Secretary Brown's last annual statement putting the European share upon mobilization at four-fifths of manpower and three-fifths of tanks and tactical aircraft. Nevertheless, the American contribution by way of linkage to overall deterrence, organizer of strategic consensus, and provider of heavy, hard-hitting units, is indispensable within present politico-strategic conceptions. As this century wears out it will surely become impossible, however, to ignore the question of whether this relationship can last forever, given the vast improvement in the ratio of European to American GNP. An answer that shifted more responsibility to Europe would have clear implications for the disposition of nuclear power in the world, and no agreed progress on these lines will be practicable on the timescale of NATO's more immediately pressing problem of military refurbishment. This task itself, however, requires a delicate balance between American public views on burden-sharing and European fears that the United States will push them into excessive and politically counterproductive military efforts. The more doctrinal reform and technological innovation could reduce both dependence on American reinforcement and the role of nuclear weapons in NATO's ability to disrupt a Soviet attack, the more this potential clash of national interests would be mitigated.

The balance of European–American military effort also overhangs the strategic problems of the Third World and the Persian Gulf. Once again, the dependence of the Western European nations upon the US and their virtual complete lack of any military capability of their own to influence areas of vital interest to them, seem a historical anomaly. It is too early to decide whether this is an aberration or the inevitable fate of affluent, industrialized medium powers in a nuclear world. It is not too soon, however, to see a further source of European-American tension. Efforts to draw Europe into collective overseas military efforts with the US are well recognized as difficult; despite a brief period of parallel European and American military operations in the Third World during the period of decolonization, one

must recognize that there is no tradition of amiable collective action. The common stake in the Gulf is now more obvious, but the appropriate politico-military strategy is not. Once again there is a balance to be struck between not allowing European public opinion to evade reality and driving it into defeatism and appeasement. While there may be deterrent value in joint operations, there can also be political value in diversity of approaches. Perhaps, to borrow categories from another debate, 'interoperability', not 'standardization' of policy is required.

The final picture that emerges is one of likely inadequacy in American capability for discharging security concerns, with or without Allied help. This inadequacy, measured not by perfectionist standards, but even by calculations of mere prudence will persist for several years even if the US sustains her new-found zeal for security matters. This should not be allowed to breed either defeatism or hysterical hyperactivity. Bankruptcy would have been the fate of most world powers in history if all security cheques were presented at once. Inadequacy was the normal state of the UK in her imperial heyday. It has been the condition of the US throughout the era of the '2$^1/_2$ wars' if that phase had ever been taken seriously. With luck it will suffice for years to come. The USSR, it is true, can take the initiative as the expansionist or wrecking power, and the US must respond. But the USSR has her own problems and must also await her opportunities, which by no means always present themselves in the form the USSR would like. The practical agenda, both for the future and for the crises that will occur within it, is not the construction of unquestionably adequate capabilities for every contingency, but the incremental management of a problem here, reduction of a risk there, in a process that will not make the world safe for American democracy – merely safer.

NOTES

[1] J. F. Dulles, 'Policy for Security and Peace', *Foreign Affairs*, Vol. 32, 1954, pp. 353–64.
[2] Cf. Robert W. Tucker, 'American Power and the Gulf', *Commentary*, Nov. 1980; 'The Purposes of American Power', *Foreign Affairs*, Winter 1980–81.
[3] Carnegie Endowment for International Peace, *Challenges for US National Security*, Washington DC, 1981, p.91.
[4] The reluctance of the United States to contemplate use of nuclear weapons is wholly understandable, and though it is never officially declared, one notes the emphasis of the LTDP and slow progress on Item 10 before the SS-20 uproar prompted a follow-up to Helmut Schmidt's IISS speech, the excitement over new conventional technology, Senator Nunn's 1974 Report to the Senate, and such pieces as Dr Fred Ikle's 'NATO's "First Nuclear Use": A Deepening Trap?', *Strategic Review*, Winter 1980, p.18.

America's Alliances: Europe

DAVID WATT

No man is an infallible judge of his own interests, but for all that, nobody else is likely to be as assiduous or perspicacious in forming the judgement. This rule applies to nations as well as to individuals, and it follows that there is something impertinent about an English commentator being made to prescribe for the future security of the people of the United States. British interests are vested in saying that American interests are vested in Europe, and it would need superhuman detachment on the part of an Englishman to say the opposite. I can only re-emphasize this interest frankly at the outset of this Paper, and hope that if American readers detect that I am saddling them (contrary to my intention) with characteristically European calculations and needs, they will find the distortions suggestive rather than merely irritating or sly.

It has been a reality of the American international situation for most of this century that the stability of the European continent is, in the most general sense, important to the well-being of the United States. Another way of putting this would be to say that, after the end of the nineteenth century, the world-wide power of the European empires was so great that any war between them or any undue concentration of power on the continent was bound to affect the Western hemisphere and more particularly to affect US interests – which were themselves widening all the time. American isolationism, before 1900, was a plausible, though decreasingly possible strategy; after 1900, it was self-deception, akin to Gaullism, and – as proved by the preludes to two World Wars – a self-deception which had subsequently to be paid for with considerable blood and treasure.

Since 1947 and the identification of the Soviet threat as the chief menace to American interests, it might be thought that the emphasis had been changed radically from a Eurocentric to a global perspective. Until very recently this has not happened. It is true that the disappearance of the European empires has narrowed somewhat the global significance of European instability as such. And of course the US has acquired many interests elsewhere. But, for nearly the whole of the post-war period, the containment of Soviet Russia has been seen in the US above all in terms of the hard-learned lesson of preventing an undue concentration of hostile power in Europe, which has itself been seen as the central, critical arena in world politics. The broad geopolitical consequences of a Soviet suzerainty of the whole north-Eurasian landmass from the Chinese border to the shores of the Atlantic have of course been regarded as horrific. But it is the huge marginal increase in Soviet power represented by control of the great industrial centres of the West, and the fearful trauma, equivalent to the fall of Constantinople in 1453, that would be caused by the collapse of the European Christian culture that has really haunted the imagination of successive American Administrations since the onset of the cold war.

Whether anything has happened or is soon likely to happen to alter this post-war American perspective radically is the first question of this Paper. In theory, two changes – or a combination of them – are possible. The US could decide that Europe is less worth defending either because a free Europe has ceased to be valuable to her, or because the overall cost in terms of men, money and nuclear exposure, or lost opportunities elsewhere, has become too high.

First, then, what is the current 'value' of Western Europe to the United States?

America's Interests – The Strategic Stakes

Western Europe is at present a 'prize' which it is desirable to deny to the Soviet Union. Western Europe is also a part of the means of its own defence. Its free existence is moreover a thorn in the side of the Soviet empire. The prize is a bit less glittering perhaps from the geostrategic point of view than from the economic; but if the Soviet Union could neutralize (leave aside control) France, Germany and the United Kingdom, she would have achieved some very important ends. What is now an American *glacis* would have been turned into a Soviet *glacis*. Some important actors on the international stage would have been eliminated. And, on the reasonable assumption that NATO had broken up in the process, the Soviet frontiers would have been made markedly more secure. In addition the Soviet Union would have consolidated her existing empire and provided a fillip to her flagging reputation as a power on whose side it pays to third-world countries to remain. To prevent this shift in the balance of world power must clearly be one of the most important aims of US policy, not so much because geopolitics is a zero-sum game (it is not) as because even in positive-sum games an imbalance of power of these proportions between the protagonists is dangerous.

The most reliable and cost-effective means of achieving this end is the preservation and, if possible, the improvement of the North Atlantic military alliance. NATO may have its defects but it has proved an effective and, for Europeans and Americans alike, relatively cheap way of meeting the Soviet military threat. American public opinion naturally, and legitimately, sees the situation in altruistic terms. Americans, from the generosity of their hearts, are defending European interests. The European perspective is equally legitimate, however – the military contribution of the Allies on the Central Front in men, money and matériel, even though given for self-interested purposes, has enable the US to defend a vital strategic interest of her own for nearly 35 years at a fraction of the cost that would otherwise have been incurred.

Moreover for most of this period two individual members of the Alliance have contributed to the wider purposes of the US as well. The British until 1970 imposed a measure of stability on the Gulf and on large areas of South-east Asia and Africa; the French had a considerable presence in North and West Africa. This contribution has not always been encouraged or appreciated (if one may put it delicately) by American Administrations, but it has now assumed a fresh importance. The increase of Soviet activity outside Europe, coming at the same time as the decline in French-British influence, has left the US with new and unwelcome security problems in the Third World. These are marginally relieved by the residual political links and influences of the old colonial powers as well as by the economic dependence of the developing countries upon Europe, but the US is understandably anxious to share these burdens to a greater extent than in the past. If the European Allies should decline to get involved, or reinvolved, in this responsibility, then the US would have to consider whether this dereliction undermined the importance of her own stake in keeping the Soviet Union out of Western Europe – a 'trade-off' to which I shall return later.

Economic Stakes
The US has a profound interest in the maintenance of a prosperous, free-market economic system in Western Europe.

Direct interest. US economic prosperity is deeply affected by the inter-penetration of the American and European economies. The interconnections are myriad and extend to all sections of economic activity. Some general examples must suffice:

- Of all US investment abroad nearly half (or about $90 billion in 1980) is in Western Europe (double the American investment in Canada and four times that in Latin America);
- European investment in the US (about $40 billion) now amounts to more than 70% of all overseas investment;
- The US is currently running a trade surplus with Western Europe of about $20 billion (compared, for instance, with a $38 billion deficit with Asia);
- American exports to Western Europe are worth at present over $50 billion a year, of which a third is in machinery and as much as 10% in agricultural produce.

Indirect interest. The European economies, taken together, now have as great an influence on the world economic environment as that of the US. The US and Europe have about equal shares of the total GNP of the world's market economies. The EEC in 1979 provided 35% of world exports (as opposed to the US 11%), and

36% of world imports (as opposed to the US 13%). In the same year the majority of world reserves were held in dollars (65%) but 31% were held in European currencies or ECUs. From a geostrategic point of view, it is vital to the US that the weight of these economies should be thrown, as at present, broadly behind purposes congruent with American interests. These interests include the maintenance of a free-trade system, close collaboration in the orderly management of the world economy, encouragement of free-market systems in the Third World, and joint economic pressure when feasible and appropriate, against hostile political forces whether in the Communist bloc or the LDCs.

Security interest. It is important to the US that the European economies should be in a position to support a sustained military contribution to the Alliance. There are political as well as purely economic aspects of this requirement. If the European economies are thrown into difficulties, from whatever cause, there will be problems in meeting the defence budgets simply because of competing pressures on public expenditures. But there will also be difficulties of a deeper kind arising from the turn of public opinion. Times of depression or very high inflation (or both) tend to foster economic and then political nationalism, as well as pressure against defence expenditure. To the extent that this nationalism reflects sharpened competition for employment and growth between the advanced industrial countries, it may pose difficult dilemmas for American policy makers. An uncompromising attack on the problems of the US domestic economy may produce anti-militarism and lower security in Europe.

Psychological Stakes

It is hard to assess what gratification (as opposed to hard strategic or economic advantage) the European Alliance gives to the US. Earlier this year, visting Texas to deliver a lecture on the Atlantic Alliance, I was interviewed separately by two intelligent young television and newspaper reporters who both prefaced their questions with an embarrassed confession that they had not had time to look up what the Atlantic Alliance was. The generation which watched the Alliance win World War II (and win the peace after it) is passing, and, as has frequently been observed, domestic power in the US has tilted towards states which have less concern with Europe than do those of the Eastern seaboard. The fact that so many American families are of recent European origin in some ways only seems to increase the distance because they so often make the limited criteria of their ethnic loyalty – Zionism, Irish Republicanism, Ukrainian nationalism, or whatever – the overriding test of the value of the Alliance.

On the other hand, successive American administrations, caught between their global perception of American interests and the tendency of American public opinion to relapse into a narrower continental outlook, have emphasized that the US is acting on behalf of something called 'the free world' of which she is the acknowledged leader and of which the European countries are the chief followers and beneficiaries. This claim to responsibility provides not only the moral strand to foreign policy that American people have demanded since the foundation of the Republic, but the consolations of companionship and friendly approval. World power is an ungrateful role, but doubly so for a people that particularly likes to be liked. If what can loosely be called the 'moral support' of European governments were withdrawn from the US because the Soviet Union had overrun them, the US would no doubt continue her global mission undaunted (assuming no nuclear Armageddon had made all missions irrelevant). However, if the European Alliance simply melted spontaneously away because Europe no longer believed that the cultural and political values she had hitherto shared with the US were worth defending – at any rate at the economic price implied by a formal military pact – then the blow to American self-confidence would be grave. The political consequences of such a peripeteia are unpredictable, but it is at the very least plausible to suppose that administrations would find more difficulty than ever in mobilizing public opinion behind any foreign policy that was not narrowly nationalistic and therefore ultimately self-defeating.

The 'cost' incurred by the US in protecting these interests can to some extent be computed precisely. The material cost of keeping 'x' men in Western Europe, providing them with suitable logistic support and reinforcement capability, and developing and deploying weapon systems for them on sea and land and air is known to the last dollar and cent. There is, of course, a methodological problem involved in deciding which military measures the US would think it prudent to take anyway if Western Europe were a neutral bloc, or (to take a more extreme supposition requiring slightly different calculations) if the Soviet Union actually controlled it. The American nuclear missile armoury, for instance, or the US fleets now deployed in the North Atlantic and the Mediterranean would presumably be rather different in size and composition under such circumstances, but they would certainly not be eliminated. Nevertheless, making some arbitrary assumptions, we could say that the military defence of Europe is a drain on the real resources of the United States of such and such a size; and if that was all there was to it, we should probably conclude that although this cost was increasing at a considerable rate, it was well worth paying, and indeed that the advantages were cheap at the price.

The problems arise, rather, in the matter of policy costs. Theory proclaims the truism that it is impossible to enter an alliance, even as its leader, without accepting some limitations on one's freedom of action. Where joint operations requiring allied co-operation are concerned, whether in the military, political, or economic fields, nothing can be achieved without agreement, preceded by consultation, debate and persuasions. But even where an individual partner has the possibility of unilateral action it may be wise to refrain, either a) because he wants to trade off his restraint for some long-term reciprocal benefit or b) because his action would attack the interests of his allies so much as to cast doubt in his allies' mind about the value of the alliance or c) because, although he intends to press on anyhow, a postponement may give him time to blunt the edge of his allies' opposition.

All these constraints have a cost in certainty and in time needed for decision-making. But there are also important political costs. In the case of constraint a) – for instance, a tariff cut – there will be the temporary cost of interest which the protagonist hopes will be out-

weighed later on, but he may have to pay a prohibitively high domestic price within the timescale of democratic elections in the meantime. In the case of restraint b) the cost will be more permanent, and the benefit (namely the continuation of the Alliance) may well be difficult to 'sell' to public opinion, and may even be seen by governments as being insufficiently high to warrant the sacrifice.

Rising Costs

Translating this theoretical discussion into the realities of our present situation, we can see that from the point of view of the US, the policy costs of the European connection have been rising quite rapidly in the past ten years. The first reason for this stems from the disappearance from within the Alliance (as from the super-power relationship) of the overwhelming preponderance of American power. In a partnership as unequal as, say, the NATO of the 1950s, the West Europeans could argue, but, in the last resort, they had little other choice than to accept American protection on American terms. The Bretton Woods system, the GATT (General Agreement on Tariffs and Trade), and the military structure in NATO itself, were all designed on the assumption of and to some extent to promote, the perpetuation of US supremacy. The oil price increase of 1973 and the collapse of the dollar altered the economic and, more important, the psychological balance of the Alliance. The fact that the American economy was proved as vulnerable and perhaps even more vulnerable than the European, gave Europe new bargaining power in the economic field but also broke the more general European (and in particular German) idea of their dependence and inferiority vis-à-vis the US. Since 1973 the European Allies have assumed, what never really sunk in before, that in general the US needs Europe as much as Europe needs the US, and in some fields the boot is even on the other foot. They have acted on this assumption by approaching intra-alliance bargaining with the United States in an entirely new spirit of self-assertiveness, even where, as in the case of security matters, their real dependence on America is as great as ever.

The second substantial factor that has apparently raised the policy cost to the US has been the divergence of views that has gradually opened up between the US and most of the West European governments on how to pursue the central purpose of the Alliance – namely the containment of the Soviet Union.

It is fashionable to see this split in terms of interest and to some extent this is right. The reasons why West European public opinions are encouraged to make a less straight-forwardly 'worst case' analysis of the Soviet threat than American public opinion include the following:

– Dislike of high defence expenditure has encouraged wishful thinking about Soviet motivation both in Europe and the Third World;
– Economic and cultural links with the Communist Bloc have produced a stake in 'detente at all costs';
– Fear of a nuclear war limited to the territory of Europe by an implicit agreement of the super-powers has caused hope to be placed on arms control;
– Fears that sharp military confrontation and super-power rivalry in the Third World will harm European economic interests in those regions.

Nevertheless the fact that these motives are to some degree self-interested does not necessarily mean that they are invalid; nor does it mean that they are exhaustive. There are other differences of perspective arising from historical, cultural, or even purely intellectual causes. The British and French Establishments, for instance, are instinctively conscious of their ability not only to understand the complexities of regional politics in the developing world, but also to react with suitable sophistication to them. They have no similar confidence in the reactions of American administrations, which are bedevilled by the need to placate a cantankerous Congress and a volatile public opinion. In the view of many Europeans (not by any means on the Left) the Reagan and Carter Administrations have been caught in the nationalistic slipstream of Vietnam and Watergate. Until this is past it will be impossible to rely unquestioningly on the international judgment of American leaders , for it will be constantly distorted by two vulgar

errors which appear to be embedded in the American collective psyche at this time – first, that virtually all aspects of world politics are to be judged in the terms of the contest between the US and the Soviet Union, and the second, that in order to win this contest it is essential to re-establish military superiority.

European Futures

It is not absolutely necessary for the US to approve, to forgive, or even altogether to understand these European interests and preoccupations, but it is essential that their existence should be recognized, for, taken together, they constitute the most important components in any American cost-benefit analysis of the Alliance. American policy-makers must also establish a view about how Europeans are likely to develop in the next few years and decide to what extent they can be influenced by American policies and persuasions. This is not an easy computation – depending as it does on many variables in the domestic politics of the European countries, as well as on the behaviour of such unreliable actors on the international scene as OPEC and the Soviet Union. My own guesses, on the main points, are as follows:

– On the psychological front, I fancy that the American ascendancy is permanently broken. The relationship is and will remain very much a questioning and two-sided one. The EEC may or may not make further advances in economic integration but there will probably be progress in establishing a common European position in a number of political and semi-strategic matters. This position may not always be welcomed in Washington;
– Europe is not about to make vast new commitments to defence expenditure in NATO – at any rate unless and until the economic situation improves or the East-West conflict markedly worsens. On the other hand, unless the US grossly mishandles the relationship, they are not about to give up their current levels of defence expenditure or abandon NATO or 'go neutralist' in any serious sense of that term. The combination of a Labour Government, led by Mr Tony Benn, in Britain, a left-wing SPD Govern-

ment (without Chancellor Schmidt) in Germany, a left-wing socialist regime (without President Mitterand) in France, and a Communist government in Italy, might portend the break-up of the Alliance, but not one of these looks in the least probable. There will, however, continue to be a powerful groundswell of public opinion throughout Europe, especially in Germany and the Low Countries, in favour of detente, East–West trade and arms-control measures; and it will tend to become more powerful and more anti-American if the US frustrates or appears to oppose its ends. A Soviet intervention in Poland would transform the situation in the short run and might perhaps reunite the Alliance in a tough anti-Soviet position; but the underlying ambiguities would tend to reassert themselves before very long;

– The vulnerability of Western Europe to the developments in the Third World, especially the oil-producing parts of it, has sunk in in most European countries. On the other hand, most governments, even the British, will remain sceptical about the Soviet capacity to control events in those regions, and will continue to fear that the instinctive reactions of the Reagan Administration will make matters worse rather than better. The most intelligent conclusion to be drawn by Europe from this perception (as well as the most desirable from the point of view of the Alliance) would be that she should accede to American demands for more assistance including military support in trying to control global instability, but use the opportunity to set up a form of consultative machinery that would give them a genuine influence on American policy. The chances are, however, that unless the Administration shows considerably more disposition than at present to allow its freedom of action to be impaired, Europe will conclude that its interests would be better served by maintaining its own freedom in its dealings with the Third World and by not becoming too closely identified with American policy;

Economic issues will continue to be a constant transatlantic irritant, and will provide a perpetual temptation for all parties to play an opportunistic three-sided game with Japan. But there will not be much dis-

position in Europe to apply direct 'linkage' between these and security arrangements – that is (to take an absurdly crude example) to say to the US: 'reduce interest rates or we will leave NATO'. Nevertheless the indirect linkage will continue to exist in that the largest single economy in the West will be held partly responsible for economic distress; and economic distress is a poor foundation for good security.

A Better Alliance

If these predictions are roughly correct, the US can in theory rely upon having, at the very minimum, a cut-rate economy version of the Alliance throughout the 1980s and 1990s, since Europe is willing to allow itself to be defended on its own territory and to make a contribution in men and money sufficient to make this defence physically possible. This would fulfil the basic geostrategic purpose of keeping the USSR from invading Western Europe, and would continue to protect a vital economic interest. Unfortunately such a model is highly unsatisfactory in several ways. It cannot be relied on to support the wider purposes of the US outside Europe; it does not perform the psychological function required by American domestic politics; and because its psychological base is weak on both sides, it does not provide a satisfactory framework for resolving awkward and inevitable differences of opinion about what really is needed for the defence of Europe, whether in cruise missiles, ERW (Enhanced Radiation Warheads) trade sanctions or anything else.

The crucial question for American policy makers, therefore, is whether it is possible to procure a more *de luxe* version of the Alliance at reasonable cost. There is naturally a strong temptation to try to get one on the cheap, mainly by browbeating Western Europe into greater efforts and better behaviour. This prescription has proved effective in the past and is being fairly liberally applied at present. The dire reactions of American public opinion to allied sins of omission is constantly cited, and more direct threats of US troop withdrawals from Europe are hinted at. The trouble is that this procedure, though useful and effective up to a point, requires very delicate handling in the US if it is not to excite public opinion to the point at which the prophecy becomes self-fulfilling. It has also proved dangerous in Europe (particularly in West Germany) where it can produce acute neurosis and, by increasing doubts about American credibility, actually provide grist to the neutralist mill.

The alternative course is to attempt to put together a new kind of transatlantic relationship, close enough to co-ordinate a broad strategy for global security between the US and Western Europe, but loose enough to take account of the fact that under the conditions of the 1980s, each side of this dialogue will often find it hard, and at times impossible, to agree. This will not be easy. For one thing, there exists a large establishment with a vested interest in declaring that the existing NATO structure is capable of coping with the problem and in opposing any new machinery for fear it should affect the old. The fact is that NATO, by the will of most of its members, is unsuited to tasks wider than military operations in the European theatre. And, as the cruise missile and neutron warhead controversies have shown, it is even unable to provide the kind of framework in which highly emotive issues relevant to European defence pure and simple can be put into proper perspective. Then there are serious problems about who is to take part in this new dialogue and how. The smaller European countries are understandably resentful of the idea of a 'directorate', and to the extent that they are excluded they have a better excuse for limiting their commitment. Yet it is hardly realistic to expect the US to accept limitations of her freedom to pursue her interests as she sees them throughout the world, except when she can expect those with whom she is consulting to accept joint responsibility for the implementation of any decisions that are reached. This difficulty would more or less dictate some kind of 'variable geometry' – a structure which has its own drawbacks.

The main difficulties, however, are those that arise from the holistic nature of American foreign policy. American public opinion has always tended to believe that 'he who is not with us is against us', and has judged its international relationships in terms of commitment (which is, incidentally, why 'linkage' is an almost inevitable element of the American relationship with allies and opponents alike). Its criteria of commitment at present do not make allowances for fundamental differences of opinion about how to cope with the Soviet Union, and the thought of setting up a structure in which the discussion of such differences would be a necessary, protracted, and by no means certain prelude to action is not an appealing one. It is doubly unappealing when most of the putative partners in the discussion have recently been utterly dependent on the United States and are in one crucial respect dependent still. Why *should* the US consult anybody or hold its hand out before giving Colonel Gaddafi a bloody nose, or sending (or not sending) military aircraft to Israel, or supporting guerrillas in Angola, or supplying China with defence equipment, or making contingency arrangements to intervene in the Persian Gulf, or even lifting the grain embargo – especially if all President Reagan hears from his major allies, at any rate at the outset, is a lot of good reasons why he should not do any of them, even though he regards them as being in the American interest?

That is a question to which it is extraordinarily difficult for any European to find a reply that does not, in the present atmosphere, sound like special pleading. Indeed there is a European school of thought which would argue that one ought not to try. Why not acknowledge that the European nations are now primarily regional powers, with very limited ability to affect the super-powers either in Europe or elsehwere? I hope it will be apparent from what has gone before why I do not agree with this proposition. It would leave the US alone in the world, and the Europeans with little or no influence whatever over American policies that could mean life or death for them. The implications of this stance are ultimately neutralist, which is why the 'economy' version of the Alliance is unstable at the European end as well as the American.

It is strongly in the American interest that this minimalist view should not gain ground in Europe, not simply because the US actually needs the political, economic, and to some degree the military co-operation of the Europeans outside Europe, but also because the support of her friends may save her from psychological traumas and consequent errors of a potentially very costly kind. The costs to the US of actually encouraging the Europeans to concert their own foreign policy and of trying to make a new approach to co-ordinated decision-making on a transatlantic basis naturally have to be considered. They represent a considerable investment in time, freedom of action, domestic political capital, and above all patience. On the other hand the price need not necessarily be so very high. There are large tracts of policy where agreement would in practice be perfectly easy, many others where it might eventually be arrived at, and others still where an agreement to disagree harms nobody. The question is whether the irreducible number of important disagreements that can be foreseen – for instance on Israel, on the Gulf, on economic sanctions, on Southern Africa – are thought to make the investment pointless.

America's Alliances: Asia

TOM B. MILLAR

United States' interest in Asia – the term 'Asia' here refers essentially to East and South-East Asia – was first demonstrated eight years after the Declaration of Independence, when American ships arrived in China and began to develop the processes of trade. Thus, when the convict colony in New South Wales was established a little later, American traders en route to China detoured south to sell rum and other less fortified but more fortifying comestibles to the new settlers. Portuguese, Dutch, English and Russians had preceded the Americans in China but in Japan Europeans were repeatedly rebuffed until in 1853 Commodore Perry, with a judicious combination of power and diplomacy, opened the door to Western interests although not (because of the character of the Japanese) to Western colonialism. Genuine (as distinct from subsequent imputed or rhetorical) American imperialism took control of the Philippines at the end of the nineteenth century, and these three countries – China, Japan and the Philippines – absorbed almost all American mercantile, messianic, military and political effort towards Asia until after World War II.

American involvement in, and attitudes to, the three countries differed widely. Never quite able to reconcile conscience with authority outside her own continental environment, nor to acknowledge the political implications of economic influence, the US became an increasingly reluctant imperial power in the Philippines, handing over the reins of government to the Filipinos substantially in the mid-1930s, and totally immediately after World War II, while retaining military bases to support her strategic interests and a massive economic involvement. American attitudes to China were a step down the imperial ladder. While having, as it were, one hand on the knife that 'carved up the Chinese melon' and the other tugging at the coat-tails of the carvers (the European powers and Japan), the United States became emotionally involved in China –

remote, exotic and alien as China was – in ways that she had not and still has not been anywhere else, combining many of the 'civilizing' and patronizing attitudes of an imperial power with a strong sense of altruism and disinterestedness.

Japan was of a different, more competitive, more combative order. Japanese migrants to California early this century appeared more threatening that their Chinese predecessors. Theodore Roosevelt's timely and statesmanlike contribution to ending the Russo-Japanese War left the Japanese believing they had received less than the appropriate rewards of victory. Successive American Administrations whittled down the profits of Japanese bullying of China, defined an inferior status for Japan at the Washington Naval Conference, and stood between Japan and the fulfilment of her Greater East Asian Co-prosperity Sphere, eventually destroying the empire with a *coup de grace* which annihilated two Japanese cities and their populations in torrents of fire and radioactive dust.

These situations, condensed and imperfect though their narrative may be, are as much a part of the accumulated sets of American alliances and relationships in Asia as are the immediate post-war events that seemed so dramatically to impel them: the establishment of a Soviet empire in Eastern Europe; the eruption of Communist insurgencies in South-east Asia; the assumption of power in China by a Communist government which saw America as an enemy; and, shortly afterwards, North Korea's attack on the South with Soviet arms and Chinese encouragement and later participation. The country which, after generations of isolationism, had come to bear so heavy a burden in World War II, and which, with little apprenticeship had assumed the leadership of the West, saw no alternative to defending in Asia, with whatever friends she could gather, the values for which she had fought and for which she was still defensively deployed in

Europe. The Korean War made a virtue of intervention;[1] it, and the South-east Asian insurgencies, produced the alliances[2] that were the legal and political bases for intervention. The Vietnam War demonstrated intervention's vices and its costs. One of the greatest vices was the narrowing of political vision which war tends inevitably to produce, so that the US and her partners failed for so long to see and for even longer to take advantage of the split between the USSR and Chinese People's Republic which has now been the central strategic fact of Eastern Asia for more than twenty years.

Threats and Alliances in Asia

All America's treaty relationships with Asia date from before the Sino-Soviet split, and most of them still exist. Apart from the first US-Japan Security Treaty (a pre-requisite for the Peace Treaty), none of them was foisted by the US on a reluctant Asian ally. On the contrary, with varying degrees of enthusiasm, American aid and protection were actively sought as well as positively offered. As with almost all treaties, the objectives of the parties were by no means identical and have changed over the years; and each treaty is but a part of a collection of agreements and arrangements between the partners, a flexible and fuzzy skeleton around which a larger although not necessarily more solid edifice has been built.

Briefly, in the case of South Korea, the Treaty supplemented and later replaced the completed UN commitment (of which the US was the mainstay) with a bilateral arrangment. The Treaty gave the United States the right to keep forces and bases in the Republic, and committed her in general terms to the Republic's defence. The Treaty incorporated a form of words used in the ANZUS Treaty (see below) and repeated in almost all subsequent US-Asian Treaties, namely that, in the event of an armed attack on either party or its territories in the Pacific (the Atlantic being a separate strategic zone), each would 'act to meet the common danger in accordance with its constitutional processes' (i.e. would do something to help but would not necessarily be committed to specific military actions in advance). The objectives of the parties in this case were identical – to prevent a second Korean War, or to defend the South should such a war occur.

The Treaty with the Philippines was to give the new nation a general sense of security in a region troubled in many places, including within the Philippines itself, by overt and covert expressions of Communist military power. A similar purpose was conveyed through the Treaty with Australia and New Zealand (ANZUS), although its rationale and ostensible primary purposes were to reassure the two antipodean states against Japan which, under the Peace Treaty, was afforded 'the inherent right of self-defence', i.e. of rearmament. The US Security Treaty with Japan, signed concurrently with the Peace Treaty, and which imposed no reciprocal obligations upon Japan, authorized the United States to retain forces and bases in Japan (without which it would have had great difficulty in fighting the Korean War) and to use such forces to 'put down large-scale internal riots and disturbances'; it committed the US to Japan's protection from her long-time enemy, the Soviet Union; and it enabled an exhausted Japanese polity and economy to recover their strength without devoting scarce resources to costly military preparedness. The Revised Treaty of 1960 was much more recognizant of Japan as an independent sovereign state.

The South-east Asia Collective Defence Treaty, known by its organization SEATO, had as many objectives as it had members. For the United States, it was designed to foster collective effort in the region in order to keep Communist military forces north of the Seventeenth Parallel of latitude in Vietnam. One can make a case that this objective was largely achieved for a decade, and US military aid to Vietnam was within the terms of a Protocol to the SEATO Treaty. For Thailand, SEATO was intended to ensure American help and protection from external and domestic Communist forces. For Pakistan, it had a general anti-Communist aim, but was even more expected to provide arms and psychological defence against India.[3] For the Philippines, it provided a sense of collective security – partnership with a wider group of regional and great powers. For France, it offered a rearguard for French evacuation, a post-colonial protection of remaining French interests. For Britain, it gave security to Malaya's northern flank. For Australia and New Zealand, it interposed the US between

Asian Communist countries and Australia's northern neighbours. SEATO is now defunct except for residual US, Australian and New Zealand unilateral commitments to Thailand.

The United States' commitment to the Republic of China (Taiwan) in 1954 merely formalized the protection she had given Chiang Kai-Shek's forces when they fled the mainland. This protection ceased soon after the US and the People's Republic finally established diplomatic relations, except for arms aid granted under separate arrangements.. Bilateral treaties with Pakistan in 1955 and 1959 were part of the web of Baghdad Pact (Central Treaty Organization) arrangements intended to contain the USSR on her southern borders, but again they enabled Pakistan to exert greater pressure on – or offer greater resistance to – India. While the Central Treaty Organization went into disrepair and eventually lapsed in 1979, the US agreements with Pakistan have space for continuing military aid, as in the recent $3-billion arms agreement.

None of the US-Asian Alliances offered absolute American support in all or indeed any circumstances. Each meant different things at different times, and each came to be affected – at both ends – by the assorted American traumas over and after Vietnam. When President Nixon began moves to withdraw the United States from the war, he gave notice to allies and partners (at Guam in July 1969 and to Congress in February 1970) that they must accept primary responsibility for their own defence. This wholly reasonable requirement nevertheless ran contrary to regional expectations which earlier US Administrations had encouraged. Thus an undertaking by Nixon to maintain existing US treaty commitments had an uncertain ring to it, and a pledge to provide a 'nuclear shield' to allies or other nations whose independence the US considered vital, was not as reassuring as it was presumably intended to be. American abandonment of Vietnam, her unilateral 'shocks' to economic and diplomatic relations with Japan, the substantial reduction of her commitment to Taiwan, and President Carter's readiness to withdraw all ground forces from South Korea, were all reasonable in American terms, but the view of these actions from the region was generally less benign than Washington would have wished.

Whereas since 1950 there has been a remarkable continuity to the American commitment to Western Europe and to the stability of the confrontation there, there have been major discontinuities to, and changes in, American commitments in East Asia. No wars [4] have been fought in Europe. Two large wars and several smaller ones have been fought in East Asia. No alignments have changed in Europe. There have been major realignments in East Asia, with Communist states at each other's throats: China confronting Vietnam and Vietnam occupying Cambodia. The main causes of change in East Asia have been the shift in the Sino-Soviet relationship from one of cooperation to one of hostility, the slow realization by the US of the political and military limits to the deployment of alien power in a hostile environment, and the clash of intraregional nationalist forces. A major byproduct of these changes, and of US withdrawal of forces from Vietnam and of recognition from Taiwan, has been the *rapprochement* between Washington and Peking that has changed the whole East Asian strategic picture.

About forty Soviet divisions and an array of missiles confront the People's Republic of China, which nevertheless feels that the balance of forces are in her favour: she does not *depend* on the US or any other country. North Korea has no assurance of Chinese support, and has had undoubted warning of American resistance, were she to launch a second attack southwards. The US is now willing to sell arms to China, although how many China will feel able to buy is another question, and will depend partly on the terms. Japan is engaged in providing sophisticated equipment to the People's Republic. Both Japan and the US are helping to 'modernize' the lethargic Chinese economy. China and Vietnam are competing for hegemony over South-east Asia, with Vietnam in the ascendant in Indochina. Vietnam's occupation of Kampuchea depends on Soviet aid, the price for which is access to Vietnamese bases. Taiwan, doing very well economically, is not under immediate threat and is a threat to no-one.

The Association of South-east Asian Nations (ASEAN), which as an economic entity exists rather more in the perceptions of outsiders than in the practices of its members, is a basically anti-Communist political community divided over the question of whether China is a buffer to Vietnam or Vietnam a buffer to China. The United States has depleted her forces in the Western Pacific to meet threats to the oil life-line in the Indian Ocean under what came belatedly and euphemistically to be known as a 'swing strategy'. Alone of the East Asian powers, Japan has barely changed her objectives or her dilemmas. She is determined to stay out of all political quarrels. She is prepared to sell almost anything (except arms) to almost anyone. She is reluctant to spend unnecessary money on arms, or to countenance nuclear weapons. She also wants the benefit of super-power protection with the minimum cost of client status. She wants greatly to translate economic power into political influence. She would like, but does not demand, to be loved, but she does want to sit at the top table.

US Interests and Japan

America's interests in the East Asian region remain essentially what they were in 1950: to protect trade, which is now equal in value to trade with Europe; to prevent the expansion of Soviet power; and to help to maintain international peace and security and goodwill towards the United States.

It is interesting to review America's treaty relationships, which were established during the early Cold War years, at this time of apparently heightened (if much more complex) confrontation, when the Soviet Union has general nuclear equality with the United States and perhaps selective strategic and tactical superiority, and when the term 'Cold War', after a period of disfavour, is coming back into vogue and its vocabulary into the conventional rhetoric of a hard-line Republican Administration. (The vocabulary has never been out of vogue in the USSR.)

When Dean Acheson, on 12 January 1950, publicly drew the American defence perimeter through the Aleutians to Japan, the Ryukyus and the Philippines, he must have assumed the inclusion of Japan (and her remaining dependencies) to be temporary while she was being restored to national health and international respectability. Thirty years later, there is no question that both objectives have been remarkably achieved. Japan's economy is the third largest in the world. Japan is a stable democracy able to accommodate dissent and to manage the transfer of power with minimum disruption. Her ministers are carefully listened to in international assemblies. She has significant armed forces clearly dedicated to self-defence. Why then is Japan still a host to American military power? Why is the US-Japan partnership in 1981 the 'keystone' of American Pacific policy, as Henry Kissinger [5] and others have called her? What are the interests to which this policy is directed?

From the American perspective, there are two main answers, one positive, one negative. The first is that the United States feels that she must retain a secure military position in Japan, so valuable to US strategic capacity in the whole Western Pacific, while the Soviet Union remains an unsatisfied power with increasing military strength, ready to use force to attain her ends. The second is that successive American administrations have wanted to give the Japanese a sense of security that did not depend primarily on their own military efforts for the US fears that a rearmed Japan could have a more assertive and independent foreign policy which, while it would presumably not be pro-Soviet, could well trouble and destabilize the region, awaken apprehensions of some new 'Co-prosperity Sphere', and act positively against American interests. The US might reasonably fear that a more independent and more nationalistic Japan could opt for an independent nuclear weapons capacity. A third consideration is that Japan is America's largest overseas trading partner, and political alignment makes trade easier and trade problems (even those as formidable as with Japan, which is putting thousands of Americans out of work) easier to discuss.

As indicated, Japan's perspective on these matters has been far more ambivalent. She has risen revitalized, repoliticized and respectable from the ashes of Hiroshima and the traumas of defeat. She had proved during fourteen years of war that to pursue economic ends by military means was ultimately a grossly uneconomic proposition; she has proved subsequently that peace hath her victories much more profitable than war. She has a special sensitivity to Soviet pressures, and to the situation on the Korean peninsula and thus has been grateful for

American protection, as well as for American civil and military technology, trade and cultural and educational offerings. But she has otherwise showed little enthusiasm for the more dramatic manifestations of her ally's Pacific policy – the long hostility with China; nuclear test casualties; the war in Vietnam; the *Mayaquez* incident; the ubiquitous, undiscriminating, fulminatory confrontation with the USSR; and now the sale of arms to the People's Republic.

Kissinger, in his *apologia pro sua vita in domo albo*, has written warmly of the ways in which the two nations, so culturally dissimilar, have been able to work together. Nevertheless, the differences on security questions are becoming more obvious. Successive US administrations have pressed Japan to make a greater contribution to the security of the East Asian region, but none has pressed harder, or more specifically, or perhaps with less sensitivity to the Japanese electorate, than the present one. After thirty years of what is quite clearly a military alliance, the use of the term in the recent Suzuki-Reagan communiqué brought such a reaction in Japan as to cause the Prime Minster to disown the term and the Foreign Minister to resign.[6] The Japanese position is that, in military respects, the increased Soviet naval build-up in the Pacific is primarily the responsibility of the United States; that the protection of Middle East oil supplies is also the responsibility of the United States, with such other Western help as she can obtain; and that if implementing the second damages the capacity to maintain the first, the US should do something about it or she will cease to be a credible ally and Japan will look to alternative means to ensure her security. What those alternative means would be, is not spelled out.

The Americans, harassed by their allies in Europe and staggering with world peace on their shoulders through the shifting Middle Eastern sands, find Japan's position difficult to understand. While no country has been as reprehensibly efficient as Japan at both having her cake and eating it, I still see the role of American pressure on Japan as desirably of a different order from American pressure on Western Europe. Certainly Japan can do more in her own defence, perhaps pay more towards US protection, and may contribute technology to US arms and equipment; but in absolute terms Japan is already spending a great deal on defence, and there is a line of public acceptability of defence beyond which no Japanese government can be pushed without endangering its position or altering the whole political fabric. More than this, Europe and Asia are two totally different strategic theatres. In East Asia the only country confronting the USSR on land is China. The USSR is quite capable of invading China but must be far less certain that she could extricate her forces once engaged there. Lines of communication are long and vulnerable. She has one ally, Vietnam, from which she is separated by several thousand kilometres, and another, North Korea, which has proved in almost every way much more of a liability than an asset and still has strong links with China. The United States, on the other hand, has a valuable ally and forward bases in Japan, a base and frontier post in South Korea, a friendly power in China, and major bases in the Philippines. Provided the US does not 'swing' too high a proportion of her forces to the Atlantic or the Middle East, the total anti-Soviet naval and air forces are a match for their Soviet opponents except for submarines. By any analysis, the Soviet strategic position must now be accounted comparatively far weaker in Asia and the Pacific than in Europe, the Middle East and the North Atlantic, and worse than it has been in the past.

In the event of a hot war other than along China's borders, the Soviet navy would have a vital role to which Japan's geographic location is most relevant. That is why Japan, with her high industrial and technological capacity and her naval, air and land bases is so necessary as an ally of the United States. The belated acknowledgment of this in Japan has led to joint US-Japanese contingency planning for the defence of Japan and her environment. The more this is done and discussed in the Japanese media, the more nervous some Japanese will become, but also the more support there is likely to be for the Alliance.[7] The essential ambivalence of Japan may thus be increased, not reduced, in the years ahead. She wants to be protected against the USSR, conventionally and with a nuclear umbrella. She wants the economic advantages of the US relationship. She also wants to take a profitable part in the development of Siberia. She does not want to be committed by her ally, or by her now friendly Chinese neighbour, to policies which will add to the possibility of conflict or tension with the Soviet Union. She does not want to arouse old resentments or new fears in South-east Asia. Despite the fact that neutrality would have many imponderable and potentially greater costs than alignment, one cannot rule out the idea that some future Japanese government might prefer it on nationalistic grounds.

Relations with China
According to Moscow Radio and other Soviet sources, the normalization agreement between China and the United States, the Japan-China Friendship Treaty, and the US-Japan Security Treaty combine to form a kind of military alliance between the three powers directed at the Soviet Union. This suggests either a misunderstanding of Japan, or (more likely) deliberately heavy-handed diplomacy. The existing Treaty with the United States is commitment enough for most Japanese and too much for some. An agreement that could drag Japan on the coat-tails of Beijing into conflict with the USSR would be quite unacceptable. Equally one cannot conceive of China entering an agreement that would align her with wider American interests in the Pacific. Nor, despite the present temporary Republican majority in the Senate, is it at all likely that the United States would extend the commitment of her already much overstretched forces in Asia.

There is nevertheless a community of interests among the three states, brought about largely by their common suspicion of the Soviet Union. This community is by no means total. Each has interests and ethics not shared with the others. China wants from the West (US, Western Europe and Japan), on the best terms possible, access to capital, to civil and military technology, to education and to trade, with the objective of rescuing China from the inertia into which she has drifted by the unequalled pressure of population and resources, by inflexible economic policies and the appalling waste of the Cultural Revolution and its aftermath. No other countries, and certainly not the Soviet Union, can provide what China needs in anything approaching the desired quantity.

There are three points of contention between China and the United States. Whatever it may privately feel or even express to Washington, and despite its approval of the US-Japan Treaty, the Chinese government cannot publicly support the American military presence in South Korea. For reasons of ideology and *realpolitik*, it must keep as friendly a relationship as possible with North Korea. Again, it finds present US policy with respect to Taiwan highly objectionable. It has repeatedly expressed concern at the continued American supply of arms to Taiwan, and will go on urging that the supply cease. Moreover, the Chinese rigid policy of confrontation towards Vietnam has seemed to Washington (although perhaps not to the Reagan Administration) to play into the hands of the Soviet Union, encouraging them to obtain more or improved facilities in Vietnam, from which to monitor Western naval activities in the South-west Pacific and the eastern Indian Ocean region. Under the present government of China, which has a degree of fragility, these three issues are unlikely to affect the broad lines of policy towards the United States. China is unlikely to have a significant *rapprochement* with the Soviet Union, although she has already made moves to a less combative relationship. China is not in a hurry over Taiwan and, if the United States would only play the game gently, she would have the best of both worlds under the present arrangements. Because of US domestic pressures, the US cannot abandon Taiwan, but she can encourage (though not compel) a slow rapprochement between Taiwan and the People's Republic. Nor can she abandon South Korea so long as the South Koreans feel vulnerable to the larger armed forces in the North and Japan is so sensitive to the security of the Peninsula. To abandon either South Korea or Taiwan could encourage each to obtain nuclear weapons – a highly destabilizing procedure.

Other Commitments
The only remaining US commitment to mainland South-east Asia is to Thailand, under an Understanding reached in 1962 between Secretary of State Dean Rusk and Thai Foreign Minister Thanat Khoman. This effectively provided that the commitments of the SEATO Treaty were individual as well as collective.

(Australia and New Zealand expressed similar views.) No-one expects the United States to send gound forces again to fight in this region, but military aid is regularly and readily given and would be available urgently in a crisis, as for example in the event of a major Vietnamese assault upon Thailand from Cambodia. As such an assault would serve nobody's interests, could prompt Chinese retaliation and would arouse ASEAN hostility, it must be considered a fairly remote possibility (as distinct from smaller operations to secure the border and harass Pol Pot forces). American access to facilities in Thailand could help with reconnaissance over the vital Indonesian and Malaccan Straits and adjacent waters.

Just as US bases in Japan are essential to the American strategic position in the northern Pacific, so bases in the Philippines (at Clark Field and Subic Bay) are essential to her position in the South Pacific. Terms on which the bases are maintained have been renegotiated several times, most recently in 1979, as a concession to Filipino *amour propre* and to provide weightier contributions to the Filipino exchequer. Although nominal control of the bases rests with the Philippines, the United States has unimpeded operational control.

This is acceptable to both governments, but the Philippines has many of the characteristics of a revolutionary society. The costly war with Muslim nationalists in the South, aided by Libya, shows no sign of abating. To replace the US bases elsewhere in the region would involve enormous expense. There is no present indication of any popular or government move to this end, but this possibility must be kept in mind.

The ANZUS Treaty, and associated agreements covering communications, defence space research and missile warning systems, have the support of both the Government and the Opposition in Australia and New Zealand. In Australia there is a slowly growing public debate on the Alliance, especially on the possibility that facilities on Australian soil might be the targets of Soviet nuclear weapons in the event of global war. Concurrently, the Conservative Government has made repeated declarations of support of US policy towards the Gulf. For some years Australian maritime reconnaissance aircraft have patrolled the eastern Indian Ocean. American B-52s have now been given staging rights at Darwin. An Australian offer to 'home port' US naval ships at the small facility at Cockburn Sound, near Fremantle, has not been accepted. Joint naval exercises (including also New Zealand ships) have been held in the Indian Ocean, and while the wording of the ANZUS Treaty – which is deliberately confined to the Pacific[8] – has not been changed, *de facto* it is clear that the Alliance operates also in the eastern Indian Ocean. The United States would undoubtedly like Australian military participation to range further west than the present or an alternative Australian government would consider discreet. Australia remains the one stable, conservative, friendly, economically advanced country on the 'westabout' route from the US to the Middle East.

The final US-Asian Treaty with Pakistan (now minus its eastern component, Bangladesh), is barely relevant to the region of East and South-east Asia. It is relevant to US-India relations, and here the US is on the perpetual horns of an almost unresolvable dilemma, which the Soviet-Afghanistan invasion emphasizes, but the dilemma will be exacerbated, not resolved, by massive arms aid to a Pakistan moving towards her own nuclear explosion.

The Unpredictable 1980s

Over the past ten or twelve years, a revolution has occurred in American attitudes to security in the Asian-Pacific region – a revolution forced on successive administrations by the stubborn facts of international politics. Who would have predicted in 1969 that the United States by about now would be selling arms to Communist China, would have ended her Security Treaty with Taiwan, would have been thrown out of Iran, or would have to start considering alternatives to Clark Field and Subic Bay? Common ideology is no longer the strategic pillar nor the test of political sympathy it was once believed to be. In Asia, as elsewhere outside Europe, the US takes her friends where she can find them, and where there is a community of interest.

Yet just as the past was unpredictable, so is the future, especially in the context of leadership changes in several countries. Assessing the continuity of American objectives, I foresee the following possible problems for US-Asian alliance policies in the rest of the decade, and offer some modest prescriptions:

- Japan will continue to be sensitive to the many pressures within and upon her, and excessive American demands could turn Japan in upon herself, with unpredictable results.
- China must be considered a fragile political society, which will determine her own future policy directions and her relations with her neighbours irrespective of US aid, and US aide – while welcome (if the terms are right) – will but scratch the surface of China's immense problems.
- As in China and Japan, so in the ASEAN states individually and collectively, nationalism and regionalism are ultimately stronger forces than those reaching across the sea for aid or protection. Despite some scattered voices, there is little desire in the East and South-east Asian region for an Asian-Pacific 'NATO', some new, wider security agreement backed by American power. It just is not politically feasible, and is almost certainly undesirable. This fact should not be seen as an obstacle to the exercise of US power, but as an influence directing that power into positive economic and political directions, for there is no doubt that every non-Communist government in East and South-east Asia wants the US to be able to deploy significant military power in the region.

As to prescriptions, it seems to me that the objective of American policy must be the reduction of tension through political normalization. For example, the objective of policy towards Korea should be the establishment of two separate Korean states, both members of the United Nations, at peace with each other and having normal diplomatic relations with all their neighbours. If one accepts that objective, then, while the American tripwire in South Korea should not be prematurely removed, US diplomacy should be aimed at building the relevant bridges. Bridges will not be built while the emphasis is on confrontation. Similarly, it should be an American objective to have Vietnam in good relations with the Western powers, China, Japan and ASEAN, and not almost wholly dependent on the USSR. The ASEAN states, whether directly allied to the US (Philippines, Thailand) or the recipients of US military aid (Malaysia, Indonesia) or development aid (Indonesia) must feel that the US wants to help, not control them. The US should not adopt the animosities of any Asian partner, nor expect that such partners should share all American perspectives and priorities.

This is not an argument for abandoning present alliances. It is an argument for keeping them in good order while seeking the political means for reducing tension, tackling the massive economic problems, and thus helping to make the alliances less necessary.

NOTES

[1] The basis for intervention in Korea was of course UN Security Council Resolution S/1501, together with subsequent resolutions of the General Assembly, although President Truman had decided to intervene before the Security Council had met.

[2] The texts of US security treaties with the Philippines (30 August 1951), Australia and New Zealand (1 September 1951), Japan (8 September 1951 and 19 January 1960), South Korea (10 October 1953), the SEATO powers (8 September 1954), the Republic of China (2 December 1954), and Pakistan (24 February 1955 and 5 March 1959) are given in the annex to T. B. Millar, *Contemporary Alliances*, Canberra Studies in World Affairs, No. 2, Australian National University, 1981.

[3] The United States added a protocol restricting military help in the event of Communist aggression. Both the US and Australia made clear to Pakistan that they saw their obligations under SEATO as not relevant to Indo-Pakistan conflict, but the US could not prevent American arms from being used in such a situation.

[4] Suppression, by the tanks of their 'allies', of political dissent in East Germany, Hungary and Czechoslovakia, is not considered to be war.

[5] *The White House Years*, Henry Kissinger (London: Weidenfeld & Nicolson, 1979).

[6] Japan also did not like well-publicized American pressure for substantially increased defence spending. Former US Ambassador Edwin Reischauer's indiscreet 'revelation' that US warships carrying nuclear weapons have visited Japanese ports over many years, added to the popular uproar in Japan, where the fiction that such visits did not occur was firmly maintained as an act of policy. In this case the Foreign Ministry got ahead of the politicians, and the Prime Minister dropped the ball.

[7] Public opinion polls show increased Japanese support for the US–Japan Security Treaty over recent years, including among Opposition parties.

[8] The Treaty covers the metropolitan territories of the parties, which in Australia's case must include the long coastline which is not in the Pacific.

American Policy towards the Soviet Union in the 1980s: Objectives and Uncertainties

PIERRE HASSNER

Postulates and Obstacles

Anyone who is reckless enough to accept as impossible an assignment as to write on the goals and uncertainties of American policy towards the Soviet Union in the 1980s should at least – to use one of Secretary Haig's contributions to political discourse – caveat his answers in so many ways that the caveats risk filling the whole of the Paper. This is even more so when the writer, aware of his own characteristics, has to top it all with a caveat about his caveats.

To speak of direct US-Soviet relations at a given point in time is difficult enough. To speak of the same problem in the dimension of prescription and prediction, of desirable goals and of the likelihood of their being implemented in the 1980s, means talking not only about Soviet-American but about every other possible subject having any connection at all with international politics. It involves one's ultimate beliefs concerning what the United States and the Soviet Union are respectively about; it concerns the essence of their regimes and their likely evolution; it concerns the bipolar or multipolar structure of the international system, and the respective importance of its key dimensions such as military power or economic interdependence or such as the balance of power and world order; it involves passing judgment on the sources of instability in the Third World and on the respective trends towards autonomy and/or 'Finlandization' in Western and in Eastern Europe.

Even attempting to define the question involves taking sides in every one of the debates – from the philosophical to the tactical – which are dividing the foreign policy community as well as the Western Alliance.

The obvious difficulties due to the richness of the subject are compounded by two major problems, one at the level of questions, the other at the level of answers.

For any prescriptive or policy-oriented paper, the obvious first question concerns *whose* interests are to be pursued. Any European but also many an American is bound to ask whether what is good for the United States is automatically good for the Western Alliance, for world peace and for the advancement of freedom, justice and prosperity for all, including the Soviet people. If there is no automatic coincidence between these various interests and goals, the question at least of priority, if not of exclusive choice, inevitably arises. A West European of East European origin, and of a broadly-left-of-centre orientation, must, then, be acutely aware that American administrations are not elected primarily to satisfy his own preferences and aspirations.

Even believing, as I do, that there exists, at least objectively and in the long run, a reasonable degree of convergence between the various goals mentioned above, I cannot fail to warn the reader about the other complicating feature, that which renders my inevitably subjective answers even more so. This concerns my personal position in the debates between hawks and doves, or, to use another terminology adopted by Shahram Chubin in relation to conflict in the Third World, between geopoliticians and regionalists.[1] While the attitudes of many in the various debates tend to be congruent (e.g. believers in detente, economic interdependence, arms control, co-operation with Soviet reformers, a regional, preferably non-military approach to third-world conflicts versus believers in the unchanging character of the Soviet regime and of the East-West conflict, in the priority of restoring the strategic balance and, possibly, in acquiring a strategy of victory, in applying pressure to the Soviet Union, in a primarily geopolitical approach to the Third World), I belong to the minority whose belief in the priority of sticks or of carrots, of conflict or co-operation, and whose position on the pessimism-optimism scale tends to vary fundamentally according to issues and to regions.

In a nutshell, I see myself as a moderate hawk on the Soviet Union and in the strategic debate, and as a moderate dove on everything else (from Central America and Southern Africa to the Arab–Israeli conflict and to attitudes towards the Left in Western Europe).

On the one hand, I believe in the fundamentally alien and hostile nature of the Soviet regime and of its foreign policy, and my hunch is that Western arms controllers and believers in economic interdependence tend to overestimate the common ground between them and their Soviet counterparts or the importance and clout of the latter. On the other hand, I believe that the sources of instability, conflict and revolution in the Third World, or even of divergence between Europe and the United States are more often domestic, national, regional or linked to the North-South cleavage than caused by the Soviet Union, that the believers in the primacy of geopolitics and of the Soviet threat overestimate the common ground between their perceptions and those of Arabs and Israelis, Africans and Latin Americans, Europeans and Japanese, and overestimate the extent to which these Americans can make them abandon or shelve their own priorities in favour of a strategic consensus and a rearmament effort based on the East-West conflict.

In 1976, I formulated the general problem in these terms:

I consider the East-West dimension to remain as it has been since the second world war, the most crucial dimension of world politics in an double sense. First the spiritual tradition of the West embodied, however imperfectly, in the political form of constitutional government is under threat from illiberal trends and regimes; secondly, the most powerful and dangerous representative of those trends and regimes is the Soviet Union who is, militarily, in an ascending phase. The overlap between these two realities – i.e. the direct or indirect destruction of Western democracies by Soviet power – represents the point of maximum danger in East-West relations. Even within their framework, however, one should be careful to speak of overlap or interaction in precise circumstances and in various forms, rather than of identification between the threats to Western democracy and the expansion of the Soviet Union; the latter – or even communism itself – is by no means the sole nor very often the main originator or beneficiary of the former: too quick an identification of the internal crisis of the West, or of the decline of human rights in the world, with the Soviet threat may lead to catastrophic mistakes in defining their respective causes and remedies. This is all the more so since in the perception of many, perhaps most people in the West, the East-West dimension as such has lost precedence in favour both of narrower and of broader concerns.[2]

Five years later, with the help of a number of Soviet actions, the perception of the precedence of the East-West dimension has gained considerably, at least in the United States. But so, by the same token, has the danger of mistakes which would fall into the Soviet trap out of too exclusive a concentration on the Soviet role.

Nothing, then, is more necessary for American policy than a struggle on two fronts, avoiding both the illusions of liberals bent on minimizing the Soviet danger and the role of military force and on exaggerating the hopes of detente, and the illusions of conservatives bent on exaggerating the former and on minimizing the latter, as well as, more generally, on neglecting the autonomous processes of change in the Third World and the opportunities offered by favourable evolutions within the Communist world itself.[3]

To emphasize the essential complementarity of the two perspectives and, in particular, to react against the European, particularly German, obsession with carrots and the American current obsession with sticks, means to align oneself with the theory – if not with the practice – of the right wing of the Carter Administration as opposed either to its liberal wing or to the dominant trend of the Reagan Administration. But this is not a particularly encouraging reference. Nor was another combination of carrots and sticks, that of Henry Kissinger, which for my taste relied too much on carrots for the Soviet Union and on sticks for all other anti-*status quo* forces, ultimately successful. And this is where my caveat about my caveats comes in.

My analysis of international problems as well as my intellectual and political prejudices put me in the 'on the one hand, on the other hand' school rather than in the 'either/or' school. But I am fully aware that a stress on complexity and on endless distinctions and qualifications cannot be the guiding principles of any foreign policy, least of all the American one.

In fact what has been characteristic of American attitudes has been an alternation of belief in detente and in cold war, of wanting to feel good, i.e. to feel moral, with Carter and of wanting to feel good, i.e. to feel strong, with Reagan, going back to the classical oppositions of idealism and realism, and of isolationism and interventionism. Beyond the inevitable difference of perspective between the nuances of the analyst and the choices of the statesman, there is the special opposition between the particularly complex nature of the world's problems and the particularly American yearning for simple solutions.

Concerning the present, such different analysts as James Q. Wilson and D. Yankelovich with L. Kaagan have noted the problem caused by the 'gap between the Reagan mandate and the constraints of modern geopolitics' or 'the ways the public's convictions about how to restore the national honor collide with the geopolitical realities of the 1980s'.

Public Opinion and Public Constraints
However, one must also remark that, whether in the early days of the Truman Doctrine or under the Carter and Reagan Administrations, the general public has tended to be more moderate or discriminating, more weary both of inaction and adventure, than the policy-making elites have tended to give it credit for or

have tended to be themselves. The succession of fashions or orthodoxies seems more characteristic of the latter than of the former. On the side of the public, it is rather the fragmentation of interests according to ethnic, regional or socio-professional lines which is striking. One could fear, then, not only that any complex policy which would be both consistent, flexible and at any rate specifically tailored to Soviet realities, but any long-range policy at all, might be impossible. Instead of one policy, one would have anarchical combinations of, on the one hand, broad historical tides and moods exaggerated by the fashions and idiosyncrasies of establishments and counter-establishments and, on the other, the fragmented and diverging interests of various sections of the American public (corporations interested in East-West trade, farmers opposed to embargoes, Jews giving priority to the emigration of their Soviet brothers etc.).

The same cannot be said of Soviet policies but it may be that there, too, domestic factors, from the biological to the economic, are more important than reactions to American policies. American and Soviet policies towards each other may be more the result of their respective feelings of weakness or strength, or withdrawal or reassertion, towards the world and towards themselves, than of the interaction of deliberate strategies directed at each other. Hence if they are at different phases of their respective cycles, if as S. Bialer convincingly puts it, they are 'out of phase with each other'[5] in more senses than one, there is a danger, if not of catastrophic misunderstandings, at least of lost opportunities, as was the case, according to some very respectable analysts like Richard Löwenthal and Myron Rush, in 1953 during the post-Stalin succession crisis when the West, and particularly J. F. Dulles, were sticking to policies prepared in the earlier phase, or reacting to previous American failures more than to current Soviet opportunities.

A Basic Continuity
There is a saving grace, however. Both the nuances of analysts and the vacillations of policy-makers may be less important than the broad constraints dictated by the double reality of the balance of power and of the closed character of the Soviet regime. The consequence of

this double reality is, I submit, that both in the past and in the foreseeable future it is very hard to imagine an American policy towards the Soviet Union which would be very much other than a 'variation on Mr X'. We do not know enough about who does what, when and how in the Soviet system to be able to manipulate successfully (at least in any direct way) either the factions within the Politburo, or the struggle for succession, or the conflicts within the Soviet elite or even the priorities of the Soviet budget, except in the most exceptional circumstances. The very important changes and divisions which occur within the Communist world are the result of its own evolution, or of our consistency in defending what we do know, i.e. our own interests.

Of the three possible directions which an American policy towards the Soviet Union can take – containment, roll-back and co-operation – the most basic one can only be containment accompanied, as was stated in the original text of George Kennan, by the hope that in time internal contradictions, if denied the outlet of expansion, will transform the Soviet empire. Both roll-back and co-operation have a role to play, particularly as we shall see in certain specific areas, on certain specific issues and in certain specific circumstances. But except in the most extreme cases, this role, in the present period, must still come second to the defensive one of containment.

Is this, however, so different from the actual practice of American policy towards the Soviet Union since World War II? After all, while every administration since 1952 has wanted to go beyond containment, none of them has succeeded. John Foster Dulles started with announcing roll-back or liberation as a political, and massive retaliation as a military, alternative to containment; he ended with something less than containment in both respects. President Kennedy wanted to re-establish the balance at every level and to combine it on the one hand with negotiation with the Soviet Union and on the other hand with support of the rising forces for change in the Third World; he ended with a major success – Cuba – and a major failure – Vietnam – which were both linked to the policy of containment.

The Nixon–Kissinger policy can best be understood as an attempt to adapt contain-

ment to new circumstances, those of a weakened American consensus, a more multipolar world and a greater Soviet interest in economic and technological co-operation: hence direct military containment was to be made more complex and supplemented by proxies and allies and by sanctions and rewards. Whether this was or was not believed to lead, one day, to a condominium or to the co-optation of the USSR as a junior associate in a concert of conservative powers is less relevant than the fact that such dreams disappeared in favour of an unsuccessful attempt just to hold the line.

The Carter Administration started by attempting to go beyond containment or at least beyond a military territorial version of it in two directions at once: by challenging the Soviet empire on the sensitive issue of human rights on the one hand and, on the other, by downgrading the role of US-Soviet relations and of geopolitical considerations in other parts of the world or on other issues, and by challenging the Soviet Union to join this global and North-South emphasis or become irrelevant. Again, it ended by giving priority to the correcting of a geopolitical military balance which had worsened even further.

Finally the Reagan Administration, while it is quite clear in restoring US-Soviet relations and the geopolitical balance to first place and in emphasizing its resolution not to tolerate any farther advances not only of the Soviet Union but of any country or movement associated with her in any way, seems to show signs of wanting to go beyond that by practising a limited roll-back against what it sees as more recent or more exposed parts of the empire (Nicaragua, Angola, Libya, Ethiopia, Cambodia, perhaps even Cuba and Vietnam) and, so to speak, an ideological roll-back by seeming to look forward to a fundamental change in the nature of the Soviet regime as a precondition for any genuine negotiation, at least on arms control.[6]

Of course, it is too early to judge but, so far, whatever tentative and distant hopes of roll-back may have emerged seem to be due more to the Afghan and Polish peoples than to US policy, which seems reluctant to exploit them.

The Art of Containment
It does seem that the policy of containment is more solidly based in the nature of things than

any of the short-lived alternatives to it. Nor has the United States been altogether unsuccessful in pursuing it.

Of course, from the outset the question of its direct or indirect, universal or geographically limited, military or socio-economic character has made it impossible to speak of containment without specifying 'containment of what and through what means' which immediately leads to a less favourable appraisal.

One can attribute most of America's failures either (as in Vietnam) to a too rigid application of military containment in Asia, or (as in Africa after 1975) by paying insufficient attention to containment in front of Soviet intervention by directly organized proxies.

The question of when a country or a movement is to be considered a proxy of the Soviet Union, and whether, in that case, one should try to detach it from Moscow or to destabilize it, is obviously a crucial one for which no general formula exists but which successive American administrations have not seemed to handle skilfully. On the other hand, as far as containment of direct Soviet expansion between 1948 and the invasion of Afghanistan is concerned, the US record is nothing to apologize for.

Yet while containment is the necessary condition of any American policy towards the Soviet Union, it is more and more difficult and less and less sufficient. The social, economic and political crisis of the West and of the Third World make not directly Soviet and not directly military challenges more serious, and military and Soviet-oriented responses, although still necessary, both less effective and more costly. The economic crisis of the Soviet empire increases its need for co-operation with the West, its political crisis makes a certain type of roll-back, for the first time since the 1950s, a less totally inconceivable proposition. Its likely succession crisis, if Seweryn Bialer or Myron Rush are correct each in his way, increases the range of possible reactions of the Soviet leadership and hence of both dangers and opportunities for the West.

What precise combination of a defensive (or containment), an offensive (or roll-back) and a co-operative (or detente) policy is more likely to minimize the dangers and maximize the opportunities for the West and be sustainable in the long run depends both on changing and partly unpredictable circumstances and on permanent and partly undemonstrable assumptions.

My own are based on a view of the Soviet Union which is very much in agreement with this formulation of Seweryn Bialer: 'It is this combination of the traditional dynamic of an ascending power with the dynamic of a power that represents the world outlook different from and competitive with the other powers that makes the balance of power policies unlikely to succeed, limits the scope of bilateral US-Soviet agreements and makes long-range solutions inherently unstable.'[7] The other side of the coin is, of course, that this same duality makes balance of power policies necessary and limited bilateral US-Soviet agreements and short-range solutions both possible and desirable.

If there is any general rule, it would lie in the two distinctions between long-range and short-range and between centre and periphery. The ultimate aims and conceptions of world order of the United States and the Soviet Union are inherently incompatible: in the last analysis their conflict *is* a zero-sum game except for the very important qualification, recognized, I think, by the USSR, that victory of one over the other is not worth a nuclear war. The Soviet long-range ultimate aim is the controlled disintegration of the West, and I think it is entirely proper and desirable that the Western long-range ultimate aim should be the controlled disintegration of the Soviet empire and of any totalitarian regime. But 'ultimate' and 'controlled' means that both sides have an interest not only in avoiding nuclear war but (for reasons of political contagion and economic interdependence) also avoiding the anarchic and unpredictable collapse of the other, and that, to that extent, each may, in the short run, have an interest in helping its adversary to overcome a crisis. A range of issues, from preventing nuclear proliferation to the regime of oceans, can involve the common interests either of the planet or of the two super-powers notwithstanding their basic conflict. About third parties or third areas, Harry Gelman's formulation that for the Soviet Union, the competition with the United States in the Third World may be seen as a non-zero-sum game in the short run but is seen as a zero-sum game in the long run[8] is very apt and corresponds to the nature of things; but again it allows, precisely for the short run, the possibility, given an adequate military balance and combination of economic incentives and disincentives, of reaching some agreements limiting mutual involvement of excluding certain means like direct military presence.

The new and hopeful factor is that even within the empire itself, there are countries and regions where the costs of keeping them down militarily and those of helping them weather their economic crisis, as well as their *de facto* vulnerability to Western influence (mainly through economic dependence as in Poland but also through military and political help to resistance movements as in Afghanistan and Kampuchea) are such that a new, delicate political balance may be struck, and lead to a special semi-autonomous status. Such a 'semi-Finlandization' of Poland or 're-Finlandization' of Afghanistan would neither be a mutual satisfactory stable solution nor signify a total Soviet withdrawal and the liberation of the people concerned; it would entail dangers for the parallel 'Finlandization' of Western Europe; it would, nevertheless, have immense historical significance in that it would dispose of the notion of the irreversible march of history, of the 'dynamic *status quo*', which are the very legitimizing basis of the Soviet empire and Soviet policy and have to some extent been accepted by most conservatives in the West, through various notions going from a '*cujus regio ejus religio*' conception of spheres of influence to a dogmatic belief in the impossibility both of evolution and of revolution in Communist regimes or in totalitarian as distinct from authoritarian ones.

Perhaps the most decisive question is that of the extent to which each is capable of living with this combination of zero-sum and non-zero-sum games, of short-run and long-run considerations. There are two paradoxes here, one at the level of the two political cultures and the other within the American and Western political debate.

The first one is that the Soviet Union, whose ultimate view of the world is essentially manichean, zero-sum or '*kto-kovo*'-like, seems able, tactically and in the short run, to accommodate ambiguity and diversity, at least outside its own society, in its way of handling social or national forces as provisional allies to be discarded later. Conversely, the United States whose ultimate goal is supposed to be 'to make the world safe for diversity' and whose genuine strength *is* the pluralism of her society and of her empire, often seems much more rigid and manichean in her tactics and rhetoric, much more impatient of heterogeneity and ambiguity. Hence she risks alienating forces whose interests and even outlooks are ultimately much closer to her own than to those of the Soviet Union. With the latter, she seems to have great difficulty in playing the double game of provisional, partial co-operation and of fundamental long-term rivalry. For instance, today she seems to be in danger of letting the Soviet Union walk away with the 'peace' issue and get away with the human rights issue, partly because of the double standard of third parties, partly because of unmatched and unmatchable Soviet cynicism, but partly, too, because of a gap between rhetoric and reality which is the reverse of the Soviet one.

Since even super-powers are often judged by what they say as much as by what they do, it should not be beyond the reach of the United States to avoid both cardinal sins – of completely believing her own rhetoric and of completely divorcing it from her own actions. A great power cannot afford to be entirely naive, a democratic great power cannot afford to be entirely cynical, if only because within its own society voices will always be found to set the record straight and because it will lose its own credibility without being quite able to match the duplicity of its opponent.

A Common Framework?
This raises both the most general problem of US-Soviet relations and the second paradox mentioned here, that which is to be found in the debate on American policy.

The problem is that of heterogeneity and communication or of asymmetry and reciprocity. In other words, to what extent can two opponents who have different regimes, values, and political cultures find a common language or common ground rules, whether in order to negotiate or to compete? This is at the heart of discussions of nuclear strategy and arms control, as well as of economic interdependence or social interpenetration.

Obviously no perfectly fair or intellectually coherent solution can be found, since the essence of the problem is that some common interests do exist and, to be pursued, require some common ground rules (of the type formulated by G. Breslauer in terms of the principles of *proportionality* in conflict and *reciprocity* in co-operation [10]); but the differences in assets and vulnerabilities as well as in outlook and objectives between adversaries are such that each will inevitably interpret these rules in a self-serving way.

The Soviet Union is of course a specialist in double standards or at least in asymmetrical criteria, such as the 'dynamic *status quo*' (which J. F. Kennedy translated as 'what's mine is mine and what's yours is negotiable'), the continuation of the 'ideological struggle' in the West but the barring of 'psychological warfare' and 'creeping subversion' in the East, or the manipulation of Western openness and Eastern secrecy for arms control. The United States is committed to more universal criteria but these, to the extent that they bar revolution and the use or threat of military force and favour the use of economic power and the management of interdependence, obviously favours the wealthier, *status-quo* power against the challenger. Hence the extent to which America has an interest in playing more according to the Soviet rules or in trying to make the USSR play more according to Western ones in an open and legitimate question.

What is paradoxical, though, are the answers given to this question in the present Western debates. Those who tend to play down the differences between the United States and the Soviet Union and to emphasize a common interest in arms control and economic interdependence are also those who recommend that the United States should behave differently to the Soviet Union. They tend to minimize the importance of new weapons systems or of military intervention when they come from the Soviet Union but to find them highly destabilizing and dangerous when they come from the United States. They ask the latter to adopt a depoliticized attitude to arms control and economic relations, so as to teach, so to speak, the Soviet Union by the force of example to become really what she already is potentially, i.e., a genuine partner in the struggle for peace and prosperity.

The current fashion, however, goes in the other direction. After twenty years of trying to teach the Soviet Union how to think about deterrence and arms control, America is tending to turn around and to wonder whether she should not learn from her and adopt her way of thinking about negotiations, about warfighting and about victory in nuclear war. This is one of the sources of the 'countervailing strategy', announced in PD59 and it is a trend of thought which runs through the writings of authors like Robert Ranger and, above all, Colin Gray. Yet it, too, is not devoid of a paradox parallel to the earlier one.

Those who ask the United States to imitate the USSR are precisely those who stress how alien the latter are and how incompatible her aims and methods are with those of the West. While they are entirely right in stressing the advantages which a belief in the primacy of politics gives the Soviet Union over an excessively technical or legalistic American attitude, they tend to assume that the Soviet position relies on a more accurate perception of reality concerning nuclear war or the chances of military intervention in the Third World (which is neither obvious as such nor consistent with their maximalist view of the role of totalitarian ideology in shaping Soviet perceptions). Furthermore, they tend to assume that a democratic, open, pluralist society or alliance can adopt the same military or political strategy as a totalitarian one, without being itself transformed in that same direction and lose some of the characteristics which make it worth defending and which may even be one of its strengths in the competition itself. Just as the less anti-Soviet analysts hope to change the USSR by the force of example and unilateral restraint, at least to the extent of making her behave more in accordance with a Western code of conduct, so the more anti-Soviet ones hope to change the US by following the Soviet example and abandoning some traditional restraints, to make her behave more in line with Soviet methods and strategies.

Both sides, I think, try in a rather distorted way to grapple with a genuine problem: that convergence between the Soviet Union and the United States is both necessary and impossible, that a viable world order presupposes a degree of Soviet conversion to Western standards and that a viable East–West competition presupposes a degree of Western conversion to Soviet methods. Just how far the first can be pursued without falling into self-destructive Utopia and the second without falling into equally self-destructive cynicism is *the* problem of US-Soviet interaction, a problem complicated still further by the fact that whatever bilateral understandings may be worked out are apt to run into difficulties coming from other centres of power or from international anarchy.

Issues and Perspectives

Four issue areas spring to mind where this problem of the proportion between conflict and co-operation and between asymmetry and reciprocity is likely to arise and to make some kind of ground rules both difficult and necessary: arms and arms control; economics and interdependence; confrontation in the Third World; and relations with and between each other's allies, particularly in Europe. Two general issues encompass them all as well as their mutual relations: that of superiority or parity; and that of linkage. In each case, I cannot offer any solution or prediction, but only a plea for the rejection of artificial alternatives in an excessively polarized debate.

Arms and Arms Control

In the military realm, it is clear that the basic reality is that of conflict and competition between two adversaries who have not only incompatible aims but fundamentally different outlooks, and that any notion of 'situational security'[11] where both sides would see the threat as coming from the system rather than from each other, or of a stop to the arms race, is to be discarded as Utopian. But it is just as clear that this makes some kind of dialogue even more necessary and its explicit extension to strategic intentions and principles, as proposed by Christoph Bertram [12], even more desirable. While strategic arms control in the form of complex packages on the SALT I and SALT II model is obviously incompatible both with technological and with political trends, the fact

that the two greatest powers are talking about their central weapons systems is indeed the revolution Kissinger said it was. Even though it was misleading to see in this dialogue the centre of their relationship, it may produce not only some contribution to the avoidance of misunderstandings but also some tangible results which, however partial, temporary, and inspired by contradictory motives, may indeed eliminate or slow down some costly or destablizing military developments – whether in terms of weapons systems, of nuclear proliferation or of confrontation in a given region.

If the competition continues, so does by definition the search for superiority. Both general or overall parity and parity at every level and in every region are impossible to define, to codify and to maintain, and may not even be desirable. Each super-power has defensible reasons for claiming a right to superiority in certain respects: the Soviet Union because of her potential struggle on two fronts, the United States because of the problem of protecting non-contiguous allies. It is indeed true that strict parity and mutual vulnerability at the intercontinental level creates problems for extended deterrence (which makes the doctrinaire attachment to strategic parity of certain Europeans, particularly the Germans, a rather masochistic exercise) and that a strict balance at every level would have a decoupling effect which would run directly counter to a Western posture based on deterrence by the threat of escalation. The only viable meaning of parity is that of a rough balance of imbalances, where each side has superiority in certain systems and certain regions corresponding to its geopolitical situation and to its strategic doctrine but where none of these levels and regions, each of whom has its own structure and reality, can be looked at in isolation from the others.

There are two senses, though, in which parity is here to stay. First, at the nuclear intercontinental level, both sides are vulnerable and neither possesses a disarming first strike capability. While mutual vulnerability is neither equal nor absolute nor necessarily desirable, the search for a disarming first strike capability is probably vain and certainly dangerous and each side is entitled to be reassured by the other that its programmes are not aiming at this objective.

Second, the Soviet Union, without being now or necessarily in the future a match for the United States in every region or necessarily controlling those parts of the world where it is establishing a presence, has nevertheless become a global power. The proud and often-repeated statement according to which in no region of the world can decisions be made any longer without taking the point of view of the Soviet Union into consideration is almost literally true. This does not mean that Soviet ambitions are limited to this recognition of global status nor, conversely, that the Soviet Union can and should never be excluded from a negotiation (even G. Breslauer notes approvingly the Rhodesian settlement); but it does mean that the freedom of action of the West in, say, the Mediterranean will never be the same again. While there is no reason to volunteer to give Moscow an access anywhere in the name of an abstract principle, neither is there any realistic long-run prospect of having Moscow accept its exclusion from such regions as Southern Africa or even Latin America.

The upshot of both phenomena – of the growth in Soviet strategic nuclear power and of its capacity for conventional power projection – is that whatever efforts the United States may make and whatever success she may obtain in keeping or regaining partial superiority, containment can no longer mean either massive retaliation or local denial along a fixed front. It must involve flexibility, retreats and counter-offensives, threats and incentives, coalition-making and bargaining – in short the linkage of military and diplomatic or economic means.

For arms control, too, a measure of linkage is inevitable. Again, all extreme positions are unacceptable; strategic arms control cannot be separated from the general climate of US-Soviet relations, as many arms controllers and, at one point, the Carter Administration would have liked. Nor can it be made the decisive factor commanding their character, through a kind of circular 'reverse linkage' by which arms control is supposed to be pursued for the sake of detente and detente for the sake of arms control. But, conversely, it makes just as little sense to decide, as Secretary Haig interpreted by former Director of Political Military Affairs Seymour Weiss seems to do, that arms-control agreements will be sought 'only when Soviet conduct world-wide seems reasonable' and hence that 'either the Soviets will have to do an abrupt about-face, abandoning a consistent policy of more than 50 years of hostility towards the West, or there will be no arms control agreements'.[13]

All three positions are unfaithful to the difficult but indispensable daily task of disentangling and combining the technical and the political, the co-operative and the conflictual, the short-range and the long-range dimensions of the relationship. Although there may be important structural differences between the military, economic and diplomatic aspects of the relationship, they do have one thing in common; in none can the Soviet Union be simply ignored, but in none can relations with the her be based either on expecting to transform her into a trusted partner in the management of world affairs or on demanding from her unconditional surrender.

In all three, however, and particularly in their combination, one can make modest, probably unspectacular and almost always ambiguous progress by practising what Richard Löwenthal has called 'inherent linkage'[14]; making the progress of arms control conditional, as indeed it should be in the nature of things, on a progressive reduction in Soviet secrecy and unpredictability, and making the progress of economic co-operation conditional on progress in arms control or at least on greater restraint in arms-building and the use of force. The same goes for European security and communication between societies. The aim of the West cannot be to make generalized and official linkage the conditions of its dealings with the East, but it must make the degree of progress in these dealings dependent on the degree of success in challenging the rigid compartmentalization on which Soviet policy relies between a military economy dedicated to dominating the West and a civilian economy which it wants the West to finance (thereby helping the military economy itself), or between economic relations and socio-cultural ones, or between the rules of the game outside and inside the empire. In this, the West should be helped by the fact that these rigid compartmentalizations are not only unnatural but they are being challenged by the functional requirements of the very relations the USSR is interested in, and they are one of the main sources of the crisis which is gripping her economy and society.

Economic Relations

That this crisis exists and that the Soviet leaders are aware of its seriousness is one of the few certainties we can all agree on. Beyond that, on its consequences for the Soviet system, on the role of East–West economic relations, and on the nature of a desirable and realistic American or Western policy on this issue, we enter a hornet's nest of debates among specialists and among allies where, again, I can only express an instinctive preference for the middle ground.

About the prospects for the Soviet economy, even those Western analysts like Seweryn Bialer, who have, for the past and the present, been on the more optimistic side concerning the performance of the system and the satisfaction of the population, stress the fact that the coming years will be a 'harsh decade' dominated by the 'politics of stringency' – which, if one follows the Tocquevillean line that a worsening period succeeding a period of improvement is less accepted than the original situation, would only lead one to predict an even more explosive situation.

I think they are right to predict that both the collapse of the system and a fundamental reform and reorientation of priorities are less likely, even if encouraged by Western pressures and a military spending war, than half-hearted reform and a process of 'muddling down'. This is all the more so since, for the last two decades, the general picture of Soviet society which I find most plausible is already – in spite of the performance of the arms industry and of the improvement in some consumer goods – one of degeneration, social and moral demoralization, and a creeping paralysis of administrative services. This picture of the Soviet Union rapidly moving towards underdevelopment in some crucial respects has been based in particular on her dramatic health crisis, including an unprecedented rise in mortality since 1970 – which had been at the centre of Emmanuel Todd's analysis in 1976[15] and has been documented with great preprecision by Davis and Fesbach.[16] The causes are somewhat mysterious and the consequences even more

so. Whether one tends to predict collapse, like Todd, or rather inertia and decline, the sudden and violent character of the phenomenon should give pause to Western determinists and activists alike.

Yet puzzlement and confession of ignorance are not a policy. East–West economic interaction, whatever its consequences, will go on. Whatever the political objections of American governments, it is clear that a policy of complete blockade is impossible, that East–West economic co-operation is found beneficial or even indispensable by powerful constituencies not only within the Alliance (including in particular the West German Government) but within the United States as well, from farmers to Caterpillar Tractors. Even globally it is not as one-sided an operation as its opponents make it appear; both in quantitative economic terms and in terms of social vulnerability, the East depends more upon the West than vice-versa. On the other hand, in terms of the political manipulation of economic interdependence, it is clear that Communist economies have greater freedom of action, particularly in a crisis, and that vested interests are more likely to be irreversible and influential within the capitalist West. The latter has no other alternative than the uphill fight of attempting some kind of political control, co-ordination, and, if possible, steering of the process.

But what should the political objectives and instruments of this attempt be? Should one try to sharpen the economic crisis of the Soviet empire, and is this best done by denial or (as happened involuntarily in Poland) by offering tempting alternatives to necessary reforms, or by increasing the costs of military competition? Or should one, on the contrary, try to encourage a positive outcome or containment of the crisis, on the theory that an acute crisis may produce dangerous reactions and that less hardship will have a better chance of producing a positive political evolution? Or, finally, should one practise direct political linkage and tie economic relations (or at least credits and long-range investments) to political changes in Soviet military, foreign or human rights policy?

All three attitudes have their place in a coherent Western policy, but to varying degrees and in varying cases.

To sharpen the crisis by increasing the costs of present behaviour is probably too uncertain, too difficult and too dangerous a game to be practised on the grand scale which would be needed centrally to affect Soviet policy. Thoughts which have been re-emerging in that direction after twenty years in connection with the arms race should be dampened by the experience of earlier speculations and half-hearted attempts. On the other hand, increasing the costs, including economic ones, of specific actions like the invasion of foreign countries is highly desirable, It seems to be practised in the case of Kampuchea and Afghanistan, and should be done even more and applied with a vengeance in the case of Poland. One caveat, there, has already been mentioned; one should be sure *whose* costs are being increased and what the degree of possible autonomy of the given country and hence of effectiveness of the opposite tactic of buying it off may be; this may apply to Angola, Ethiopia or Nicaragua. The other caveat is that, even in the first category, the punitive strategy must leave the door open to its own success, i.e., to modification in case Soviet behaviour is itself modified.

The reliance on the process of interdependence leading to modernization and economic reform, themselves leading to political changes, is of course the preferred course of American liberals and the official policy of many European governments, particularly the West German one. While the more extreme forms of the argument – as proposed for instance by Samuel Pisar – are both naive and disingenous, its partial, long-range relevance cannot be laughed out of court. It has had some degree of confirmation in the case of small countries like Yugoslavia and Hungary. Serious studies have documented the potential role of 'economic modernizers' within the Soviet elite and the political relevance of their views.[17] Again as an outsider, I am more attracted by the tripartite division – into 'sectarians, reformists and activists' – proposed by S. Bialer following F. Griffiths, and I would stress that the encouragement of economic reformists can be meaningful and positive only if it goes hand-in-hand with the discouragement of military activists. And this brings us back to the third option, direct political linkage.

Again, in its tit-for-tat form, it would be both the most desirable and the most difficult course. No country, particularly no great power and even less one with the Soviet Union's psychological, cultural and ideological constitution, can be expected to accept for whatever economic reasons having its policies openly and continuously dictated by its adversaries. On the other hand, both direct and exceptional bargains in a crisis, and longer-range but less explicit and more discrete shifts of priorities are feasible. The fate of the Jackson-Vanik-Stevenson Amendment and of the immigration of Soviet Jews show both that it can be done and how it can be bungled. The Soviet Union did in effect, modify her behaviour towards a category of her own citizens in order to please the American Congress. But the incentives attached were so meagre and, when the USSR did give positive signs, the American side was so reluctant to recognize them that ultimately everybody lost in the operation, beginning with the Soviet Jews.

Beyond the obvious lessons of the need for flexibility, face-saving devices, and real incentives and rewards, there remain two general strategic questions attached to any policy of linkage. Should one give priority to long-range regularity and structural change, which, in order to work, implies a degree of irreversibility? Or to the freedom of rewarding or punishing the other side's behaviour, which implies only short-range and reversible agreements? I cannot attempt to settle for either priority. But, in both cases, whether for the long-range indirect modification of priorities through interdependence or for the immediate modification of behaviour through leverage, it seems that Soviet allies or satellites are more realistic targets than the Soviet Union herself, and Soviet foreign actions more than Soviet domestic structures.

In the case of Poland, neither unconditional trade and credits nor a simple cut-off of economic relations nor a policy of sanctions nor sticks without carrots are likely to produce results. The West was clearly wrong to finance Prime Minister Gierek's economic policies for more than 10 years without any controls. It was also wrong not to launch a massive aid programme between August 1980 and December 1981 in order to try to save the experiment. It would be wrong today to continue either a policy of 'business as usual' or one of total disengagement. Only a policy of both sticks *and* carrots, of refusing any economic relations (including the rescheduling of Poland's debts) other than direct and controlled humanitarian aid to the population so long as repression continues but promising a new 'Marshall Plan' for Poland if a number of minimum political conditions are fulfilled can offer some hope of exploiting the Soviet Bloc's difficulty in living in autarchy for a long time to come.

Third World and Alliances

This brings us back to my general point about zero-sum and non-zero-sum games, centre and periphery, long-range and short-range. Both the risks and opportunities of shifts in the strategic and the economic balance between the two super-powers are important above all for their respective relations with the Third World and with each other's allies.

As strong a believer in the dangers of Soviet superiority as Colin Gray has written: 'Moscow does not need strategic nuclear superiority over the United States; all it needs is a robust strategic nuclear counter-deterrent to hold the ring square for Soviet forward diplomacy in the Third World. A strategic counter-deterrent checkmates the erstwhile Western strategic advantage and allows the Soviets to use non-strategic military and diplomatic tools effectively in the international arena.'[18]

Even within the Western Alliance, the crisis brought by the deterioration of the balance concerns much less the deterrence of a Soviet attack on the United States than the credibility of extended deterrence through the threat of escalation, and hence the danger of a strategic decoupling between the United States and Western Europe.

Similarly, the United States is in no danger of direct economic dependence upon the Soviet Union. But to the extent that it is dependent on foreign sources of energy and raw materials, it may be threatened by Soviet control over crucial regions of the Third World. Of course, here again, the danger is much greater for Western Europe and Japan, and, again, it is Western Europe, particularly the Federal Republic, who may be reaching a politically sensitive threshold in its reliance on

East-West trade and particularly on Soviet natural gas.

Conversely, to the extent that the combination of rising economic and political costs and of military dangers may induce a modification in Soviet offensive behaviour, this is likely to occur primarily concerning Soviet military involvement in the Third World, directly or through her Cuban, Vietnamese and East German proxies. To the extent that a retreat – negotiated or not – is conceivable, it would involve places where it is these proxies who are engaged rather than the Soviet Union herself.

Dreaming even further, to the extent that there are Soviet-dominated regimes where the degree and character of this domination may be altered, this would concern those states where this domination is recent, not yet well entrenched and, in spite of the trend towards increased reliance on military control, not fully backed by the Red Army. Libya would be an example but, if one accepts Harry Gelman's formulation that even in the cases of North Vietnam or South Yemen,'there are still no non-contiguous Soviet puppets in the world today',[19] there may be several others.

Finally, even among contiguous satellites, the costs of empire may just conceivably lead to a semi-retreat – but in that case the regional environment (Pakistan in the case of Afghanistan, Western Europe, particularly the FRG, in the case of Poland), including allies of the United States, would be an important consideration behind this evolution and would be affected by it. More, for instance, than the SALT dialogue, it is the strategic interests of the super-powers in the Third World and the evolution of their alliances which may be decisive for the fate of their relationship. The crux of the problem is the interplay between the evolution of their relations with the third parties and with each other.

This is why, primarily in the *Third World*, the notion of a code of detente or of ground rules for competition can only derive whatever limited validity it may have from the success of a threefold policy; local containment, global linkage and adaptation to changes in third parties and to the limits of control by external powers.

Any generalized understanding based on universal principles and on intentions is bound to fail, at least in the long run, for, given the primacy of competition and the incompatibility of designs, it can only be either so vague and ambiguous as to be meaningless or so hypocritical (such as the 1972 'no unilateral advantage' formula) that each side will violate it. To the extent that it sanctifies the *status quo* and bans revolution, the Soviet Union will see her sacred duty in violating it and the United States will do the same with a mixture of bad conscience and of resentment.

To the extent, however, that a given balance is clearly established in a given type of situation, a truce or a *modus vivendi* (as distinct from a permanent treaty or compromise[20]) can consolidate it for as long as the existing conditions obtain; it can prevent unnecessary confrontations in situations of the same type. The point is that the burden lies not on a meeting of minds or on a solution of basic conflicts but on avoidance of direct confrontation based on a mutual and provisional assessment of incentives and disincentives, clearly recognized for what it is.

The first precondition for that is the establishment of a local military balance, keeping Soviet power either from direct invasion or from influencing even domestic developments through the political projection of its shadow. The proportion of local forces, of direct American presence, or of proxies or allies, of course depends upon circumstances.

To the extent that these are too unfavourable, some form of linkage with the global balance of military and economic power has to be established. This can take the form of a plausible, implicit or explicit threat of vertical or horizontal escalation, by establishing a link with other regional theatres (such as between the Gulf and NATO via Turkey as proposed by Albert Wohlstetter) or with the possibility of central war via the presence of nuclear weapons, or with possible local confrontations in areas where the Soviet Bloc is more vulnerable (such as Cuba) – although the world-wide balance of local vulnerabilities through exposed positions would not necessarily favour the West.

This is one more reason why 'containment-through-linkage' should also include the positive form of economic incentives. Indeed, increasing the costs of military action and the benefits of economic interdependence are two sides of the same coin, the inducement of restraint. Surely Richard Löwenthal's warning from 1976 to 1978 that 'possible major Soviet decisions are being prepared in a situation in which the Soviets have the impression that they have nothing to hope and nothing to fear from the United States, and indeed from the West in general'[21] have found at least *prima facie* confirmation in the Soviet actions of 1978 and 1979. The lessons could be drawn for the cases of Poland, of possible Soviet actions in the Gulf, and, more broadly, for some rough parallelism between the moderation of the arms competition and the encouragement of plans for long-range economic co-operation. But the success of such a policy of combined military containment and economic linkage presupposes that both containment and linkage have to be flexible and graduated. Every Soviet action has to be met at its own level, but some forms of confrontation are compatible with the pursuit of co-operation in other areas and others not, some forms of escalation are encouraging restraint and others are discouraging it. Some application of Breslauer's rule of proportionality and some balance between his criteria of geography, alliance and means [22] (with, I submit, a priority of the latter) is in order.

This is where the Reagan Administration's policy in Central America and its generalized rhetoric on terrorism seem certainly dangerous and probably, to the extent of my knowledge, misplaced. For the Soviet Union to give arms to Central American revolutionaries through Cuba and Nicaragua (as the United States does, and should do more, to Afghan resistance through Egypt and Saudi Arabia), for it to encourage the destabilization through terrorism of West European democracies like Italy or Spain, and for the Red Army to invade Afghanistan or Poland, are at least three different types of action which lead to different types of conclusions about their policies and demand different types of responses, none of which are helped by the indiscriminate use of the 'terrorist' label.

Similarly for the case of Cuba or Nicaragua, the nature of their regimes and their harbouring of Soviet missiles or submarines, their help in weapons and training to ideological relatives in Central American civil wars where the other side is being armed and trained by the United States, and their sending of tens of thousands of troops to Africa to keep down their former allies of the Eritrean Liberation Front, are fundamentally different – if only because of the differences in the geographic, strategic, national and political context.

This is where the third – and by no means the least important – dimension comes in: that of third party realities. Even for the deterrence of direct Soviet intervention in a country other than a Western ally, the degree of national resistance is an obvious factor in the degree and even the nature of Western response. In all the other cases, the popular support of each side has, even more obviously, to be given just as much attention as its international alignment. There *are* revolutionary situations in the world, and there will be more, particularly in dictatorships, whether pro-Western or pro-Eastern, whether authoritarian or totalitarian. If each time a movement attempts to use force to overthrow a tyrannical government that declares itself pro-American, it is considered as terrorist, and each time it receives help from Moscow or Cuba while the West refuses to help it or helps its oppressors, it is considered a Soviet proxy, the United States will have been more effective than the Kremlin itself in promoting the extension of the Soviet empire.

On the other hand, even though Moscow has no particular compunction about letting down an allied revolutionary movement to safeguard its own national interests in a crisis, this may be a pyrrhic victory for the West if, in the long run, it reinforces the vicious circle of anti-American rebellion and pro-American repression.

This does not mean, of course, that containment of the Soviet Union has to come second to North-South relations or to abstract principles of democracy, nor that the mutual impact between the East-West balance and local domestic evolution should be underestimated. It does mean that the only effective anti-Soviet policy is a truly two-pronged one, dedicated both to keeping the Soviet Union at bay militarily *and* competing with her through economic and diplomatic means, for the allegiance of third forces (who, often, are closer to Moscow ideologically but know that Washington can do more to further their interests) and for the promotion of settlements including, as in Zimbabwe, movements led by past or possible future allies of the Soviet Union.

While almost everybody would agree that the ideal solution in the Third World is the encouragement of forces which would be both reformist, democratic, efficient and pro-Western or at least genuinely non-aligned, it is obviously true that very often the choice is between supporting a corrupt, tyrannical, unviable ally or abandoning him and accepting that his successor may be a Gaddafi or a Khomeini, if not a Castro or a Karmal. But again only pragmatic circumstances, such as the degree of decay of a regime, its geopolitical situation, the degree of Soviet control over its opponents, etc., can dictate from case to case a priority of short-term security (for instance in the Gulf) or of long-range evolution (e.g. in Central America).

Even for *Europe*, and for members of the two Alliances, the duality of short- and long-range considerations and the dilemma between the dictates of security and those of domestic evolution may obtain in a different form.

On the Soviet side, the role of the external environment is becoming more and more crucial for the fate of the empire. On the one hand, detente and the reliance on economic relations with the West have contributed to the destabilization of Eastern Europe, at least in the case of Poland; on the other hand, given the economic crisis of the satellites and that of the Soviet Union herself, the costs of keeping domination in an autarkic empire are becoming enormous and would be close to unbearable if the military costs of an invasion of Poland and of preventing reactions in other East European countries were combined with those of being alone in carrying the burden of supporting their economies because of a breakdown in economic relations with the West. To that would be added the political consequences for Soviet diplomatic enterprises in relations with Western Europe. Hence what appeared before 18 December 1981 as a 'no win' situation between letting the Polish renewal continue or intervening militarily. The Soviet Union has, for the time being at least, succeeded in evading the dilemma by the semi-fiction of a semi-autonomous Polish military coup, which has minimized reactions both in Poland and abroad and increased Western division. Yet economic realities, i.e. the impossibility of making an economy like that of Poland recover without a measure of consent from the population and of help from the West, produce a more basic dilemma for the Soviet Union which is bound to increase and this will, in turn, face the West with a dilemma of its own.

The USSR both fears and needs the influence of the West for controlling her empire. Hence the West acquires, almost against its will, a say in the manner in which this empire is run. It has a chance of making the USSR accept the unacceptable, i.e., a kind of co-management of the periphery of her empire between herself, local forces and Western creditors.

An alternative policy is of course conceivable, both for the Soviet Union and for the West. Each may find that its interest lies in avoiding contamination and opting for an attempted return to Stalinist rule through terror-cum-autarky which would seem to be the only alternative. On the Western side, however, while some in the United States may find this preferable – for at a minimum it would discredit the Soviet Union abroad and at a maximum it would provoke her collapse – this option would certainly be unacceptable to Western Europe which, both for the sake of Eastern Europe and for its own safety, would find it both inhuman and dangerous.

If, then, both sides do gamble on evolution with – as in the whole process of European security – conflicting ulterior motives, the borderline between the desirable and the dangerous becomes extremely thin. The USSR would certainly like to see the West collaborate unconditionally in its own domination over its empire and, in the process, be both compromised in the eyes of the victims and be slowly induced, in fact, to join their ranks. This, of course, would be a disaster not only for the US but for Western Europe, whose attempt at 'Finlandizing' Eastern Europe would cause it to be 'Finlandized' itself.

Hence the necessity of maintaining intra-Western cohesion and strength, and of pursuing a policy towards Eastern Europe which would not rely on the automatic effects of economic help but would never lose sight of political objectives nor lose contact with its potential allies within the societies of the region.

On the other hand, the Soviet Union cannot be expected to accept a process so contrary to precedents and to her instincts (even though she hopes to control it and eventually to stop it or to reverse it) without not only economic benefits but some politically face-saving counterparts, which are only conceivable within the framework of the resumption of the 'European security process' in one form or another. Some, particularly in Germany, would like it to continue unconditionally, that is without being affected by the events in Poland. This would be both wrong and unrealistic. Anything even remotely resembling 'detente and business as usual' must be made dependent on a clear Soviet willingness to compromise with society in Poland and the rest of Eastern Europe and on a clear Western willingness to combine moderation and restraint with firmness and a willingness to interrupt the process in some circumstances. Even then nobody, in Europe as well as in the US, should be blind to the dangers of this process as well as to its opportunities. In particular if the US exaggerates its dangers and becomes isolated from the process while Europe exaggerates its opportunities and becomes involved in this process alone, both sides are likely to lose.

What may well be occurring today is a further episode in a play whose first act had already taken place in the 1960s. At that time, both Zbigniew Brzezinski and Henry Kissinger were writing that 'de Gaulle has a vision but no policy, the United States has a policy but no vision'.[23] Only today, the German Social Democrats seem to have replaced de Gaulle.

After the invasion of Afghanistan, many in the Federal Republic, including Helmut Schmidt, have been so struck by the attachment of both West European and East European governments to the preserving of detente, in spite of the hardening between the two super-powers, that they have hailed this community of reactions between the middle powers of Central Europe as the emergence of a new Europe. I have criticized the illusions and the false symmetries attached to this view which were soon to be demonstrated by Gierek's fall and Honecker's hardening.[24] However, even the Polish events have been interpreted by the proponents of these notions as further proof that in Europe the ideological

101

competition, hence the Cold War, was over, that what existed now were only national realities, that these were forcing the two super-powers into a global competition but were drawing the two Europes together away from this global competition and towards 're-Europeanization'.

This view has been exposed in a particularly forceful and extreme way by Peter Bender.[25] In my opinion he pushes it to absurd lengths both in terms of false symmetries between the two sides and in terms of policy recommendations. (For instance, in order to encourage Moscow to give up its rule over Eastern Europe, Western Europe should have neither missiles nor radio stations reaching the USSR.)[26] He himself points to the precedent of de Gaulle's ideas for a 'Europe from the Atlantic to the Urals' in the same direction of Western Europe's detachment from the US as a precondition for Eastern Europe's detachment from the USSR.[27]

Clearly the same reasons which provoked de Gaulle's failure (an over-estimation of the leverage of a weak and disunited Western Europe and an under-estimation of the Soviet Union's ideological charater, and of her determination to keep what she has) are valid today. They may be even more so, since the Soviet Union is militarily much stronger and the need for Western Europe to reinforce its security link with the United States correspondingly more urgent, whereas (even though some, in the left wing of the SPD and some isolated voices like Peter Bender himself or in France, Michel Tatu and in Italy, A. Gambino,[28] are beginning to speak of the need for an autonomous European defence to implement an autonomous conception of detente and to influence Eastern Europe) the main thrust of these trends, particularly in West Germany is, much more than in de Gaulle's case, to make Western Europe weaker and more dependent, economically and militarily, upon Moscow's good will.

And yet, who can deny that the secular trend is, indeed, in the direction foreseen by de Gaulle and rediscovered today, namely that of the increasing costs of empire, of the increasing psychological gap between the two Europes and their respective super-powers, and of the increasing human and economic ties between them? Each of these trends has progressed spectacularly in the last fifteen years, in parti-cular in the case of Germany, and can be expected to increase in the 1980s and 1990s.

However, the two cardinal sins which are being committed by those new left-wing Gaullists are, on the one hand, to jump from social trends and perceptions to political conclusions while neglecting the more persistent geopolitical realities, and, on the other hand, to confuse a long-range historical perspective with an immediately operational policy direction.

Obviously, the right attitude is to act neither as if the long-range perspectives were never to materialize nor as if they were already here.

In the short run, the priority is both to restore a credible balance in front of the growth of Soviet power (which means strengthening the Atlantic Alliance) and to influence the evolution of the Soviet empire in the way described above. In the long run, both processes may indeed be channelled in the direction of a stronger Western Europe having a more autonomous dialogue with a weakened Soviet Union and encouraging a more autonomous Eastern Europe.

For the United States this means, in the short run, being more engaged in Europe, in the re-shaping of European defence, in the European security dialogue (so as to stop the growing influence of the Soviet notions of 'military detente') and in discrete and peaceful but active engagement in Eastern Europe. At the same time, with a view to the long run, it means accepting with good grace, and even encouraging, a more united and independent Western Europe having special ties with and a special role in Eastern Europe.

Conclusion

This leads us to a more general conclusion. Today, the Soviet–American competition has never been more dominant either in geographical scope or in terms of the difference of military power between them and all other countries. Yet, in the longer run, the costs of empire are bound to increase for both, the emergence of new national and social centres of power is bound to make for more pluralism within countries, within alliances and within the international system as a whole. This is not necessarily and entirely a reassuring perspective: more pluralism may mean more anarchy, which in turn, one day, may mean more tyranny or at least a reassertion of domestic authority and of global empire. Meanwhile, whereas the power of the United States may be, again, in an ascending phase, her control over events will continue to decline. But a more pluralistic world, even if it means less satisfaction for US 'possession goals' or national interests in a narrow sense, still gives her many chances for using various channels for influence connected with her social system. At any rate, it does not conflict with America's ideology or with her 'milieu goals' or her conception of world order. It is, on the other hand, anathema to those of the Soviet Union.

And this is the ultimate paradox of our subject. The Soviet Union is prepared, by her national tradition and by her ideology, to work for a long-range future. Yet today, she may experience the zenith of her historical ascension, although not of her capacity for an active militarist and dangerous foreign policy. Now that she has become a global power, all her long-range goals seem to evade her, hence the temptation of making as many short-term gains as possible while there is still time. On the other hand, the United States is emerging from twenty years of tragedy and retreat and can look forward to national and global evolutions which, if she can only combine strength and moderation, if she can only avoid going from one extreme to the other every few years, should, during the 1980s and 1990s make her come out on top, at least as compared to the Soviet Union.

The outcome, however, is still in doubt. For the long-suffering Soviet people and the old apparatchiki who rule it have one virtue in common, and that is the quality which goes most against the grain both of any democratic system and, in particular, of the American character and experience. It is the quality of patience.

NOTES

[1] Shahram Chubin, 'The United States and the Third World: Motives, Objectives, Policies', in *Third-World Conflict and International Security*, Adelphi Paper 167, (London: IISS, 1980) pp. 19–34.

[2] 'East–West Relations Today', *Survey*, Autumn 1976, p. 63.

[3] For an elaboration, see my 'Tenir les deux bouts de la chaîne', *Commentaire*, Spring 1981.

[4] 'Assertive America' by Daniel Yankelovich and Larry Kaagan, *America and the World 1980, Foreign Affairs*, Vol. 59, No. 3. pp. 711–13.

[5] S. Bialer, *Stalin's Successors*, (Cambridge: Cambridge University Press, 1980), p. 277.

[6] See the comments by S. Weiss on Secretary Haig's remarks on arms control, *The Wall Street Journal*, 1981, reproduced in Wireless File, Paris, 28 July 1981, no. 143.

[7] 'Soviet Foreign Policy: Sources, Perceptions, Trends', in S. Bialer (Ed.) *The Domestic Context of Soviet Foreign Policy*, (London: Croom Helm, 1981), p. 435.

[8] H. Gelman, *The Politburo's management of its America Problem*, Rand, R2707NS, April 1981.

[9] For an analysis of process and for the questions of 'who is Finlandizing whom?', see my 'The New Europe: from Cold War to Hot Peace', *International Journal*, Winter 1971–72 p. 1–17, and 'Europe: Old Conflicts, New Rules', *Orbis*, Fall 1973, pp. 895–911.

[10] G. Breslauer, 'Why Detente Failed', unpublished paper.

[11] I. Smart, 'Alliance, Deterrence and Defence', *Yearbook of World Affairs*, (London: Stevens, 1972), p. 125.

[12] C. Bertram, *Arms Control and Technological Change: Elements of a New Approach*, Adelphi Paper No 146, (London: IISS, 1978); and 'Rethinking Arms Control', *Foreign Affairs*, Winter 1980–81, pp. 352–65.

[13] S. Weiss, *op. cit.*, in note 6, p. 5.

[14] R. Löwenthal, 'Dealing with Soviet global power', *Encounter*, June 1978, p. 91.

[15] E. Todd, *La Chute finale: Essai sur la décomposition de la sphère soviétique*, (Paris: Laffont, 1976).

[16] Christopher Davis and Murray Fesbach, *Raising infant mortality in the USSR in the 1970's*, United States Bureau of Census, p. 95, no. 74, September 1980; see also the comprehensive, but perhaps over-dramatic, review article by N. Eberstadt, 'The Health Crisis in the USSR', *New York Review of Books*, 19 February 1981.

[17] Erik Hoffmann and Robbin Laird, *Soviet Economic Modernizers and Contemporary East–West Relations*, USICA, R17-80, 28 August 1980.

[18] Colin Gray, 'Understanding Soviet Military Power', *Problems of Communism*, March–April 1981, p. 66.

[19] H. Gelman, *op. cit.*, in note 8, p. 66.

[20] For this distinction, see Gerhard Wettig, *Instrumentarien der Entspannungspolitik*, Berichte des Bundesinstituts für ostwissenschaftliche und internationale Studien, 17, 1981. pp. 14–26.

[21] Löwenthal, *op. cit.*, in note 14, p. 90.

[22] Breslauer, *op. cit.*, in note 10, p. 7.

[23] See Zbigniew Brzezinski, *Alternative to Partition*, (New York: McGraw-Hill, 1965) and Henry A. Kissinger, *The Troubled Partnership*, (New York: McGraw-Hill, 1965).

[24] See my 'The Soviet Union and the Western Alliance', *The Problems of Communism*, May–June 1981, pp. 48–50.

[25] Peter Bender, *Das Ende des ideologischen Zeitalters: Die Europaisierung Europas* (Berlin: Severin and Siedler, 1981).

[26] *Ibid.*, p. 261.

[27] *Ibid.*, pp. 166–72.

[28] See his 'Ma l'Europa non è un satellite', *L'Espresso*, 19 July 1981.

The Soviet Union in the American Perspective: Perceptions and Realities

WILLIAM HYLAND

Schizophrenia is defined, in part, as 'a psychotic disorder characterized by loss of contact with the environment and . . . expressed as a disorder of feeling, thought or conduct'. This approximates to the attitude of the United States toward Russian Communism, the Communist Party of the Soviet Union and the Soviet State. In simpler terms, the US has displayed and still displays the symptoms of a split personality when confronted by the USSR.

On the one hand, there are those who are convinced that they completely understand the nature of the Soviet problem and its remedies: they tend to be of the school that sees the Soviet state as an expansionist, neo-imperialist movement driven by an all-encompassing ideology that must be resisted at every turn and in virtually every place. In this view the Soviet Union is an inherently hostile and implacable foe, not subject to the persuasive force of politics and diplomacy. The contest is primarily a military one.

The contrary view is that the USSR is not much different from other states. To be sure, she is motivated by some ancient Russian drives for security and tends towards authoritarianism, but she is essentially pragmatic and opportunist in her foreign policy. Ideology is largely irrelevant and, while a difficult and obstreperous state and unusually devious in her conduct, is nevertheless subject to the traditional means of international politics, diplomacy, bargaining and compromise. Hence the conflict is soluble.

Of course, the vast majority of analysts and statesmen consider themselves to be in the large middle ground between these ends of the spectrum. But American policy has tended to oscillate towards one end or the other.

Some reasons for the erratic nature of Soviet-American relations can be found in fundamental American attitudes toward foreign relations. A sustained involvement in world affairs has never held much appeal for the United States. When confronted with a protracted contest with the Soviet Union there was a tendency to expect an early settlement, or the mellowing of Soviet Communism, or its eventual collapse. The problem was simply to find the right sequence of actions and proclamations.

Moreover, the US is uncomfortable with prolonged ambiguity in international affairs. There has been a compulsion to define the problem in crude alternatives: co-existence, containment, confrontation, or co-operation. Seeking partial settlements, settling for tacit accords, manipulating a balance of power, defining spheres of influence, all these require long experience in the grey zones of international politics.

Finally, Americans are ambivalent toward military power. Large standing armies, high defence budgets and limited wars rub against deeply-engrained American domestic resistance, on both the left and right. Even in the nuclear age, the idea of mutual deterrence and a 'balance of terror' have been difficult to explain and accept.

Does this mean that the problems between the two super-powers result from a muddled American perception, from misunderstandings and, as one study concluded, plain 'bad luck'? The view that the US has failed to perceive the true essence of Soviet policy is also perpetuated by the USSR, who charges:

Inaccuracy of many American perceptions of the Soviet Union is hardly surprising given the fact that there may be no other country in the world the US perceptions of which have for such a long time been formed on the basis of so one-sided and distorted information. That is why they are so tinted with strong biases and prejudices.[1]

That there are biases and prejudices in any policy is scarcely a novel insight. That such biases have resulted in systematic distortions would be a serious charge, suggesting that the Soviet–American contest was a series of ghastly errors. Is that the reality?

Containment and the Cold War

There is little doubt that the American relations with the Soviet state have been 'tinted' with prejudices from the start. In a rather remarkable public letter in 1920, the Secretary of State, Bainbridge Colby, wrote that, as long as the Bolsheviks governed, a 'free and unified Russia' would not be able to take its place in the world. The Communist regime negated:

Every principle of honour and good faith and every usage and convention underlying the whole structure of international law; the negation in short of every principle upon which it is possible to base harmonious and trustful relations, whether of nations or of individuals. There cannot be any common ground upon which (the United States Government) can stand with a Power whose conceptions of international relations are so alien to its own, so utterly repugnant to its moral sense.[2]

The point of the quaint vignette is that the mind-set that eventually led to containment and the Cold War was not an invidious conspiracy of President Truman, but a natural evolution of the suspicions produced by the Revolution, its unacceptability on 'moral' grounds, and the lingering hope that someday 'Russia' would reassert herself. A further characteristic was the equation of international standards with personal ones. Thus 'trust' was a major criterion; 'can we trust the Communists?' was a question that would echo for decades.

As the hope or belief in a Russian counter-revolution faded, and the USSR was finally accepted by the US as a 'legitimate' member of the international community, three other themes appeared that would also reverberate through the history of US-Soviet relations:

– There was the view that the Communists had turned out to be not all that much different from various reformers, socialists and other left wing movements; communism was mellowing. This was propagated mainly by American liberals (including the American Ambassador) and even endured the purge trials. Later it was to resurface in the wartime diplomacy of Roosevelt and symbolized in the appellation of 'Uncle Joe';

– There was also a strong view that the threat from the USSR was not Russian imperialism in a new guise, but international subversion. The Litvinov negotiations prior to the establishment of diplomatic relations in 1933 were dominated by American apprehension over Soviet interference in American affairs: hence a wall of guarantees and prohibitions was erected against subversion, but little thought was given to the USSR as a participant in European diplomacy;

– Before the war relations were cordial but minimal. However, there was a strong though muted hostility to the USSR among the professional corps of Sovietologists (e.g., Bohlen, Kennan, Henderson, *et al.*) and this was also to be another characteristic of American policy: there was a gap between the desire to American political leaders for normal relations and the suspicions of the community of Sovietologists (not a unified group, of course).[3]

Although the United States entered into the wartime alliance with substantial reservations about the USSR, President Roosevelt's natural enthusiasm, coupled with his fear that he would suffer the fate of President Wilson and the Versailles Treaty, led to substantial political co-operation. The files of the US Embassy and various enclaves in the State Department in Washington are littered with warnings and admonitions about the USSR but the dominant perception, expressed primarily by President Roosevelt and by Harry Hopkins, was a pragmatic one: the USSR could be dealt with; it was largely a problem of communications and persuasion.

Strangely enough, the opposite view accepted the same starting premise about the nature of Soviet policy: it was no longer impelled by a strong revolutionary impulse, but was a resurgence of Russian expansionism blended with residue Communism. Thus Kennan, returning to the USSR in 1944 after a long absence, noted that Stalin had now realized that the world revolution had little chance.[4] Kennan's conclusions and those of others who accepted his basic view are well known; they gradually evolved into the theory of containment. What is important about this interpretation is not only the prescription for American policy, but the assumptions that were made about the Soviet Union: that the USSR was an expansionist power, but internally weak; that it was subject to influence from abroad, mainly through forceful resistance; and that in the face of the logic of containment, Moscow would adjust to the new realities of the international order, because, unlike Hitler, the Soviet leaders were not committed to a timetable of conquest. This general formula was not seriously challenged because to question the concept of Soviet expansionism would have seemed hopelessly and dangerously naïve in the late 1940s, and to suggest that the USSR would not evolve would have been hopelessly fatalistic.

Out of this new view came an operational nexus between negotiations for a possible settlement and the advisability of waiting for change in the USSR. During the war it was argued, especially with the dissolution of the Comintern, that she had already changed and therefore co-operative relations were fully justified. After the war, the opposite view prevailed: the Soviet Union would have to change before any accommodation was possible.

This latter position was challenged by those who continued to see the USSR as the Russian empire only slightly disguised. Walter Lippmann, for example, rebutted the containment theories by evoking historic Russian ambitions, in order to argue that it was quite possible to negotiate a European settlement.

What was the reality?

As one would expect, the reality was probably a blend of these two interpretations. Stalin was far less bent on a limitless expansion than envisaged by the advocates of containment in the US. He tended, if anything, to see confrontation as developing later, perhaps in a decade. His treatment of the true believers – Tito and Dimitrov – suggested an acute awareness that there were limits to Western toleration. Similarly, he was quite hesitant in the Far East, advising China that she had no real prospects of

defeating the US. True, in Europe Stalin seemed bold and dangerous yet the most plausible explanation of his strategy was a series of controlled probes and tests to determine the true balance of power and the actual extent of Soviet influence. Thus in Czechoslovakia he found that the limit of his forward movement had not yet been reached, but in Berlin he found certain anachronisms would have to be tolerated.

There remains the vexing problem of the Korean War. According to Krushchev, it was sanctioned by Stalin. There is little doubt that the military equipment came from the USSR or that Stalin persuaded China to intervene. Yet there is no evidence that he planned to take the USSR into the war, or that he planned to attack Western Europe, which was the great fear of American policy-makers of the period. Thus it is a fair conclusion that the US misread Stalin's ambitions and misconstrued the nature of his foreign policy. Yet this is a misleading judgement. What was happening was the creation of a sphere of influence in Europe. Stalin overplayed his hand and accelerated the process but the outcome would probably have been much the same. From the vantage point of 30 years, it is clear that Stalin on the one hand, and the major Western powers on the other, were ultimately content to settle down to a measure of political stability in Europe. In this sense, the containment policy was correct and to a degree vindicated. Stalin was checked in Germany. He accepted the limits imposed by the 1949 Berlin Settlement, let Yugoslavia go its own way with impunity and watched numerous setbacks imposed on local Communists. Most significant, he never entertained any genuine interest in a European settlement that would have entailed Soviet disengagement or withdrawal. In this sense, the Lippmann school was probably wrong: there was never a real alternative to partition.[5] But it also seems true that both schools over-estimated the mellowing influence inside the USSR. Indeed, the opposite proved correct: the *gulag* mentality was intensified and matters proceeded from bad to worse. One can only wonder what would have happened if Stalin had not been felled by a stroke and died a few days later.

Political leaders are wont to believe that we learn from history, but history is usually more elusive. Thus, a relevant commentary on American perceptions of the Cold War is provided by a recent survey of six standard American high school textbooks, which concluded that:

> . . . several of them fail to give a coherent picture of the Cold War, fail to explain the interrelationship of events, fail to show how Western perceptions and policies were created by actions of the Communist powers and fail to make clear the defensive nature of American foreign policy in the post-World War II period.[6]

From Co-existence to Confrontation

Indeed, this short conclusion about American teaching of the Cold War illustrates a doleful lesson: that American policy became burdened by a sense of guilt about the period and could not overcome the feeling that it was all some ghastly misunderstanding, or, as a very recent Congressional survey put it:

> Looking back over the Cold War, it is obvious that many mistakes – compounded by misunderstandings, misconceptions and plain bad luck – were made on both sides. Finding the way back has not been easy. The road to genuine detente is strewn with the debris of the past.[7]

Thus the death of Stalin revived the contention between the differing interpretations. Containment was attacked as both ineffective and unrealistic; from a different political vantage point it was assailed as passive and self-defeating. The same themes were sounded again, though played with new variants. One school argued that the Soviet empire could be rolled back by the re-assertion of Western might, i.e. containment taken to its logical and most extreme conclusion. Hope that the USSR would evolve was illusory, it was argued. There were no essential differences in the policies of Stalin and his successors.

The opposite view, however, began to prevail. The USSR was indeed changing; the 'thaw' was evidence. That it was amenable to a settlement was demonstrated by the withdrawal from Austria and by the Korean Armistice. It was time for summit diplomacy, to strike that overall bargain that should have been made in 1945–6. 'It would be a mistake to assume that nothing could be settled with Soviet Russia unless or until everything is settled', Churchill argued. An irony of the period was that the great container, George Kennan, emerged in 1957 as the champion of the European settlement that Lippmann had urged a decade earlier in 1947, while John Foster Dulles, the liberator, turned out to be the conservative determined to avoid a diplomatic engagement until the West had gathered its strength.

Did the West in fact miss a major opportunity for a settlement in the 1950s?

Central to any answer is an appraisal of the policies of Nikita Khrushchev. The traditional American penchant for nostalgia seems to have captured the memory of Khrushchev. He is seen as an almost benign, fatherly figure, only trifle impetuous. In fact, he was dangerous, overly sensitive to a crude appraisal of the balance of power and an inveterate gambler. The idea that he could or would have settled the European problem is a myth that seems bound to grow. For example, a recent appraisal of Eisenhower, who seems to be enjoying a revival, concluded: 'The Eisenhower Administration may well have missed a genuine opportunity for detente in the months following Stalin's death'. While it may be that some Soviet concession may have been made under firm pressure or because of the internecine warfare within the Kremlin, disengagement from Germany and Eastern Europe, implying the abandonment of a major military position, seems highly unlikely. Khrushchev did not become the First Secretary of the CPSU to preside over the liquidation of Stalin's empire.

Yet this period had an impact on Western policy that may have inadvertently led to the great missile crisis in Cuba. The notion of a lost opportunity gained ground, especially in Germany, and to some extent in the United States. It lingered on despite the reality of the suppression of the Hungarian revolt. When Khrushchev challenged the West during the missile gap and Berlin crisis, there were strong voices urging negotiations and compromise over Berlin. Even Eisenhower, who was sceptical at first, finally came around to the view that if he could only meet Khrushchev (in 1959) he could use it as an opportunity 'for one great personal effort before leaving office, to soften up the Soviet leader even a little bit'.[8] In the actual meeting he told Khrushchev that he had the chance to 'go down in history as one of the truly great statesmen of all times' if he would help Eisenhower end the Cold War.

In his memoirs, Khrushchev frankly admits he wanted to force a change in American policy by exploiting the new missile-gap assumptions about the balance of power and to force, once and for all, Western recognition of the Communist gains in Europe. But this was only a minimal aim which indeed might have been satisfied through diplomacy. In addition, Khrushchev also wanted to establish Soviet ascendancy in Germany, to defeat the policy of Adenauer and Dulles. This was vaguely recognized, but usually subordinated to a more complicated analysis about the ratification of the *status quo* in central Europe. Had that been all there was to it, there would have been no missiles deployed in Cuba. At bottom it was a change in the balance of power that Khrushchev wanted and that was why he proved more dangerous than imagined.

In this sense the outcome in the Cuban crisis was unfortunate. It demonstrated that the West was still predominant and that the USSR could be defeated by superior will. It vindicated Kennedy's military build-up in 1961–62, but it turned the Soviet-American contest into a test of nerves (i.e. who 'blinks' first) rather than a protracted strategic conflict. It led to a belief that the Soviet problem was, after all manageable and that once the worst was over, the USSR under Krushchev and even Brezhnev could be amenable to new forms of political *rapprochement* – mainly through expanded trade and through arms control – both symbolized in the first wheat sales and in the Limited Test Ban Treaty in 1963–64.

The Road to Detente

The decade from the conclusion of the Cuban crisis through the first Nixon-Brezhnev Summit is a difficult period to analyse.

The first part – until about 1970 – was not really dominated by the super-powers. It was almost as if both welcomed a diversion, the US in Vietnam and the USSR with an internal rebuilding and the split with China. Nevertheless

two very strong perceptions were nourished in this period in the United States. It was believed that the Soviet Union wanted and needed a great increase in economic intercourse with the West, and that this would prove the key to a genuine relaxation of tensions. Second, that the two powers shared the same apprehensions about the nuclear arms race, and the same aspiration for stabilizing it. Thus the Johnson Administration pursued both aims, spurred on in part by the judgement that the Soviet system was entering a period of genuine crisis, demonstrated by the remarkable coup against Krushchev. Since the entire system was at risk, diplomacy might go beyond the traditional objective of a political settlement and seek a gradual easing of the Soviet domination of East Europe. This was 'bridge building' in the US, and in West Germany it was the policy of *kleine Schritte*. Both in effect harked back to the earlier theme of lost opportunities, that it would be possible for the Soviet Union to evolve and for the balance of power in Europe to change. Indeed, the world-wide balance could be stabilized by a balance of nuclear arms, in which the survival of each side would be guaranteed by doctrines and strategies of mutual assured destruction.

It was in this period, however, that the US and the West in general failed to perceive the real trends in the Soviet Union. Well after the Soviet economic reforms were killed, the West insisted that trade was essential to promoting a liberalization inside the USSR. Premier Kosygin became the symbol for these hopes for 'positive' change. Moreover, even after the build-up of Soviet missiles was well underway, the US persisted in believing that build-up would reach some acceptable plateau from which to negotiate a final settlement. American military estimates were based on this firm assumption. Thus Secretary MacNamara argued that the US should have stopped its own build-up sooner had he realized how far behind the USSR was lagging.

How can one explain these lapses?

In part, the explanation was the enormous preoccupation with Vietnam. As the war worsened and prospects for any acceptable outcomes receded, the Johnson Administration saw the USSR as a latent ally; North Vietnam was seen as an extension of the

108

main enemy, China. And this view was nurtured by the Soviet conciliation in the Non-Proliferation Treaty negotiations and the negotiation for a summit in the Summer of 1968. Vietnam also had the effect on President Johnson, as it later did on President Nixon, of forcing an inordinate preoccupation with proving the Administration's peace credentials. Thus arms control and relaxation with the USSR were to become a major feature in the efforts of both Administrations to demonstrate their peaceful aims.

Neither the Western interest in trade with the East nor the rising expectation about arms control were new in the late 1960s. They were elements of earlier assessments dating back a decade. There were two new factors, however, that markedly changed the American and Western perception of the possibilities of a new relationship with the USSR: the worsening of the Sino-Soviet split in the Spring of 1969; and the advent of a Social Democratic Government in Western Germany and the sharp changes in Germany's eastern policy that followed.

The new *Ostpolitik*, which had its origins in the mid-1960s, when the Grand Coalition was formed in Bonn, was the culmination of years of rethinking the Soviet problem in Germany. It epitomized the school of thought that the USSR was susceptible to major changes if the right formula could only be found; the main theme of the new Eastern policy was 'transformation through *rapprochement*'. This time, however, the analysis was butressed by the new geopolitical realities along the USSR's eastern frontier. As one analyst of German policy noted in 1969:

> Caught between the German problem and the Chinese problem it (the USSR) would have to decide which was the more important. Possibly as a consequence of this choice, Poland was given permission to attempt a new approach to West Germany, while the Soviet Government also attempted to improve its own relations with the Federal Republic.[9]

Thus the pressure on Moscow from the East became a key element in the reasoning that led West Germany into her phase of detente, and, somewhat later, led the US in the same direction. This was a significant difference in perception compared to the earlier phase.

The second difference between the Nixon-Kissinger period and the earlier period was in the expectation about Soviet behaviour. Neither President Nixon nor Henry Kissinger expected much internal change in the USSR nor did they consider such a change either a prerequisite for, or an objective of, improved relations. Mr Kissinger was sceptical of the thesis that internal changes could be induced by foreign policy (bridge building) and, especially, whether American policy could be geared to any assumptions regarding changes in Soviet society.[10] In essence President Nixon and Mr Kissinger were willing to settle for a new balance of power with the USSR and they hoped to create political and economic incentives for Soviet acceptance of a rough *status quo*, guaranteed in part by Sino-American *rapprochement*.

Detente and its Critics

Thus in a broad sense 'detente' was not only the opening of a new era reflected in Sino-American relations, but also the closing of an old one, reflected in a settlement of the German and Berlin problems. Europe remained divided, but with more ties between the two halves. Strategic arms would be limited, though not definitively. Trade would be expedited, but with qualifications. Other trappings of normal bilateral relations would be developed. The anti-containment programme of the late 1940s and late 1950s would be fulfilled, but not on the basis of disengagement.

While detente had its origins in the East, it was still Eurocentric. Thus its most permanent effects were in Europe, and detente became a European phenomenon which proved to be one of its principle weaknesses. What was not settled in 1972–73 – the high point of detente – was how the super-powers would relate in third-world conflicts. The relationship was therefore vulnerable to non-European crises – in the Middle East in 1973 and in Angola in 1975. In the former case the US took advantage of an opportunity to exclude the USSR from the area, whereas in Angola the Soviet Union precluded American influence through a forceful intervention. In these circumstances the relationship with the Soviet Union was increasingly reduced to SALT and arms control. Indeed, the essence of the Carter policy was to allow the gap between the geopolitical context and arms-control accommodation to grow to the point that SALT was highly vulnerable to even minor episodes (such as the discovery of a Soviet brigade in Cuba) let alone the massive impact of the Soviet invasion of Afghanistan.

The critics of detente have centred on one general theme: that the period was based on an illusion or, more precisely, on a series of illusions, some conciously perpetrated by the US Government, some reflecting a naïveté, and some reflecting pure softheadedness – all, of course, at complete variance with a supposed Soviet reality.

Surely, this entire period, dating back to 1963, cannot be written off as a mirage. The principal perceptions all had a kernel of reality. The Soviet Union *was* apprehensive about China; they *did* want a settlement with the West in Europe; they *did* want and need Western economic assistance; they *did* want nuclear parity; and they *did* want a period of relaxation after a period of internal Krushchevian turmoil. In short, there *was* a basis for the Western policies that came to be called detente.

The failures were errors of omission rather than errors of commission as most of the critics have charged. First and foremost, the US executive authority was critically weakened at a crucial moment when the new policy toward the USSR was in mid-flight. Second, critics from both the left and right formed a bizarre coalition against detente and radically escalated the demands on American policy: free immigration from the USSR; internal liberalization; genuine disarmament; and abandonment of the liberation struggle. In other words the profound transformation of a system which only a decade earlier had seemed immutably hostile. Politics seldom work that rapidly or radically. The opponents of detente indulged in illusions of about the same magnitude as they charged against the proponents.

The greatest misjudgement was in the military field. The experts and the political leaders knew that the era of parity was dawning. What they underestimated was the political impact. What in the 1960s and early 1970s had seemed primarily a geopolitical contest conducted under American strategic superiority was transformed into a military contest measured in exceedingly complex and arcane symbols (missile throw-weights and hard-target kill probability). Thus a new perception was born – namely that an unfavourable military balance was eroding America's global position, and that the Soviet Union herself was coming to believe it and was acting more audaciously in Ethiopia, Yemen, Vietnam and Afghanistan.

It seems increasingly likely that the invasion of Afghanistan has, in fact, meant the 'end of detente'.[11] A new era is developing, and a new American consensus seems to be taking shape. It has been expressed in a number of weighty pronouncements by elite groups, including a Presidential Commission, the Council on Foreign Relations, the US UN Association, and a group of American, French, German, and British institutes of foreign relations.[12] The new consensus seems to run along the following lines:

- The Soviet Union has 'dangerously' threatened strengthened its military position; this shift in the military balance forms the principal challenge to the US and to the West; Soviet military power poses a threat to its neighbours, and will be projected to more remote areas. The West must be prepared for the actual use of Soviet military forces.
- The change in the balance leads to a Soviet willingness to take greater risks, to act with increasing assertiveness, and a new 'boldness'. Soviet policymakers in any case see a close linkage between military power and political influence.
- The main area of conflict is in the Third World, because of an inherent turmoil and because of Soviet opportunism in exploiting it.
- There is little reason to expect much change in Soviet policy; new leaders will be conservative and opportunistic.
- Soviet internal weaknesses, however, are growing, but Soviet refusal to contribute to a stable world order is rooted in all the structures of Soviet politics. Hence the outlook is not at all promising.

'This means', the Presidential Commission concluded, 'that the world will continue to be a place of some potential danger for the United

States and that the Soviet Union will remain our prinicpal antagonist in the realm of international politics'.

As this theme of a new balance of power becomes more and more entrenched in American political life, a counterpoint has inevitably appeared that suggests a more complex perception. While the USSR is truly a formidable military power, in all other respects it is supposedly dwindling. Consequently the Soviet Union may well take new risks while the moment is optimal, but over the long term it has entered an 'historic decline'.[13]

Thus the US has come virtually full circle. It is returning to a form of containment, even if the rhetoric and syntax are different. Moreover, the policy rests on a judgment that the USSR is fundamentally weak and that once thwarted its strength will erode. On the basis of the record a certain scepticism is in order.

NOTES

[1] Georgi A. Arbatov, 'Accuracy of US Perceptions', US Senate, Committee on Foreign Relations, *Perceptions: Relations Between the United States and the Soviet Union* (Washington DC, USGPO), p.297.

[2] John Lewis Gaddis, *Russia, the Soviet Union and the United States. An Interpretive History* (New York: Wiley, 1978), pp. 94–95.

[3] Hugh DeSantis, *The Diplomacy of Silence: the American Foreign Service, the Soviet Union and the Cold War, 1933/1947* (London: University of Chicago Press, 1980).

[4] George F. Kennan, *Memoirs 1925–1963* (London: Hutchinson, 1968–1973), p.516.

[5] A.W. DePorte, *Europe between the Superpowers: the Enduring Balance* (London: Yale University Press for the Council on Foreign Relations, 1979), pp.141–165.

[6] Martin F. Herz, *How the Cold War is Taught: Six American History Textbooks Examined* (Washington DC: Ethics and Public Policy Center, Georgetown University, 1978), p.75.

[7] US Senate, *op.cit.*, in note 1.

[8] Robert A. Divine, *Eisenhower and the Cold War*, (Oxford: OUP, 1981), p.137.

[9] Philip Windsor, *Germany and the Management of Detente*, (London: IISS, 1971), p.188.

[10] Henry A. Kissinger, *American Foreign Policy*, (New York: Norton, 1977).

[11] Robert G. Kaiser, 'US-Soviet Relations: Goodby to Detente', *Foreign Affairs and the World 1980*, pp. 500–521.

[12] *The United States and the World Community in the Eighties. President's Commission for a National Agenda for the Eighties* (Washington DC, USGPO, 1980). *The Soviet Challenge: A Policy Framework for the 1980s*, The Commission on US-Soviet Relations, Sponsored by the Council on Foreign Relations (New York, 1981). *US-Soviet Relations: A Strategy for the '80s*, Report of a National Policy Panel of the United Nations Association of the USA (New York, 1981). *Western Security: What has Changed? What Should be Done?*, a Report prepared by the Directors of Forschungsinstitut der Deutschen Gesellschaft fuer Auswartige Politik (Bonn), Council on Foreign Relations (New York), Institut Français des Relations Internationales (Paris), Royal Institute of International Affairs (London), 1981. Also, 'American Renewal' *Time*, 23 February 1981, and William E. Odom, 'Whither the Soviet Union', *Washington Quarterly*, Spring 1981.

[13] See Seweryn Bialer's sophisticated analysis, *Stalin's Successors*, (Cambridge: CUP, 1980), pp. 1–2 and p. 281 ff.

Index